Kids Who Hate School

Kids
Who Hate
School

A Survival Handbook on Learning Disabilities

Lawrence J. Greene

Humanics Limited * Atlanta, Georgia

HUMANICS LIMITED
P.O. Box 7447
Atlanta, Georgia 30309

Library of Congress Card Catalog Number: 82-81896

PRINTED IN THE UNITED STATES OF AMERICA
ISBN 0-89334-035-9

Edited by Roberta Dunton and Christopher Simer
Cover by Laurie Svenkeson
Design/Typography by Daniel R. Bogdan
Photograph by Steven Greenburg

This book is dedicated to the 6000 kids with whom I have worked over the last thirteen years. Each and every one of them tested my resources every bit as much as I tested theirs. I hope they have derived as much from this process as I have.

CONTENTS

ABOUT THE AUTHOR _____

After completing his graduate studies in the School of Education at Stanford University, Lawrence Greene pursued his clinical training in learning disabilities in Chicago. For the last thirteen years he has been the Executive Director of the Developmental Learning Center in Saratoga, California. In addition to his diagnostic, teacher training, program development and counseling responsibilities at the Center, he has found time to conduct workshops for school districts and to teach courses for parents and teachers at California colleges. Mr. Greene has also taught at the Esalen Institute in Big Sur, California, and has trained teachers and learning disabilities specialists as part of the Continuing Education Program at San Jose State University.

ACKNOWLEDGMENTS _____

I am indebted to my exceptional staff for their support, counsel and criticism. Their many remarkable talents have made this book possible. I am especially indebted to Leigh Jones-Bamman who served as my research assistant, fact-checker and critic. Her support and incisive criticism have been invaluable.

AUTHOR'S NOTE ⸻

The case studies and anecdotal material that are included in this book are drawn from my thirteen years of clinical experience as a learning disabilities specialist. All the educational data that pertains to the particular learning problems I discuss is correct and accurate. Certain facts and background information have been changed, however, to protect the identities of the children and their families.

I have used the male gender to refer to the learning disabled child throughout this book. I employed this usage as a matter of convenience only. In no way is it meant to reflect or attribute an inherent inferiority or superiority to either female or male children.

INTRODUCTION _____

He is eight years old and so far the most significant thing he has learned in school is how to fail.

He can barely read, seldom finishes a project he starts and has difficulty concentrating. His handwriting is illegible. When his teachers speak in class he doesn't listen. When they give instructions, he is confused. Distractible, inattentive, fidgety, overactive — each day he falls further and further behind.

His parents love him, of course, but their patience is wearing thin. They are convinced that his problems would disappear if only he would try harder. As the months pass, they become more and more desperate. His teachers are equally perplexed. Despite their efforts, they recognize that the child is not learning properly. Each day the boy's self-image sinks a bit lower. School becomes intolerable, and with increasing frequency he finds refuge in his daydreams. The boy's name is Mike, and he is one of the 8,000,000 children in the United States with learning problems.

Eight years later, Mike is sixteen and six feet tall. He can still barely read. In fact, little has changed during the last eight years. Except now Mike has a probation officer assigned to him by juvenile court and attends a continuation high school on an irregular basis. His parents and his teachers expect very little of him, and his school counselor and his probation officer are happy when he simply decides to show up at school. Repeatedly disappointed, his parents have become resigned to their son's erratic behavior and unreliability. Although Mike has made several halfhearted attempts to find a part-time job at a hamburger stand and a car wash, he has had no success convincing anyone to hire him. Any prospective boss can see that he would be a high-risk employee. Frustrated, angry, and defeated, Mike has lost all self-confidence. No longer able to communicate with his parents, he feels as if he's an unwanted guest in his own home. Most of the time he is hostile and turned-off to anything that requires effort or perseverance. He is irresponsible, uninvolved, and already a failure in his own eyes. His prospects — like his confidence — are nonexistent.

Although the entire process of destroying Mike's self-esteem spanned ten years, the seeds of destruction were first planted in kindergarten. Unable to learn like the other children, Mike inevitably concluded that he was somehow different from his classmates. While most of his classmates pro-

1

gressed from one learning experience to the next, Mike progressed from frustration and failure to despair.

This book is not written for Mike. He probably can't read it. In a sense this book is not even written for Mike's parents. Most likely it is too late for them to intervene in the process that destroyed Mike's self-confidence. Mike himself will ultimately have to decide what he has to do to overcome his learning problems and straighten out his life.

The primary goal of this book is to provide you, the concerned parent, with the information that you will need to be able to participate intelligently in the process of determining how best to meet your child's special educational needs. The basic premise of the book is that your involvement in your child's education is preferable to noninvolvement. This premise is especially valid when, and if, you perceive that your child's learning problems are not being dealt with appropriately.

Another major goal of this book is to help you seek out, evaluate and effectively utilize the professional resources that exist in your child's school district and in your community. These professionals, be they teachers, school psychologists, learning disabilities specialists, principals or physicians, can be important allies guiding you through the labyrinth of choices and decisions you must make about your child's education. Their input can be invaluable. But their input can also be incomplete, inaccurate, contradictory or confusing. The second basic premise of this book is that the more you know about your child's learning problem, the easier it will be for you to evaluate your options and to make the critical educational decisions that can dramatically affect the course not only of your child's education but of his entire life.

In most cases, the child with a learning problem is not permanently disabled or irreparably damaged. If his learning deficiencies are properly diagnosed, they can probably be remediated. It is not uncommon for a child's reading scores to improve by two or more grade levels in one year if he receives quality remedial assistance. Even greater gains are possible. The degree of improvement will depend of course upon the severity of the child's learning disabilities, the effectiveness of the learning assistance program in which he is placed, the child's commitment and effort, and your commitment and support of your child and his teachers.

Each year hundreds of thousands of diagnosed learning disabled children learn how to overcome their academic problems because they receive meaningful remedial learning assistance in their schools or at private learning centers. Tragically, many other hundreds of thousands of diagnosed learning disabled children are not receiving meaningful help because no help is available, or the quality of the help that is available is poor. Equally tragic is the reality that many more hundreds of thousands of children with learning problems are not being diagnosed at all. These students represent a wasted and perhaps unrecoverable national resource. Their potential achievements and contributions may be lost to society forever. But of even greater importance is the personal loss of pride, self-esteem and accomplishment these students will experience because no one has provided them with the help they so desperately need.

CHAPTER ONE _____

The Failure Cycle

ELENA: RETENTION WASN'T THE ANSWER

A shy ten year-old girl with dark hair and an impish smile entered my office with her parents. My first impression of the girl was that she had a spinal deformity. Her shoulders and neck were hunched forward. Because she avoided looking directly at me, establishing eye contact with her was nearly impossible. I knew that it was going to be a difficult diagnostic evaluation, not only because of her shyness but also because her parents barely spoke English.

I knew enough Spanish to be able to communicate with the family, and I was able to piece together the girl's background. Her name was Elena, and she attended an inner city parochial school. The family spoke exclusively Spanish at home. Although the girl had been retained twice, she could still barely read! Her parents indicated that she had no significant medical or congenital problems. Elena had been retained in kindergarten, with her parents' approval, because she was not progressing. The school and her parents decided to retain her again for the same reason after she completed first grade. Elena was now ten years old and still in second grade. Embarrassed by her height and age, she had recently begun to bend her head and shoulders forward in an attempt to camouflage her height. At the tender age of ten, she had begun lying about how old she was.

The school suspected that Elena was retarded. Although her spoken English was perfect, Elena couldn't seem to learn to read. She was highly distractible and noncommunicative. She was not a behavior problem in class, but she exasperated her teachers because she was unable to keep up with the other students. Realizing that a third retention was out of the question, the school had referred Elena's family to our center.

At first, communicating with this withdrawn little girl was difficult. Soon though, she began to respond to my questions in a most distinctive way. In her shy manner, she would answer a question and then make a little joke or even a pun. As she described her day in school or her teachers or her friends, her wit became very apparent. There was no question that she was bright, perhaps even brilliant. It was also clear that she had a serious learning problem that was unrelated to the fact that the family spoke a foreign language at home.

When I finished testing Elena, I explained to her parents that she had some fairly common learning problems. Elena had difficulty seeing words accurately while she was reading. She also had difficulty remembering words that she had previously struggled to "sound out." Each time she saw a word — even if she had read it many times before, it was as if she were seeing that word for the first time. Because reading required continuous effort, I felt that unless Elena quickly received specialized learning assistance, she would soon give up trying and become totally demoralized in school. Unfortunately, this help was not available at her parochial school.

Although Elena's deficits were significant, they could be remediated. Her superior intelligence made the prognosis for correcting her learning disability excellent. With appropriate learning assistance and short-term physical therapy to correct her posture problems, there was little doubt in my mind that she would ultimately be able to function at her proper grade level with her head erect and her wit intact. But it was absolutely critical that she receive help before any more damage was done to her already fragile self-concept.

I wish I could report that the story had a happy ending. But I don't know if it did because I was unsuccessful in persuading Elena's parents to let us work with her at our learning disabilities center. When I finished explaining the results of my tests to Elena's parents, they told me that they wanted to discuss the matter privately and that they would call me and let me know if they wished to enroll their daughter in a specialized learning assistance program at our center. The call never came. I don't believe that the cost of the program was the deciding factor because I had carefully explained to Elena's parents that scholarship assistance was available. But I never learned why they decided not to let us work with their daughter.

When the parents left my office after the diagnostic evaluation and conference, I sensed that they would never return, and I felt like a physician must feel when a critically ill patient refuses treatment. I knew that if Elena were to be spared further emotional damage her parents would have to find help for her somewhere. Her learning problems would not "go away" of their own accord. Elena would fall further and further behind in school with devastating psychological consequences. Without learning assistance, this superior human being stood an excellent chance of being permanently scarred by a problem that was correctable. Elena's self-image had already been seriously damaged. This damage would soon be irreversible.

QUITTING VERSUS STRUGGLING

Imagine a real estate salesman who works in an office where everyone is selling houses — except him. Each day he goes to work and hopes to sell a house, but despite his efforts, nothing happens. Before long, he begins to experience self-doubt and feelings of insecurity. His enthusiasm disappears, and he dreads going to work. With increasing frequency, he arrives late at the office and finds excuses for leaving early. On the way home he stops for a drink, and in the morning he calls in sick. The prospect of facing another day of failure and rejection depresses him, and he finds himself feeling resentment toward the other more successful people in the office. The after-work drink becomes several after-work drinks. He starts losing his temper with his children over minor things, and he becomes gruff with his wife. They begin to argue more frequently. Each new day without success causes his self-confidence to erode further. Finally, he decides to find another job.

Having the option to quit is one of the "privileges" of being an adult. An unsuccessful real estate agent can decide to change jobs. A child is not given this choice. Legally, he is not permitted to quit school until he reaches sixteen. But the child can decide to give up and for the next ten years simply go through the motions of being educated.

Imagine now a child of five. On the first day of school he appears to be just like the other kindergarten children. Excited, apprehensive, perhaps a bit bewildered by it all, he arrives in the classroom that first day to begin the process of acquiring the educational tools that he will need to succeed in a complex, competitive world. During the next one hundred eighty days he will be taught to obey rules, follow instructions, and interact with other children. He will be taught how to cut and to trace and to draw and to color within the lines. He will learn to raise his hand when he has to go to the bathroom. He will learn to participate in a group and to make the transition from "fun time" to "work time." After a few months, he will be taught to recognize and to write some of the basic letters. Later, he will learn how to blend the sounds of letters to make simple words. The child will be on his way to mastering the most essential skill that is taught in elementary school. He will be learning to read!

Now imagine a child who is unable to follow this script. He has difficulty obeying the rules, following instructions and interacting with the other children. Overactive and easily distracted, he finds it impossible to keep up with the other children. He can't cut and trace and draw and color within the lines because his fingers don't seem to work right. Although he is shown the letters of the alphabet and is taught how to pronounce them, he can't seem to remember the names of the letters or the sounds that they make. The task of putting the sounds together to make simple words is overwhelming.

The child looks around at the other children in the class. They understand what the teacher wants them to do and they are able to do what she asks. Their drawings have fingers and ears and clothes, and the teacher likes their work. They are able to write their names on the line and they remember to put in all the letters and spell their names correctly. They also remember the words in the songs and they remember to raise their hands when they have a question or when they have to go to the bathroom. Unlike our hypothetical child, they can sit quietly in the circle without hitting other children or making noises. They can recognize the letters that the teacher holds up and they can remember the strange sounds that those letters make. The child knows there is something very wrong *with him*! He can't get it. He must be stupid.

Every day his stupidity is confirmed. Every new task is an agony. No matter how hard he tries, he is unable to learn what he is expected to the way other children do. He begins to act silly and to become disruptive. It's impossible for him to concentrate, so he disturbs the other children. The teacher doesn't know what to do and is totally exasperated. In desperation, she calls his parents in for a conference. Unable to explain precisely why the child cannot seem to learn, she describes him as immature. The parents are equally perplexed and exasperated. The teacher promises to submit the child's name to the school psychologist for possible testing and suggests the possibility of retention. Meanwhile, the child's self-concept sinks lower and lower.

The child learns to cope as best he can. He may become shy or act out. He may continue to try to learn. But most likely he'll simply give up and accept his limitations. He has begun the process of learning to be a failure. He knows already where he stands relative to the other children in his class. Although he might not be able or willing to express what his feelings are, he *knows* that he is stupid. No evidence has suggested any other conclusion. There are no positive strokes — no happy faces on his papers like those the other children get. He begins to hate school — and himself.

Despite all the turmoil he is experiencing, his parents and his teachers expect him to continue working, trying and behaving. He is not permitted to express his frustration or to express his anger. To do so would disrupt the class. He is expected to show up in school each day and to learn, or at least go through the motions of learning. If the child is unwilling to conform to this script, he will become a behavior problem. If he is willing to conform, he has no alternative but to turn his anger and frustration inward where it will seethe and fester. Unless there is meaningful intervention, the child will be required to suffer through this process for ten years. Naively, his teachers and parents continue to hope that he will somehow magically emerge at the end of the educational production line emotionally and educationally intact.

8

Unlike the real estate agent, a child is not permitted to start coming to school late. Nor can he call in sick when he's really not sick. Mommy may be fooled a couple of times by tummyaches, but she quickly learns when he's faking. Not getting ready for school on time doesn't work either. Everybody gets angry, and he will still have to go to school anyway. Losing his temper with his mother or father is a sure guarantee of punishment — possibly a spanking. Although he may want to quit, he cannot — at least not until he reaches sixteen. Having no other option, the child arrives at school each morning and begins to build a wall around himself to protect himself from the pain. Even if the decision is made to retain him, ultimately he will be promoted to the next grade and the next, despite the fact that he doesn't have the necessary skills.

There are few safety valves for such a child. The basic choices are: to give up, to act out, to daydream, to stop trying, to withdraw. The child resigns himself to seven hours a day of frustration and learns to cope as best he can. Even though he is only six years old, doors to potential careers and professions are already beginning to close against him. The process of reducing his potential earning capacity by as much as 75% has begun. The subsequent course of the child's life is already being determined. To insulate himself from feeling inadequate, the child develops a complex system of coping compensatory mechanisms and rationalizations, which his parents and teachers see only as irresponsibility, unreliability, laziness and immaturity.

Although on the surface it may appear that the child has no options, in fact, he does. He may not be permitted to quit, but he can — and probably will — give up. He may not be permitted to scream, "I've had it. I'm not going back to that school anymore!" But he can begin to devise a system of behaviors which will help him to cope with the frustration and failure that he is forced to experience each day. The child may choose to become shy or disruptive. Or he may choose to become a clown or a bully. If he is clever he may realize that he has other talents which he can use to compensate for his learning deficiencies. He may discover that he has charm or athletic ability. Or he may discover that he is funny or entertaining or that he is good at working with his hands or fists. If he is fortunate, the compensations he chooses will help him survive emotionally. If he is unfortunate, they will only magnify his deficits.

By the time the learning disabled child becomes a teenager, whatever coping system he has developed will be operating at full throttle. His defenses against feeling inadequate will be all but impregnable. By now his personality will be formed, and his sense of self will have been defined by his experiences. If the experiences have been repeatedly negative, it should come as no surprise that the teenager's sense of self is also negative. Although that sense of self *can* be redefined, the process is arduous and tentative. Usually the only thing that will motivate a teenager or young adult to begin that process is a feeling of desperation and hopelessness.

Parents of a learning disabled teenager must resign themselves to the fact that they cannot force their child to "work on himself." The most they can do at this stage of their child's life is to support and encourage their teenager to reach out for help and avail himself of any resources that may exist in the community. These resources would include private tutoring, counseling, the church, or the local community college.[1]

FAILURE IS HABIT-FORMING

Children learn to fail in much the same way that they learn to read—through practice and experience. Failing can become habit-forming. When children are forced by circumstances beyond their control to fail repeatedly, they begin to anticipate, accept, and to accommodate themselves to failure. It doesn't take long before they lose their ability to envision even the possibility that they might succeed. Subjected to demands they cannot meet, and feelings of hopelessness and inadequacy, these children can find refuge in perceiving themselves as failures. Once they become habituated to failing, they may be reluctant to change their script. Because they perceive themselves as failures, children may actually experience distress at the prospect of succeeding. Failure-oriented children will often consciously or unconsciously structure their own failures. For instance, they may choose not to complete assignments or to hand them in. Through repeated experience they learn to accept and to expect a losing role for themselves. Even though this role causes them to suffer emotionally, being a failure does provide them at least with a sense of identity. This identity can dictate the course of their entire lives.

CONFLICTING RECOMMENDATIONS

Watching your child suffer in school is an excruciatingly painful experience. You may sense intuitively that your child is not learning properly. You may know that something urgently needs to be done to help, but you may feel powerless. Perhaps you have hesitated to become involved because you feel that you lack the expertise to know precisely what it is that needs to be done. Your confusion may be compounded by the sometimes conflicting information and recommendations that you receive from teachers, friends, pediatricians and/or psychologists. You may feel like the

---

1. See Chapter 7: "Dealing With Learning Disabled Teenagers"

person who knows nothing about cars and is told by one mechanic that his engine needs an overhaul and by another that all he needs is a new carburetor. Whom do you trust? If you are like most parents of learning disabled children, you will probably be forced to rely on your child's teacher or the school psychologist to suggest the appropriate course of action for correcting the learning disability. Sometimes the proper strategy is very obvious and all of the professionals involved are in agreement. Unfortunately, such a consensus does not always occur. It is when the appropriate course of action is not clear or when the remedial strategy is not working that parents are most likely to become overwhelmed with feelings of hopelessness and helplessness. Discouraged and confused, parents often put up defenses to keep from having to confront and deal with their child's learning problem.

PARENTS' RATIONALES AND RATIONALIZATIONS

Twelve years of clinical experience with thousands of learning disabled children have convinced me that providing help for these children requires commitments from everyone involved in and affected by the learning problem. It requires a commitment from the parents to seek help for their child either within or outside the public school system. It also requires that the parents make a commitment to support the child and his teacher while the help is being provided.

The child himself must also make a commitment to the remediation process, for, in the final analysis, it is the child who must solve his problem and who must persevere even when quitting seems very appealing.

Finally, the remedial process requires a commitment from those offering the help to provide the most effective learning assistance program that they possibly can. Unfortunately, these four essential commitments are not always made.

During these years as a clinical learning disabilities specialist, I have heard many rationales and rationalizations from parents who are resisting making the commitment to confronting and resolving their child's learning problem. Some of the most common of these are:

Laziness:	There's nothing really wrong with my child. He's just lazy.
School's Responsibility:	I pay taxes for education. The school should take care of my child's problems.
I Suspected a Problem:	I knew there was something wrong back in first grade. The school assured me that there was no problem and told me not to worry.

Immaturity:	The teacher said my child was just immature and that if we had him repeat first grade everything would be okay.
Confusion:	We didn't know what to do. So we didn't do anything.
I Made It!	I had the same problem in school, and I'm okay. (This comment usually comes from fathers.)
Patience:	He'll outgrow it.
Inconvenience:	It's too far to drive to the learning center.
Cost:	Private learning assistance is too expensive. (Please note: private assistance may not be necessary!)
Discipline:	My husband (or wife) thinks it's a behavior problem and that we're not strict enough.

As a learning disabilities specialist, I am, of course, committed to the process of providing quality remedial assistance to children with learning problems. I have, with great reluctance, resigned myself to accept these rationalizations. Over the years, I have come to recognize that it is virtually impossible to help a child unless his parents give their complete support to the child and to those providing the learning assistance. If the parents themselves are unconvinced or skeptical, or simply not committed, they will invariably communicate these feelings to the child. The child in turn will become skeptical, and he will probably resist the remedial process. The parents' negative expectations become self-fulfilling. Typically, such parents will choose to withdraw their child from the remedial program before he has made any meaningful gains. In the end, the child has experienced one more defeat. As a professional, I realize that all I can do is tell the parents what I see and what I feel should be done, and then I must let them make their decision. But the rationalizations *do* require a response.

Laziness:	Children are *not* lazy by nature. Laziness is a learned behavior and is most likely a defense mechanism. By not trying, children delude themselves into believing that they haven't really failed.
School's Responsibility:	Yes, the school *should* take care of your child's learning problems. Unfortunately, sometimes it doesn't. And you still have to pay your taxes even though your child is not being helped properly.

I Suspected a Problem: When your intuition tells you that your first grader is not learning or is struggling, *trust* your intuition. Ask penetrating questions and demand penetrating answers from the educators in your child's school.

Immaturity: Very few children are truly physiologically immature. Teachers often use the term to describe a problem which they cannot identify. Request a more specific assessment of your child's learning deficits.

Confusion: If you don't know what to do, seek advice. Ask your pediatrician. Talk to other parents whose children have the same problem. If there's a university in your town or city, speak with someone in the education department. Ask for a referral. Perhaps there is a learning disability lab connected with the university. As a last resort, look in the phone book.

I Made It! *You* may be okay and may have successfully survived your own learning problems, but *you* are not your child. There is no guarantee that he'll survive the experience as well as you did. Without help, your child may become psychologically crippled by his learning problems.

Patience: Children do not generally "outgrow" learning problems. They do outgrow school, however, and ultimately leave. Children *also* outgrow acne, but if the problem is not treated they can become severely scarred in the process of "outgrowing" it. Learning problems, if not treated, can also scar a child severely and can totally warp his perception of himself.

Inconvenience: Yes, it may be a long drive to a learning disabilities center, but six years from now it may be an even longer drive to a psychiatrist's office or to juvenile court. If your child does require learning assistance and if this assistance is not available in his public school, private tutoring may be your only recourse.

13

Providing remedial help for your child is like taking out an insurance policy. It could prove to be one of the wisest investments you could possibly make in your child's future. To survive in a competitive world, your child will require certain basic academic skills. He will have to know how to read, write and do math at a minimum eighth grade level. Such skills will unquestionably be a requisite to a satisfying, well-paying job. The requirements for college admissions of course will be much higher. Although there is no guarantee that special help will totally eliminate your child's learning difficulties, the alternative is to do nothing and hope that the problems will magically disappear. They probably won't.

Cost: At issue is a family's priorities. If the program available to your child in his public school is inadequate, you must decide the extent of your commitment to resolving the problem.

Discipline: Discipline is healthy for a child. It can build character. But discipline alone will *not* correct a learning problem.

CHILDREN'S RATIONALES AND RATIONALIZATIONS

Many children with learning problems also have rationalizations for why they don't want remedial help. Obviously, most kids can find lots of things that they would rather do than study or work on their spelling or reading or math. If they have a long history of learning problems, having to work hard at resolving them may be the last thing they want to do. Ironically, once these children begin to experience academic success at school their resistance often disappears.

Children of all ages tend to be myopic. I am not referring to actual near-sightedness, but rather to the child's inability to recognize the consequences of the choices he is making about his life. When anyone, be it an adult or a child, is too close to a problem, he tends to lose perspective. Children often feel that the easiest solution to a problem is to pretend that the problem doesn't exist or will somehow disappear. Until the child matures and develops perspective, he must rely on his parents to guide him into making choices which are in his best interests.

Most children, for example, would choose not to go to the doctor for an injection even if they were sick and needed one to get better. During the formative years, parents must make such important decisions and choices for their children. Sometimes these decisions will make a child temporarily unhappy, and although most parents do not want to make their child unhappy, sometimes they must. Although a child may cry because he is being punished for playing with matches, were his parents not to punish the child for fear of making him cry, they would be remiss in fulfilling their responsibility as parents. Any temporary upset that the child experiences must be weighed against the potential tragedy that could occur if the child does not learn how dangerous playing with matches can be. Similarly, a child's temporary resistance to learning assistance must be weighed against the potential damage to his life and self-esteem if he is allowed to forego such assistance.

PROFESSIONAL RATIONALES AND RATIONALIZATIONS

Teachers and school districts also have explanations for why it is difficult or impossible for them to provide for certain children's special learning needs. With justification, many teachers contend that they are overwhelmed with too many children in their classroom and too many responsibilities. Many classroom teachers will frankly admit that they lack the specialized skills to provide for the special needs of the learning disabled child. Other teachers will point out that essential learning assistance programs have been eliminated because of cuts in school budgets. Some teachers will even be honest enough to admit that they are simply burned out after too many years of teaching. The quality of their teaching and the intensity of their commitment to the educational process will most likely reflect their diminished energy level.

Most teachers are vitally concerned about the learning disabled child. And most teachers are acutely aware of the disastrous emotional implications of an unresolved learning disability. The typical classroom teacher has approximately thirty children in his or her class. Theoretically, each child should demand no more than three to four percent of the teacher's time and energy. A child who may require twelve percent of the teacher's time creates an impossible situation in the classroom. Were the teacher to give that child twelve percent of his or her time, he or she would be doing a disservice to the other children. The most obvious solution to this dilemma is to provide quality specialized learning assistance programs for *all* children who need them. Seldom are such programs available, however, for all of the children who need them.

15

TO INTERVENE OR NOT TO INTERVENE

Once you become convinced that your child requires learning assistance you may be faced with an important decision. If learning assistance is not available, you must decide whether or not you want to become actively involved in getting help for your child.

For many parents, the prospect of becoming involved in their children's education is frightening. They may lack confidence in their own intuition about their child's educational needs because they are not professional educators. Other parents may experience anxiety because they remember from their own childhood being intimidated by authority figures such as teachers and principals. They may feel that they have no right to meddle, or they may conclude that the teacher or the school psychologist, by virtue of professional training and education, knows what is best for their child.

As someone who has dealt with hundreds of teachers, school psychologists and principals, I can attest that despite their good intentions, their training and their education, some of these professionals may not know what your child's educational needs are. Others may be able to identify those needs but may not have the resources to meet them. In some instances, the diagnostic capabilities of a school district may be superior to its remediation capabilities. In other instances, the converse may be true.

In this age of budgetary cutbacks, it is not uncommon for learning assistance programs to be filled with children who have serious learning problems. There may not be room for the child with less severe learning disabilities. It is also possible that the program your child requires simply does not exist in your particular school district.

Quite often "uneducated, " untrained parents trusting their intuition have a far better sense of their child's educational needs than the professional does. Intuition is perhaps one of the highest forms of human intelligence. It represents the distillation of all of your life experiences. As you acquire more information about learning disabilities, the accuracy and reliability of your intuition will increase.

Intuitively you will know whether your child's educational needs are being met. This same intuition will tell you whether or not retention is a viable solution to your child's learning problems. Your intuition will also help you to decide if your child needs to be given an extensive diagnostic work-up and if your child needs to be placed in a specialized program. Having access to objective information about your child's level of academic performance is, of course, an essential component in the decision-making process. Although the recommendations of professionals are essential, it is you, the parents, who must decide what is best for your child.

The following checklist is designed to help you determine whether or not to intervene in your child's education.

PARENTAL INVOLVEMENT CHECKLIST [2]

	YES	NO
Do you feel that your child may have a learning problem?	☐	☐
Do you feel that your child's learning deficits have been accurately identified by his/her school?	☐	☐
Do you feel that adequate diagnostic testing has been administered?	☐	☐
If your child has been tested, do you feel that you fully understand the results of the tests?	☐	☐
Do you feel that your child requires further testing?	☐	☐
Is your child receiving special learning assistance for any learning problems which have been identified?	☐	☐
Is your child responding positively to this assistance?	☐	☐

A pattern of "No" answers on this inventory is indicative of a potential educational problem which may require your involvement. If you suspect that your child's educational needs are not being met, then you must decide whether or not you want to become involved in your child's education, and if so, the degree to which you want to be involved in resolving his learning problem.

Logic would dictate that if your child is struggling in school, he should be tested immediately so that his problems can be identified and remediated before he falls seriously behind in school. Unfortunately, this logical procedure is not always followed. There may be too many children waiting to be tested and too few school psychologists to test them. Or there may be too many children in the district who need special help and too few places available in the special programs.

2. Copies for your individual use of the checklists included throughout this book are available from: Humanics Limited, P.O. Box 7447, Atlanta, Ga. 30309. (404) 874-2176. Please write or call for ordering information.

If your child's school does not voluntarily recommend testing, it may be necessary for you to request that he be tested. If this request is denied, or if you determine that quality remedial assistance is not available even if a problem is identified, then you must decide whether to pursue the matter further. To do so could result in an unpleasant confrontation with the school. If you choose not to confront the school administration, your options are: 1) to do nothing and hope that your child's learning problems correct themselves; or 2) to look outside the district for private learning assistance. The choices you make can affect your child's entire future. It is important that you realize that if you decide to do nothing, you are still making a choice for which you must assume responsibility.

Diagnosis: The First Step to Remediation

JOSH: A MANAGEABLE TORNADO

Josh zoomed around the classroom knocking over chairs and pulling things out of drawers. The other five year-olds stared at him wide-eyed with perplexed looks on their faces.

When the principal called Josh's mother and asked her to pick up her son, he explained that the boy was out of control and was disturbing the other children. Both he and the kindergarten teacher felt that Josh was not yet ready for kindergarten.

With reluctance, Josh's mother agreed that perhaps her son did need more time to mature. She consented to keep him home for another year.

The following September Josh's mother once again escorted him to his assigned classroom. And once again, she received a call from the principal. He informed her that Josh's behavior apparently had not improved and that he was still out of control. He suggested that Josh be held out of kindergarten for another year. Although Josh's mother strongly objected, the principal was adamant. He would not permit the child to attend.

Determined to find a school for her son, the woman began visiting other schools in the district. She did not deny that Josh was hyperactive, but she felt that despite this problem the school district was responsible for educating her son. If the local school would not agree to provide this education, she would find another school in the district that would.

Each time that Josh's mother did find a school which was willing to accept her child, she would invariably receive a call from the principal informing her that upon further consideration, the school had decided her son could not be admitted into the kindergarten program. It was clear that the principal of Josh's original school was advising the other principals in the district not to accept Josh into their kindergarten program.

In desperation, the woman began to visit schools in other districts. When she found a strong kindergarten teacher or a program that was highly structured, she would request an interdistrict transfer. Invariably, the request would be denied by her own district.

After months of frustration, the woman discovered a remarkable teacher who taught in a school that was a considerable distance from her home. Despite being forewarned by the mother about Josh's hyperactivity, the teacher agreed to have the boy in her class. Josh's mother then inform-ed her local school district that if they attempted to block the transfer in any way she would consult an attorney. The transfer was approved.

The kindergarten teacher at Josh's new school employed a novel technique for helping Josh to control his hyperactivity. She taught this "un-manageable" seven year-old Yoga. When Josh sensed that he was becom-ing excited, he was sent to a certain spot in the classroom where he could sit down unobtrusively, assume the traditional Yoga position and quietly chant his own personal mantra until he calmed himself down.

The teacher also worked out a system of private signals with Josh. If Josh was unaware that he was becoming hyperactive, she would alert him with a signal. This signal told Josh that it was time to get himself under con-trol. A second signal would indicate that he was to go to his special "spot." The system worked perfectly. The teacher taught Josh to take responsibili-ty for his hyperactivity. Once Josh learned how to control himself, he could begin the process of acquiring an education.

RECOGNIZING AND INTERPRETING THE SYMPTOMS

The proper identification of a learning problem is the essential first step in the remediation process. But it is only a first step. The data obtained from testing and from subjective observations must then be interpreted properly if the identification process is to have prescriptive value.

Although the principal of Josh's local school had accurately identified Josh's problem, his proposed "solution" to the problem was to do nothing. By insisting that Josh be held out of school, the principal was choosing not to deal with Josh's hyperactivity.

Contrary to the principal's conclusion, hyperactivity is not the result of immaturity, and the problem is seldom solved by simply giving the child time to "outgrow" it. Hyperactivity is a physiological phenomenon which is characterized by excessive firing of the motor neurons. Although the causes of hyperactivity are not totally understood, the condition can be controlled in numerous ways. Behavior modification, perceptual-motor training, disciplined athletic training, Yoga or meditation, special diets and medication are methods which have proven effective in helping children overcome the often educationally devastating effects of hyperactivity.

Holding a child out of school until he "matures" does not cure hyperactivity. Although many children do indeed outgrow their hyperac-tivity after they reach adolescence, it is clear that hyperactive children must be educated while they are waiting to "outgrow" their problem.

Fortunately, the response of Josh's school district to his problem is not typical of the way in which most school districts handle the hyperactive child. Unfortunately, the widespread use of the term "immature" *is* typical. Far too many learning disabled children are so labelled simply because no one has bothered to test them in order to identify their precise learning deficits.

Relatively few children are actually physiologically immature. When the term "immaturity" is used by teachers or administrators to describe atypical or hard to define behaviors, the term offers little insight into the actual causes of a child's learning difficulties.

Diagnosed as unmanageable, Josh was capable of learning once he was placed in the appropriate learning context. Like many hyperactive and learning disabled children, Josh required a highly structured program, a strong and creative teacher, and a well-conceived teaching and behavior modification strategy that would help him take responsibility for his own hyperactivity.

It was fortunate for Josh that his mother was a determined lady. Had she not been, Josh might not have entered school until he was eight years old. The psychological and emotional implications of such a course of action might have proven disastrous.

LEARNING VERSUS NON-LEARNING

Nature has genetically programmed a compelling need to learn into its most complex creation — the human species. Children in particular are consumed by this need to understand how they and the world around them "work."

A four month-old infant, for example, will gaze with rapt attention at his hand as he moves his fingers. Staring at his fingers as they open and close, the child begins to realize that he is the one who is controlling his hand. This realization will have a profound impact upon the child's evolving appreciation of the process of cause and effect. Understanding this process is the cornerstone of all knowledge.

As a newborn, the infant quickly learns that when he cries, he will be fed, or cuddled or changed. The child slowly begins to recognize that he has the power to influence and affect his environment. With this newly discovered power, the child realizes that he can begin to assume more and more control of his life.

The infant also learns that the more he understands about his world, the more power he has to do and get what he wants. Everything the infant touches or puts into his mouth helps him to learn to identify, distinguish and remember the objects and the experiences which make up his environment.

When the infant turns over and begins to crawl, he discovers that he can expand his world by simply moving from where he is to where he isn't. As he crawls from one place to another, he learns to judge the distance between points and he learns how long it takes to get from point A to point B. In this way, the infant learns to integrate concepts of time and space which are essential building blocks for learning.

As the child becomes increasingly more mobile, he realizes that although his mother remains the center of his universe, there is a new and exciting world out there waiting to be explored. His sensory systems are assaulted by countless new objects that need to be examined and countless nooks and crannies that need to be investigated. Like a computer, the child voraciously consumes and stores the new information that he discovers about his world.

Compelled to learn by the nature of the species to which he belongs, the child continually attempts to expand the boundaries of his understanding. He learns how to use his fingers to open a drawer or to lift the lid on a pot. Enthralled with wonder and curiosity, the child's brain absorbs this new data and cross-references it with previously stored information. With rapture, the child discovers that all he has to do is open the door to the cabinet under the sink, and a whole new universe of potential experiences unfolds before his eyes!

When a child fails to develop the desire or the capacity to learn, it is safe to assume that there is something profoundly amiss either within the child or his environment. It is also safe to assume there is something profoundly amiss when a child enters school with the desire to learn and loses this desire in kindergarten or first grade. Unless there is intervention, this unnatural lack of a desire to learn may evolve into a profound aversion to learning with disastrous educational, social, vocational and psychological consequences.

The equation that produces a child who is academically successful consists of five major elements: intelligence, stimulation, attitude, academic skills and parental encouragement. Deficient learning may result from the absence of or deficiency in any of these elements.

If a child is exposed to good teaching and if it appears that he is not learning properly, the child most likely has some type of learning problem. Although the definition of what constitutes "proper" learning will vary, there are certain generally accepted norms for learning achievement. These norms are defined by individual teachers, professors of education in teacher training programs, school districts, state departments of education, publishers of textbooks and publishers of standardized tests.[1]

1. See the Testing Appendix.

22

A fourth grade teacher who expects his or her students to be able to solve a three place multiplication problem is basing that expectation on his or her own experience as a teacher and on the collective experience of other teachers who have contributed to the curriculum of the school and who have written the textbooks that are used in the school. If the teacher is capable of teaching the subject matter adequately, a child who is unable to master the material that is presented might reasonably be considered to have a learning problem.

Each element in the learning equation can be affected by a wide range of emotional and environmental factors. Psychological or family problems, peer pressures, language difficulties, puberty and the frequent changing of schools are but a few of the factors that can negatively influence a child's ability or desire to learn. Any of these factors can cause a learning disability.

REBECCA: A VICTIM OF NEGLECT

When Rebecca finally did make it to the center for diagnostic evaluation, she appeared to be very pleasant fourteen year-old with a keen sense of humor and a warm and friendly personality. She had missed her first appointment with me because she had gotten angry with her parents the night before we were supposed to meet and had run away.

The daughter of a dentist, Rebecca had a long history of learning disabilities. Her parents had become so disillusioned with her progress in school that they had decided to take her out of school and hire a private tutor to educate her. The strategy had proven unsuccessful, and Rebecca, who should have been in the eighth grade, was functioning at a beginning fourth grade level in most academic areas.

Rebecca's father explained that Rebecca had been mistreated by his ex-wife, whom he had divorced one year after Rebecca's birth and to whom the court had awarded Rebecca's custody. The mistreatment consisted of neglect rather than physical abuse. Rebecca was left for days on end in her crib without being changed or acknowledged in any way. During this time she received virtually no stimulation. Restricted to her crib, the child was not permitted to crawl and explore her world. The court finally granted custody of Rebecca to her father and she went to live with him and his second wife shortly after her second birthday.

It was not difficult to understand why Rebecca was struggling academically, given the sensory deprivation she experienced as a child. She had been denied attention and stimulation during a critically important time in her life, and I suspected that her emotional scars were profound. Rebecca's learning problems were serious, but I was convinced that they could be remediated with proper treatment.

Despite the lack of stimulation and attention during the first two years of her life, and despite the developmental and emotional consequences of the sensory deprivation she'd suffered, Rebecca appeared to be remarkably intact both emotionally and intellectually.

Of far greater concern to me was the relationship that had developed between Rebecca and her father and stepmother. Her parents had unfortunately fallen into the habit of nagging Rebecca about her studies and certain other behaviors which they considered to be irresponsible. Rebecca had responded by blocking out this criticism and by becoming even more irresponsible.

The situation had reached a crisis point. Understandably, Rebecca had developed a strong aversion to anything academic. Unless she was given intensive learning assistance and unless her parents refrained from continually expressing displeasure, Rebecca, in my opinion, might run away for good and disappear into the back streets of San Francisco or Los Angeles.

During our first session I succeeded in getting Rebecca to express to her father how she felt when he "put her down." At first she refused to acknowledge that she was angry, but after a few minutes of gentle prodding Rebecca finally managed to tell her parents with tears in her eyes how their continual criticism made her feel inside.

Fortunately, Rebecca's parents were honest enough to admit that they needed help in learning how to express their feelings to their daughter in a nonderogatory way. They agreed to seek counseling, and Rebecca agreed to come to the center two days a week for learning therapy and tutoring.

It was clear that if Rebecca were to prevail over her learning problems and her family problems, she would have to make a commitment to both the remediation and the counseling process. Because I wasn't convinced that Rebecca was emotionally capable of making even a partial commitment to a learning assistance program, I insisted that family counseling be the first priority. Rebecca's anger and resistance would have to be defused, and the family would have to learn how to communicate without pressing each other's "hot buttons" before any significant academic improvement could occur.

DETERMINING YOUR CHILD'S LEVEL OF LEARNING

A child's level of learning is generally determined by three criteria: standardized tests such as the Stanford Achievement Test, teacher-designed tests and assignments, and the subjective impressions of teachers.

When a child scores below the norm on standardized tests and when his grades and performance in class are poor, there is sufficient justification for teachers to recommend, or for parents to request, a diagnostic evaluation to determine if there is an underlying problem.

Standardized tests are tests which are administered to large numbers of students throughout the country. The purpose of the tests is to determine a child's level of achievement relative to other children of his age and grade level. [2]

By statistically comparing a child's performance on a standardized test with the performance of other children who have taken the same test, achievement norms are established. The process of establishing these norms is called standardization.

FACSIMILE TEST RESULT REPORT

	Raw Score	Stanine	Percentile	Grade Equiv.
Reading Comprehension	27	4	46°	3.7
Vocabulary	29	4	47°	3.8

The facsimile test result report presented above records a hypothetical fourth grader's scores on a standardized reading test. The child's raw score (27 in reading comprehension and 29 in vocabulary) represents the total number of his correct answers on the test. The stanine score (4) is a statistical representation of this score on a scale of 1 to 9. It indicates the child's performance relative to the other hundreds of thousands of children who took the exam.

The percentile score in reading comprehension (46°) is another way of statistically ranking the child relative to the other children taking the test. In this hypothetical case, out of every one hundred children who took the exam, this child scored higher than forty-five children and lower than fifty-three children. (The 99° is the highest score one can receive). Assuming that the fourth grader took the standardized exam in the beginning of the month of October (the second month of fourth grade), his raw score of 27 in reading statistically yields a grade equivalency score of 3.7 (third grade seventh month). Because the child is in the second month of fourth grade, he should be testing at this level to be considered reading at grade level. His raw score, however, indicates a grade equivalency that is five months below grade level [4.2 (grade level) – 3.7 (child's level) = 5 months below grade level].

2.   See Glossary of Testing Terms for definitions of the terms used in this section. Also, see the Testing Appendix for a description of many of the diagnostic and achievement tests which are commonly administered to children in the United States today.

In the case of teacher-designed tests, assignments and projects, the performance criteria for determining a child's level of achievement are more subjective and lack the statistical objectivity of standardized tests. This lack of statistical objectivity, however, does not detract from the validity of the teacher's more subjective performance criteria. Ideally, a teacher's projects and test questions are carefully selected and are designed to assess accurately the child's mastery of the material that has been taught.

When developing a curriculum and lesson plans, most teachers have a certain degree of latitude in choosing their academic priorities. A particular teacher may choose to emphasize writing and language arts skills, for example, while another teacher, who teaches the same grade level, may feel that reading comprehension, handwriting and spelling are the priorities. A teacher's priorities will be based upon his or her own teaching philosophy and upon the particular needs and skills of the students. At the same time, the teacher is responsible for covering all material designated in the school district's curriculum. The criteria that a teacher uses to evaluate his or her students' performance will reflect that teacher's academic priorities and academic objectives.

When a child is unable to achieve these objectives, his performance will be perceived by the teacher as deficient. The child's grades will reflect this perception.

Unless they have concrete evidence to the contrary, parents must assume that the teacher's criteria for evaluating their child are fair and valid. When a child is doing poorly in class and is having difficulty fulfilling the teacher's performance criteria, his parents must also assume that the child's difficulties reflect his own learning deficiencies and not the teacher's teaching deficiencies. This assumption, however, may not always be correct. The child may not be learning effectively because the teacher is not teaching effectively.

The child who does not learn with proficiency is generally considered to have a learning problem. When used as an all-encompassing generic description, the term "learning problem," like the term "immature," has limited diagnostic and prescriptive value. If meaningful remediation of the "learning problem" is to occur, a more precise identification of the child's specific learning deficits is essential.

THE CAUSES OF LEARNING DISABILITIES

A child's learning disability may result from one or several causes. The most common sources of a learning problem are:

1. Low aptitude or intelligence
2. Emotional problems
3. Poor teaching
4. Neurological disorders (brain damage)
5. Sensory impairment (for example: a hearing or vision loss)
6. Perceptual dysfunction (for example: poor visual memory)
7. Language deficiencies (for example: English is not the native language)
8. Language disorders (for example: speech impediments or difficulty with oral expression)
9. Cultural or environmental influences (for example: academic achievement is not reinforced by the family or subculture)

As we examine the different types and sources of learning problems, let me re-emphasize that this book is a parent's handbook. The book is *not* intended to be a learning disabilities textbook. Teachers and other professionals who are interested in a more in-depth treatment of the symptomatology of learning disabilities are directed to the many excellent textbooks which are available at most university bookstores.

PHILIP: AN ADULT LIVING UNDER A CLOUD OF FEAR

It was apparent that the man entering my office had little self-confidence. He appeared depressed and very self-conscious. As his story unfolded I could well appreciate his distress.

Philip was a mechanic who worked in a medium-sized plant. He had worked there for seven years and had been promoted several times during that period. His boss had indicated that he was pleased with Philip's work and that he wanted to promote him to assistant foreman. The promotion, however, would require that Philip pass a written exam. Unfortunately, Philip could barely read.

None of Philip's previous promotions had involved a written exam. He had worked his way up through the ranks because he had impressed his employers with both his conscientiousness and his knowledge of machines. When a machine broke, it was Philip who would invariably coax the machine back to life.

Philip explained that he had had learning problems for as long as he could remember. In elementary school, his second grade teacher had given him comic books to look at in the cloakroom while the other children read books and did their spelling and math. He simply could not read, and the teachers and the other students were convinced that he was mentally defective. Philip himself soon began to believe that he was too.

As an adult, Philip was totally dependent on his wife to read everything for him from a tax return to a prescription bottle. Whenever he went somewhere with his son he constantly dreaded having to read something and being embarrassed. Little League forms couldn't be completed on the playing field. He had to take them home for his wife to complete.

Philip's employers were unaware that he could barely read. They simply assumed that he could read because he could "read" schematic diagrams and was intuitively competent when he worked with machines. His fear of being embarrassed in front of his son was compounded by his fear of being "found out" by his employers. Not only was Philip convinced that he would be unable to pass the exam for promotion, he was also convinced that if he were ever dismissed from his job he would have to start over at the bottom of the ladder, assuming he would be able to find another job at all.

After chatting with Philip for thirty minutes, I realized that he was highly intelligent and perhaps even brilliant. The man could type one hundred words per minute with almost perfect accuracy. But Philip had no idea what he was typing. Because he could not read, he would type words exactly as they appeared. If a word were misspelled, Philip would type the word misspelled.

Although Phillip had profound perceptual problems, he had a remarkable mechanical aptitude. When shown a picture of twenty gears that were attached to each other, with the direction in which the drive gear was moving indicated, he could immediately tell you in which direction gear number twenty was moving.

My tests confirmed that Philip had severe learning problems. He was dyslexic [3] and had extreme difficulty with visual discrimination (seeing the difference between letters). His visual tracking (seeing words and letters accurately and sequentially) and visual memory (identifying words from memory) were very poor. Paradoxically, Philip's visual discrimination, visual tracking and visual memory skills were all highly developed when it came to operations involving machinery.

Had I uncovered the same learning disabilities profile in a child, I would have recommended an intensive program of perceptual activities and exercises that would have stressed visual decoding skills. Although I felt that Philip could still be helped to compensate for his perceptual pro-

3. Dyslexia is a fairly antiquated term. It generally refers to inaccurate reading characterized by letter reversals and word reversals ("saw" is perceived as "was"). (See Glossary of Educational Terms.)

cessing deficits, it saddened me to realize that had I had an opportunity to work with him when he was a child, I probably could have spared him much of the pain and despair he had experienced during the last twenty years.

I assigned Philip to a marvelously talented young woman who had just completed graduate school. She and Philip worked together for approximately eight weeks and were making good headway when Philip's wife called and told us that her husband had decided to discontinue the therapy. I later discovered that orders at the plant at which he worked had decreased significantly, and Philip had been laid off. His nightmare had become a reality.

INTELLIGENCE AND APTITUDE

Intelligence: the capacity to learn from experience and the capacity to use the knowledge gained to solve problems and to understand and retain information.

Aptitude: a specific ability, capacity or talent, or a specialized facility to learn or understand a particular skill.

Almost everything we do of a voluntary nature requires intelligence, from making a bed to solving a problem in long division to writing a symphony. Most human beings have the necessary intelligence to make a bed. Very few, however, are capable of writing a symphony.

The spectrum of skills that human beings are capable of performing is awesome. The spectrum ranges from pouring a glass of milk to designing a computer chip the size of a pinhead that can store a seemingly infinite amount of information.

Many of the functions of which we are capable and which we take for granted actually demand a degree of intelligence beyond the reach of any other species. Although typing or driving a car are fairly basic skills, these activities require coordination, spatial judgment, analytical thinking skills, memory skills and visual discrimination skills. Without average intelligence, a person would not be able to perform these tasks competently.

The complexity of any task or endeavor will determine the degree of intelligence required to perform it. Generally, the more complex the task and the more variables involved in performing it, the greater the intelligence necessary to master it.

Learning is a sequential experience. When we learn, we add on to what we already know and understand in order to be able to perform more demanding and complicated tasks. A person who wants to play tennis well or to knit a sweater which involves complex stitches must first learn the basics of tennis or knitting. As people learn, they inevitably make mistakes. The capacity to learn from these mistakes is an essential characteristic of intelligence. The more intelligent the person, the less likely he or she is to repeat the same mistake.

There is a distinct difference between general intelligence and aptitude, or specialized intelligence. For example, a person who is good at taking engines apart and putting them back together may be considered to have a good mechanical aptitude. This same person with obviously good mechanical aptitude may or may not have a high degree of general intelligence.

Some people have both a high degree of specialized intelligence and a high degree of general intelligence. The person who is capable of designing a computer program or of solving a problem in accounting will probably have both types of intelligence. A person may also be highly intelligent and lack specific aptitude. There are many highly intelligent people who are capable of writing a brilliant novel but who may not have the specialized mechanical aptitude required to repair a lawnmower engine. And the person who can solve a complicated problem in physics may not have the artistic aptitude to plan and paint a mural, or the language aptitude to master a foreign language.

MEASURING INTELLIGENCE AND APTITUDE

I.Q. (or intelligence quotient) tests were designed to predict academic success. Theoretically, the higher a child's I.Q. score, the better his chances of doing superior work in school. The test is intended to measure a child's potential; unfortunately, it doesn't always do so. There are many instances of children with high I.Q. scores who are not academic achievers, and there are other instances of children with average or even below average I.Q. scores who graduate from college, go on to graduate school and become highly proficient in their chosen professions.

An inconsistency between a child's school performance and his I.Q. scores raises serious questions about the validity of the scores with respect to that particular child. Significant discrepancies between potential and performance or between mathematical and verbal aptitude I.Q. scores must be examined and interpreted. Possible explanations for such discrepancies are numerous, with a learning problem or an emotional problem being high on the list.

A discrepancy between potential (as measured by the I.Q. tests) and performance may reflect a learning problem, an emotional problem, or simply a child's boredom in school. Such conditions can also deflate the I.Q. score, cause the child to test lower than he should, reduce the quality of the child's schoolwork, and cause him to function at a level below his potential.

When properly interpreted, aptitude and intelligence tests can be an important educational tool. The scores can help the educator identify a child's strengths and help him develop his potential. But aptitude and intelligence tests can also work at cross-purposes with a child's development, especially when they are misinterpreted, inadequately administered or used to label and catalogue a child.

The results of I.Q. tests are not sacred. In my clinical experience I have seen too many instances when the results were misleading or misused. One child with whom we were working was referred by his pediatrician to a clinical psychologist for an I.Q. test. The psychologist reported that the child's I.Q. was 65 and recommended that the child be placed in a class for the retarded. My staff was absolutely convinced that the boy was of average intelligence. Their subjective assessment was based on their firsthand knowledge that the child was grasping math concepts, performing math computations and reading with comprehension. The boy did have serious learning problems, but the staff's work with the child at our center and the feedback they'd received from the boy's classroom teacher made them seriously question the results of the test.

I concurred that the test results were suspect, and I asked an educational psychologist on my staff to test the boy. She gave the child a different I.Q. test than the one that had been administered initially. This particular test (the Stanford Binet) tended to be less biased against children with perceptual problems. The psychologist also spent a half an hour chatting with the child before administering the test. This chat was especially important because the child was very shy and had told his parents that the other psychologist had frightened him. The result of this re-testing was that the child's I.Q. measured 100. This score represented an increase of 35 points and placed him well within the average range of intelligence.

Had the boy's parents followed the advice of the pediatrician and the psychologist and placed the boy in a class for the retarded, a terrible mistake would have been made. Once the child was classified as retarded, it is likely that his parents and teachers would have begun to expect less from him. The child would probably have begun to perceive himself as retarded, and would have then performed consistently with that perception.

The emotional state of a child when he is tested can profoundly distort or skew the results of an I.Q. test. When a child has a negative association with being tested or experiences excessive anxiety, he will almost invariably do poorly on the test. If a child is convinced that he cannot do well on a test, or if he "shuts down" when being tested in certain subject areas, his performance will probably be negatively affected. In such cases, it is doubtful that the resulting test scores will meaningfully reflect that child's abilities and potential.

Other factors can also influence a child's or an adult's scores on any test. These factors include: rapport with the examiner, the type of test which is being administered, the health of the person at the time of the examination, and the willingness of the person to be subjected to testing.

Cultural biases can also distort test scores. It has been shown that children from certain cultural environments are at a disadvantage when they take certain tests. For example, a test question might read:

Manager is to baseball team as _____ is to orchestra.
   a. violin   b. opera   c. stage   d. conductor

A child living in a ghetto might not be able to relate to this analogy because violins, conductors and operas may not be part of his life experiences.

Because so may factors can negatively affect test performances, the results of intelligence tests must be cautiously and conservatively interpreted. Educational research has demonstrated that a teacher's academic expectations for a student can be influenced by his or her knowledge of the child's I.Q. scores. Teachers who know that a particular child's I.Q. scores are low will frequently expect less from that child than teachers who have no knowledge of the child's scores. And teachers who know that a child's I.Q. scores are high will frequently put forth greater effort to teach the gifted child, even if the child has difficulty learning because of a learning problem.

A teacher's expectations of a child are often self-fulfilling. The academic performance of a child who senses that the teacher expects little from him will often be consistent with that expectation. Conversely, children who sense that their teachers have positive expectations will generally respond to those expectations by producing at a high level.

Test scores must be professionally interpreted and not just recorded on a child's transcript as the ultimate pronouncement of the child's potential achievement. *Performance* rather than potential should be the primary criterion for determining the success of a child's education. It is the responsibility of parents and educators to identify the source of the child's problems when a child's academic performance is poor. Aptitude scores and I.Q. scores are but two components in the quest for an accurate and meaningful identification of those problems. The ultimate goal of the testing process is to help children reach their potential so that they can achieve life's rewards and choose from its many possibilities.

DIAGNOSTIC TESTING: A MEANS TOWARD AN END

Determining why a learning disabled child is unable to learn properly is the first step in providing help for him. In order to learn, the child's brain must be able to process information efficiently. Written and spoken words and symbols must be decoded before higher level skills, such as drawing inferences, perceiving analogies, and using symbolic logic, can be achieved.

Diagnosis is the cornerstone of meaningful remediation. Fortunately, there are excellent diagnostic procedures which permit school psychologists, reading specialists and learning disabilities specialists to identify a child's learning deficiencies with a high degree of accuracy. These tests are designed to identify the specific deficits which are interfering with a child's learning process.

Because the causes and the symptoms of learning problems vary, diagnostic testing strategies will also vary. In some instances very comprehensive diagnostic work-ups may be necessary in order to pinpoint the child's specific learning deficits. This is especially true when the learning deficits are complex or when the learning problem involves atypical components. When the learning deficits are straight-forward, an abbreviated diagnostic screening may be sufficient. Such a screening may be all that is required to identify the child's learning problem and to suggest an appropriate strategy for remediating the problem. The screening may also indicate that further testing is necessary.

Diagnostic tests are designed to measure a wide spectrum of skills, including: *aptitude, perceptual decoding, reading skills* (phonics, blending, word attack), *math skills, motor skills,* and *self concept.* [4] The test results provide a profile of the child's learning strengths and weaknesses. Although the results can be inaccurate, especially if the child has emotional problems or is hyperactive or highly distractible, they are an essential first step in the remediation process and can provide the learning disabilities specialist with invaluable insights into the child's learning needs.

Diagnostic testing reports are intended primarily to provide information to learning disabilities specialists and to reading and resource specialists. A classroom teacher with little or no training in learning disabilities would probably have difficulty interpreting this technical data. This difficulty in no way reflects on the classroom teacher's teaching skills. Few

4. See Glossary of Educational Terms for the definition of these terms. See also Testing Appendix.

classroom teachers are learning disabilities specialists, and only a very few have received training in the diagnosis and treatment of learning problems.

The diagnostic test report, however, can serve as an invaluable prescriptive tool for the learning disabilities specialist, the resource specialist or the reading specialist. Once the student's learning deficits have been identified by the diagnostic tests, the specialist can design an individualized education plan (I.E.P). Specific remediation goals can be established for the student which will provide the remediation process with focus and direction. [5]

Specialized tests might reveal, for example, that a particular child is having difficulty with reading comprehension or vocabulary because he has visual memory deficits. Although the child may be able to read grade level material with accuracy, he may not be able to remember the content of what he has read. This very same child is also likely to have difficulty with spelling inasmuch as good spelling skills require the ability to remember the letters which make up a word. He will have particular difficulty when words are nonphonetic and cannot be sounded out. Knowing the exact nature of the child's learning disability allows the learning disabilities specialist to plan remediation.

THE MARGINALLY LEARNING DISABLED CHILD

As a general rule, children with severe and obvious learning problems have a much better chance of being identified and receiving learning assistance than do children with subtle learning problems. Whereas the behavior and academic performance of the disruptive, hyperactive child will demand attention, that of the shy, hypoactive (lethargic) child probably will not. Typical learning problems such as dyslexia are more likely to be recognized and treated than the more nebulous learning problems that are characterized by disorganization, impulsivity, or poor study skills.

Many American schools have been forced by economics to adopt the mentality of a battlefield hospital where only the most severe casualties (or in this case the most severely learning disabled) are treated. The "slightly wounded" are sent back to the front lines without treatment or, at most, with a Band Aid. Far too many school districts lose sight of the fact that the "slightly wounded" are also "casualties" and need help.

5. See Testing Appendix for an explanation of the most common diagnostic tests and what they are designed to measure.

In many California school districts, a child must test a minimum of two years below grade level to qualify for learning assistance. The rationale for this policy is based upon the economic realities which often determine educational priorities. Most school districts have been forced to adjust to severely limited resources. The needs of the marginally learning disabled child are generally considered to be far less urgent than those of the severely learning disabled child, and learning assistance is usually reserved for those with severe problems. Children who are suspected of having only subtle learning problems are frequently not even given diagnostic evaluations.

Because children with marginal learning problems seldom receive learning assistance, many of them continue to perform marginally in school. Students, their parents and their teachers may confuse performance with potential and conclude erroneously that marginal performance is all that can be expected.

Children with marginal learning problems (one year or less below grade level in any academic subject) may represent as many as 25% of the entire school population. Because they have only subtle learning problems, these children are often expected to fend for themselves. Such students may require only short-term learning assistance to overcome their learning deficits. Without this short-term assistance, however, it is probable that many, if not most, will continue to experience difficulty in school.

Ironically, the responsibility to become involved in the educational process may be greater for parents of children who are marginally learning disabled. If their school district does not provide appropriate assistance, these parents may be forced to seek out-of-district testing and remediation. It is possible, however, to carry testing too far as the following anecdote reveals.

ERIC: TOO MUCH TESTING

My initial impression of Eric was that he was a bright child with a moderate learning problem. The diagnostic evaluation revealed minor motor-coordination deficits and certain other reading-related deficiencies. Eric was having an especially difficult time distinguishing between the right and left sides of his body. Not knowing the difference between right and left was causing him to reverse letters when reading and writing.

The checklist that had been completed by Eric's classroom teacher[6] confirmed the boy's letter reversal problem. The teacher indicated that Eric was not able to keep up with his class. He was easily distracted and he tended to daydream. Eric had not been given any standardized reading tests during the last six months, but the teacher estimated that he was read-

---

6. See Chapter 5: "Teacher Feedback" for a copy of this checklist.

ing at least one year below grade level. My own subjective assessment during the initial diagnostic conference confirmed this estimate.

After I evaluated the input supplied by Eric's classroom teacher and Eric's parents, and reviewed the results of my diagnostic screening, I recommended a two hour per week intensive learning assistance program. The program would focus upon correcting Eric's motor-coordination deficits and right/left confusion and would emphasize activities designed to help the child develop a greater attention span. In addition, Eric would receive remedial reading assistance to correct his reading deficits.

Eric's parents agreed to the proposed strategy and the boy was assigned to a learning disabilities teacher who would supervise his program in conjunction with other staff members. We scheduled further testing to provide the staff with more information about Eric's specific deficits.

At this point Eric's father informed me that upon the recommendation of the family physician he had previously scheduled a comprehensive diagnostic evaluation which was to be administered at a medical center. The tests would include a psychiatric and neurological work-up as well as extensive academic testing. He asked whether I felt that it would be advisable to go ahead with the evaluation. I responded that I believed that there was always value in seeking another opinion, but that I was fairly certain that the results of the work-up would confirm my own conclusions. I also expressed some reservations about the extensiveness of the evaluation that was to be done. Eric did not appear to have problems of sufficient magnitude to warrant such a comprehensive work-up.

I was certain that Eric did not have any neurological problems that could be measured by an E.E.G. (electroencephalogram). In this testing procedure, which is performed under the supervision of a neurologist, electrodes are attached to a child's head and his brain waves are measured. Irregularities or deviations from the normal pattern might indicate possible brain damage. Very few of the learning disabled children who are referred to me have organic brain damage. Subtle to moderate motor-coordination deficits may be detected during the initial diagnostic evaluation, but seldom do such "soft" symptoms actually involve organic damage. When "hard" symptoms are observed (such as a profound inability to coordinate both sides of the body), a pediatric evaluation followed with a neurological evaluation is standard operating procedure. [7]

Eric's father elected to go ahead with the comprehensive testing battery. Eric was evaluated by a psychiatrist, a social worker, a pediatrician, an educational psychologist, a neurologist, a speech and hearing specialist and a learning disabilities specialist. Each professional submitted a report. The entire report totaled twenty-four pages and the fee for the procedure was $1,300. The tests indicated the following things:

7.   See "Minimal Brain Damage" and "Minimal Brain Dysfunction" in the Glossary Of Educational Terms.

1. Eric had no neurological damage.
2. Eric's I.Q. was in the high normal range.
3. Family counseling was recommended. (Both parents were already in psychotherapy.)
4. Moderate learning disabilities were detected with no serious deficits in any area. (The specific learning deficits were enumerated in the report.)
5. Subtle coordination deficits were observed and specific perceptual-motor activities were recommended.
6. Remedial learning assistance was recommended.
7. A reduction in the amount of sweets Eric consumed each day was suggested as he was approximately ten pounds overweight.

Eric's father was presented with a precise, well-crafted diagnostic report. Although far more comprehensive than my initial diagnostic screening, the evaluation essentially confirmed my assessment of Eric's learning deficits. Thirteen hundred dollars seemed a substantial amount of money to pay for such a confirmation, especially when Eric's symptoms did not appear to justify such an extensive work-up. Eric's parents spent far more money on diagnostic procedures than they ultimately invested in having us remediate Eric's learning problem.

Extensive, multi-discipline diagnostic evaluations do serve an important function, especially when a child has a severe or enigmatic learning problem or when a child has a learning problem that is not responding to treatment. Having the input from highly-trained professionals representing a wide spectrum of disciplines can direct the learning therapist to the appropriate strategy for correcting the child's particular learning deficiencies.

It is neither necessary nor justified for all learning disabled children to undergo extensive, multi-discipline diagnostic testing. An abbreviated, highly professional diagnostic work-up can provide the essential information that parents and teachers need to design a remediation strategy. Essential information can be obtained quickly and inexpensively. The money allocated by school districts or by families for special education would be far better spent on remediation rather than testing. Testing overkill can be an expensive indulgence.

CHAPTER THREE _____

Identifying Your Child's Learning Problem

VISITING A SPECIAL CLASS

The students listened intently as I explained the rules for a fairly advanced perceptual activity. The rules were somewhat complicated and involved developing a verbal plan to direct one of the students through a maze of wooden blocks which had been set out on the classroom floor. To devise such a plan, the students needed to be able to concentrate, judge distance, orient their bodies in space, remember, and communicate precise instructions. Much to my amazement, all of them were able to do this very challenging activity with ease.

The students in the classroom were E.M.R. (educably mentally retarded). This label is applied to marginally retarded children who can master basic academic skills. The I.Q. range of such children is generally from 60 to 80. [1]

As a learning disabilities specialist, I had had relatively little experience working with retarded children. I had anticipated that these students would have far more difficulty with this perceptual training activity than my learning disabled students who were of average or above average intelligence. I was astonished by the facility with which these mentally retarded students were able to direct each other through the maze.

My purpose for visiting this class was to demonstrate some of the perceptual training activities that we had developed at our center. These activities were designed specifically to help learning disabled children process and decode sensory information more efficiently and effectively. Although the students in the E.M.R. class did have learning problems, it was clear that the learning problems of these particular students were very different from those of children with perceptual dysfunction. [2]

In contrast with the students at our center, I found that most of the students in this E.M.R. high school class possessed relatively good perceptual processing skills. None of the twelve teenagers appeared to have difficulty distinguishing between right and left, nor did they appear to have difficulty with spatial concepts or simple planning skills.

On numerous occasions I have worked with children with I.Q.'s above 140 who have struggled with the very same activity that these

---

1. I later learned that the students in this particular class were all above 70.
2. See subsequent section in this chapter entitled "Perceptual Dysfunction."

students were doing with ease. Typically, the children who attend our center are distractible and many have difficulty with spatial orientation and with directionality (knowing the difference between the right and the left sides of their bodies). Because of their perceptual processing deficits, many of our students often find this motor-planning activity very challenging. The activity was designed specifically to help the child with a perceptual dysfunction develop his concentration and problem solving skills. Although the activity was a valuable training exercise for childen with concentration, planning and spatial problems, the exercise did not address the special learning deficits of the E. M. R. students.

There are many different types of learning problems which affect a wide spectrum of children. Because of this wide spectrum of types of problems and types of children, there is a need for an equally wide spectrum of learning disabilities strategies. No one single strategy can possibly resolve all learning problems.

THE DIFFERENT TYPES OF LEARNING PROBLEMS

There is no universally acceptable and applicable definition of the term "learning problem," for no single definition could possibly encompass all of the symptoms that characterize the gamut of learning deficiencies. Learning problems interfere with the learning process, and this interference creates the need for learning assistance. The basic objective of all remediation programs is either to eliminate the source of the learning problem or teach the child how to compensate successfully for his particular learning deficits, even though the methods of remediation may vary.

Learning disabled children invariably function inefficiently. The degree to which they can be taught to function with greater efficiency will reflect the nature and severity of their particular learning problems. Another important factor in the educational equation is the child's level of intelligence. It is conceivable that a very bright child with a severe learning problem may ultimately go to Harvard Law School, assuming of course that his learning problem has been corrected. It is much less likely that a child of average or below average intelligence who has a learning problem will ultimately study at Harvard, whether his learning problem is resolved or not.

The specific symptoms of a learning disability will vary from child to child. To be effective, a learning assistance program must identify and treat the source of the child's problem. Reading, math, or spelling deficiencies are symptomatic of an underlying problem. A student who has difficulty understanding how numbers relate to each other, for instance, will have difficulty with math computational skills. To drill multiplication tables without first determining where the child is blocked and without first helping the child to overcome this block is an exercise in futility.

If we accept the premise that a lack of efficiency is a common denominator in all learning problems, then we can formulate a general definition of the term "learning problem":

Learning Problem   a response pattern in learning situations which is inefficient and which interferes with the student's ability to understand, remember, apply or integrate the material being taught.

Learning problems are generally divided into the following categories: [3]

1. Neurological Disorders
2. Sensory Impairment
3. Language Disorders
4. Mental Retardation
5. Cultural Deprivation
6. Language Deficiencies
7. Emotional Problems [4]

Each category of learning problem has its own characteristic symptoms. Some of the symptoms are subtle and may only be recognized by a professional who has been trained to diagnose learning or medical problems. Other symptoms will be more obvious and may be recognized by parents or classroom teachers. [5] These symptoms might include poor reading, spelling, handwriting, language arts, math and study skills. Other common deficits may involve difficulty communicating, concentrating, following instructions, keeping up with the class, hyperactivity and general disorganization.

A child's learning problem may involve both obvious symptoms and subtle symptoms that can reveal a great deal about the cause and the nature of the learning problem. For example, a child who has trouble following instructions and who is highly distractible may also have difficulty crossing the midline (coordinating both sides of the body) and may perseverate (repeat the same mistake over and over again as if he were locked into a certain response pattern). Such symptoms might indicate a neurological disorder and should be discussed with the pediatrician.

3. The terminology may vary in different regions of the country. See page 27 for a discussion of the causes of learning problems.

4. I'll be discussing emotional problems in Chapter 4.

5. There are many instances where parents are convinced that their child has a learning problem in first grade, only to be told by the teacher or the school authorities that he does not. Years later, it often turns out that the parents were right all along. See Chapter 1: "To Intervene Or Not To Intervene."

Certain learning deficits and behaviors may be characteristic of several different types of learning problems, and when they are evident, a fairly extensive diagnostic work-up may be necessary to pinpoint the specific disability. Generally the responsibility for making this diagnosis will rest with the school psychologist. In some instances, several professionals representing different disciplines may need to become involved to arrive at an accurate assessment, especially if the symptomatology suggests that the child has several overlapping learning problems.

Seldom is a child a "textbook case" of a learning problem. The child may have certain classic symptoms but not others. Children who have perceptual learning problems will often have difficulty with reading, but some children with perceptual learning problems will be excellent readers and have difficulty with primary math. Other children with perceptual problems have no academic deficits at all. Their primary problem may be in the area of coordination or concentration.

The following descriptions of the major different types of learning problems are intended to help you to understand and identify the nature of your child's particular learning problem. Be cautious about jumping to conclusions. The responsibility for specific diagnosis and identification should be that of the professional who is trained to diagnose and identify learning problems. Your understanding of your child's learning process, however, can play an important role in the remediation process. The more you understand, the more you will be able to support your child and his teachers during the remediation process.

NEUROLOGICAL DISORDERS

Shaw: Overcoming Minimal Brain Damage

The little boy sat at the table struggling to sound out a two letter word. Shaw had attended our center for forty two-hour sessions, and still he could barely read. Despite our intense efforts to develop this eight year-old's visual and auditory processing skills, he could not remember the sounds of the letters. We had attempted a phonics approach, a sight-word approach, neurological impress methods, kinesthetic techniques and perceptual-motor training. [6] All of our efforts were to no avail. It was clear that we were failing with this child.

Shaw was a child of above average intelligence who, in addition to his reading problem, had significant motor coordination deficits. Although he was not hyperactive, or even overactive, Shaw was highly distractible. He also had a unique habit of jerking his head slightly to the left when he was

6. See Glossary of Educational Terms.

attempting to concentrate. Highly personable and cooperative, Shaw put out 100% effort as he struggled to learn to read. It was heart-wrenching for all of us to acknowledge that despite his efforts and our efforts, he had made little progress.

When I had tested Shaw originally, I asked the boy's parents if the pediatrician had ever recommended a neurological examination. In the state of California, pediatric neurologists generally will accept referrals only from other physicians. The responsibility for the primary diagnosis and possible subsequent referral is that of the family pediatrician or family physician. Shaw's parents indicated that their pediatrician had not recommended that a neurologist examine Shaw. I suggested that they discuss the matter with him again, as I had detected significant indications of a possible neurological problem.

During the next twelve months, however, nothing further was said about the matter of a neurological work-up. Despite Shaw's parents' reluctance to follow my recommendation that they consult a neurologist, I felt that I had a responsibility to Shaw and his parents to pursue the matter. I once again advised a medical work-up and referred the parents to a medical center that I knew to have an excellent pediatric department and an excellent department of neurology. This time they agreed to follow my recommendation.

Shaw was examined by a pediatrician and referred for a neurological exam. The E.E.G. revealed minimal brain damage.[7] The neurologist spent an entire hour explaining to Shaw's parents the nature of Shaw's problem. He explained that Shaw's intelligence was in the normal range and that he felt that Shaw would be able to learn to read if he were placed on medication. The purpose of the medication would be to help Shaw to concentrate and to remember.

A period of experimentation with different types of medication and different dosages followed. At first Shaw became lethargic in class. Later, when the effects of the medication wore off, he was unable to sleep. After three weeks the doctor determined the proper drug and dosage. It was as if he had prescribed a magic potion!

Shaw began to consume books. He progressed through the beginning readers like a whirlwind. His coordination improved and he no longer jerked his head to the left when he was concentrating. Shaw's self-confidence soared. For the first time in his life he had tangible evidence that he was intelligent and capable of learning.

7. See Glossary of Educational Terms.

Although Shaw still had significant learning deficits that needed to be remediated, he was now able to progress. The improvement in Shaw's academic performance was an extraordinary morale booster for everyone involved in the remediation process. We actually saw Shaw walking down the street with books under his arm!

I must state categorically that I do not feel that medication (amphetamines) is a magic panacea for all types of learning problems. In fact, I am personally very conservative about the use of such medication. Any drug can be abused if it is prescribed indiscriminately, but in this particular case I am convinced that medication spared Shaw from remaining functionally illiterate and developing serious emotional problems as a consequence of this illiteracy.

The Facts About Neurological Disorders

Learning problems which are the result of neurological disorders manifest distinct symptoms. Generally these symptoms affect motor functioning (coordination); perceptual decoding skills (skills involved in the auditory or visual processing of letters, sounds and words); perceptual encoding skills (language expression); and behavior.

When neurological disorders are severe and involve damage to the brain or to the central nervous system (minimal brain damage), the disorders are considered to be organic. Organic problems manifest specific symptoms. The resulting deviations from normal cerebral functioning generally can be measured by special medical procedures and specialized medical instrumentation such as the E. E. G.

Although organic neurological disorders can cause learning problems, such disorders and learning problems do not necessarily go hand-in-hand. Some children may have very subtle neurological disorders and very serious learning problems. Other children may have more severe neurological disorders and very subtle learning problems, or in rare instances, no learning problems at all.

Children with severe organic neurological problems or brain damage will often have significant motor coordination deficits. They may have difficulty with such activities as skipping, balancing , handwriting, cutting with scissors and orienting themselves in space. (Please note: it is normal for children under six to have some difficulty with these tasks. And even if a child over six has difficulty doing these activities, he does not *necessarily* have a neurological problem.) When a child does exhibit significant motor coordination deficits, however, a work-up by a pediatrician is standard procedure. If the pediatrician suspects an organic disorder, he or she will refer the child to a pediatric neurologist for a more extensive neurological work-up.

44

Neurological disorders can range from the severe to the moderate to the subtle. Although organic neurological problems can cause mental retardation, neurological problems are *not* synonymous with mental retardation. Many brilliant children have minimal brain damage. [8]

There are many effective educational and medical protocols which can help a child overcome or compensate for his specific learning deficits. Perceptual training activities and sensory-motor integration activities have a documented track record for improving coordination and perceptual efficiency. Specific teaching techniques such as the Slingerland method and the neurological impress method [9] have also proven to be highly effective in treating specific types of problems.

Medication is sometimes prescribed in cases where children appear to be unable to learn because of extreme hyperactivity or distractibility. Special diets which eliminate artificial substances also appear to be very effective with the hyperactive and highly distractible student.

Listed on the following page is a simple checklist which describes some of the symptoms that *might* indicate the possibility of a neurological disorder. Let me emphasize that if your child manifests some of these characteristics it does *not* mean that he or she has a neurological disorder. If there is any question in your mind about the possibility of a neurological problem, however, consult your pediatrician or family physician. Remember, relatively few learning disabled children have organic neurological disorders.

You may not be able to evaluate your child in some of the areas listed on the following pages without input from your child's teacher. If you note a pattern of "yes" answers, you will want to consult your pediatrician.

---

8. The term "minimal brain dysfunction" or M.B.D. is not synonomous with "minimal brain damage." The latter is a more severe disability. See subsequent section in this chapter entitled "Perceptual Dysfunction."
9. See Glossary of Educational Terms.

NEUROLOGICAL CHECKLIST

	YES	NO
BEHAVIOR		
Hyperactive (excessively overactive)	☐	☐
Short Attention Span	☐	☐
Perseverates (repeats the same mistake over and over)	☐	☐
Chronically Distractible	☐	☐
Impulsive	☐	☐
MOTOR DEFICITS		
Chronically Awkward	☐	☐
Chronically Clumsy	☐	☐
Pronounced Physical Immaturity	☐	☐
Delayed Development	☐	☐
Reflex Asymmetry (different reflex responses on each side of body)	☐	☐
Poor Fine-Motor Skills (handwriting erratic, malformed or spidery)	☐	☐
Poor and Immature Drawings	☐	☐
EMOTIONAL DISORDERS		
Disinhibition (lacks socially appropriate control)	☐	☐
Lability (emotional instability)	☐	☐
Maturational Lag (emotional behaviors are not appropriate to the child's age)	☐	☐
PERCEPTUAL SKILLS		
Auditory Memory Deficits (forgets what is heard)	☐	☐
Auditory Discrimination Deficits (cannot hear the difference between sounds)	☐	☐
Visual Memory Deficits (forgets what is seen)	☐	☐
Visual Discrimination Deficits (cannot see the difference between letters)	☐	☐
Letter Reversals	☐	☐
Figure-Ground Deficits (cannot perceive spatial relationships)	☐	☐
Poor Memory for Designs	☐	☐

MEMORY & THINKING DISORDERS	YES	NO
Difficulty Thinking Abstractly (understanding ideas and concepts)	☐	☐
Poor Organization of Ideas and Concepts	☐	☐
VISUAL/HEARING/SPEECH IMPAIRMENTS		
Tone Deaf	☐	☐
Poor Articulation (inaccurate pronunciation of words/sounds)	☐	☐
Eye-Control Irregularities	☐	☐
LANGUAGE DISORDERS		
Delayed Development of Language Skills	☐	☐
ACADEMIC DEFICIENCIES		
Pronounced Reading Deficits	☐	☐
Pronounced Difficulty Keeping Up with Class	☐	☐
Chronic Disorganization	☐	☐

SENSORY IMPAIRMENT

A sensory impairment is a condition in which one or more of a person's sensory receptors is defective. Blindness or deafness represent the most extreme forms of sensory impairment.

The sensory receptors that are most directly involved in learning are the eyes and ears. Any student who has difficulty seeing or hearing is a high risk candidate for experiencing difficulty in school. Unless the student's sensory impairment is identified and corrected, or unless he is placed in a special program, he may quickly become demoralized and may erroneously conclude that he lacks intelligence.

Ruling out the possibility of an auditory or visual defect should be the first step in the process of diagnosing a learning problem. A child who has difficulty reading or copying things from the blackboard may simply need glasses. A visual screening by the school nurse or a pediatrician, optometrist or ophthalmologist will reveal if this is indeed the case. A diagnostic evaluation for a learning disability would be the next step in the identification process if the child does not have a visual impairment.

A child who has difficulty following auditory instructions or hearing the difference between sounds or letters may have a hearing loss. To rule out such a possibility, a hearing test by a pediatrician or audiologist is advisable. It is common for children to have ear infections when they are young. Although most of these infections can be controlled with medication or with tubes to permit the drainage of fluid, the infections can cause the child to experience temporary partial hearing loss. In some instances, the infection has residual effects and the child may experience permanent partial hearing loss.

Partial visual or auditory sensory impairment generally can be corrected with glasses or a hearing aid. Even children who have severe sensory impairment can frequently be taught how to compensate for their disability successfully. The key which unlocks the door to overcoming or compensating for the impairment is proper identification.

A child may have a sensory impairment and no learning problem, *or* he may have a learning problem and no sensory impairment. It is also possible for a child to have both a sensory impairment *and* a learning problem which is not directly related to the sensory impairment. A child who wears glasses to correct his visual acuity may also have a visual discrimination problem (difficulty distinguishing the difference between letters such as "b" and "d") even after his visual acuity problem is corrected. The visual discrimination problem is symptomatic of a perceptual processing dysfunction, and although corrective lenses will improve the child's vision, they will do nothing for his visual discrimination problem. Clearly, any meaningful learning assistance strategy must be based on an accurate determination of the child's particular problems and needs.

LANGUAGE DISORDERS

Andrew: Two Years Of Silence

As the little boy stared at me with his big brown eyes, I could sense immediately that there was something profoundly wrong. When he spoke, his speech was slow and had that unique tonal quality of someone who is deaf and has never heard the sound of his own voice. Andrew, however, was not deaf.

Andrew's mother explained that her son appeared to be developing normally during the first two years of his life. He had crawled and walked at the appropriate times, and he had begun to babble at the age children are first expected to begin babbling. But then suddenly he stopped making any noise whatsoever. He became cranky and seemed to manifest the symptoms of a chronic, intermittent low-grade infection.

At first Andrew's mother was simply concerned about her son's slow language development. Her concern soon turned to alarm. Andrew became lethargic and his continued silence was eerie. The mother took her son to several different doctors, but no one seemed to be able to identify the problem. His hearing seemed to be normal and there were no serious health problems. Finally one doctor suggested that Andrew should be tested by an allergist. The allergist discovered that Andrew was profoundly allergic to milk.

His mother removed all dairy products from Andrew's diet and slowly his ability to produce sounds returned. An electroencephalograph revealed, however, that the allergic reaction had been so profound that measurable brain damage had resulted. [10] The educational implications of this brain damage were not yet totally clear, and Andrew's mother had brought her son to our center in the hope that we might be able to improve his learning skills.

Andrew was attending a school for aphasic children. [11] The school, which was funded by the county, dealt exclusively with children who had serious language disabilities. Language therapy and highly specialized learning assistance were provided as an integral part of the curriculum.

Although Andrew had apparently made significant language gains at the school, his mother was concerned about his profound learning problems. Andrew was barely able to recognize the letters of the alphabet. He had a difficult time attending to tasks and his ability to follow instructions was very poor.

My diagnostic evaluation confirmed that Andrew was having difficulty not only with encoding skills (language) [12] but also with decoding skills (perceptual processing). The serious nature of Andrew's learning and language problems made it clear to me that our program could not provide for all of his remedial needs. Andrew required a full-time program which offered extensive learning therapy, speech/language therapy and occupational therapy. [13] The school he was attending offered all these resources and I recommended that he stay there. I also gave Andrew's mother the names of several other schools that provided similar services so that she could observe and compare their programs with the one that was offered at Andrew's school.

10.   It is rare that an allergic reaction to dairy products results in brain damage.

11.   Aphasia is an impairment of the capacity to use language symbols. It can include skills involved with receptive language, expressive language, written language, reading and mathematics. Aphasia will often manifest itself in an inability to communicate with spoken language. The term is often used synonymously (and erroneously) with the term dysphasia which is a less severe language disorder. Relatively few children are actually aphasic. Far more children are dysphasic and have language deficiencies. See Glossary of Educational Terms.

12.   See following section "The Facts About Language Disorders" for a discussion of "encoding."

13.   Occupational therapists will frequently employ a method called sensory integration to help brain-damaged patients organize their central nervous system functions. See "Sensory Integration Therapy" in Glossary of Educational Terms.

The Facts About Language Disorders

The capacity to affect others with our words is a gift that can easily be taken for granted. Most of us simply open our mouths and, on command, out spill the words which communicate our needs, our ideas and our thoughts.

Language is a response to either external stimuli (for example: a question) or internal stimuli (for example: an idea or an emotion).

External stimuli:	"When are you leaving on your trip?"
Language:	"After Christmas."
Internal stimuli:	How can I convince her that I'm really not upset?
Language:	"Honey, you know it really doesn't matter."

The perceptual processing of sensory information, such as spoken language or visual images, is called decoding, and the process of producing written or spoken language is called encoding. Although encoding is distinct from decoding, the two processes overlap. In most cases, encoding is preceded by decoding. When we are asked a question or when we want to describe a beautiful sunset, our brains must first sort out the sensory stimuli in our environment. In the case of a question, the stimuli consist of words addressed to us. In the case of the sunset, the stimuli consist of visual images. The data must be perceptually processed before we can express our responses to the data.

The interrelationship between encoding and decoding is especially apparent in learning situations where a child is constantly being bombarded with sensory information to which he is expected to respond. In order to respond, the child's brain must first decode the sensory input. Once this data is properly decoded and processed, the child can produce or encode the appropriate output.

Question:	What is the capital of California?
Decoding:	Receive input.
	Decipher sensory signals (words).
	Associate information.
Encoding:	Retrieve appropriate expressive language.
	Respond with written or spoken words.
Answer:	Sacramento.

To respond to the question cited in the example, the child must run the input through his brain or "on-board computer." If the question is written, then he must process the symbols which represent words visually. If the question is spoken, the auditory symbols which represent words must be processed by the child's auditory perception system. If it is functioning efficiently, the child's brain instantaneously connects the meaning of these symbols with information that has already been programmed into the "computer." Discrimination skills, memory skills and association skills are essential components in this process. Once the brain has deciphered the information, it will then retrieve other symbols (in the form of words) which it will use to express a response to the question.

Sometimes the "computer" does not function properly.

Teacher:	"What is the capital of California?"
Child:	"Buffalo."
Teacher:	"No, that's incorrect."
Child:	"Sacramento."

In this instance, the child must repeat the decoding/encoding process. Assuming that the child has learned the information, he must order his brain to search once again for the proper response. If his memory fails him he will not be able to encode the answer.

It is also possible that a student may know the answer to a question and simply not be able to express it. This inability may reflect an incomplete understanding, or it may reflect an encoding or expressive language deficiency.

Certain people have a greater facility than others in expressing themselves. This facility may reflect a particularly efficient decoding/encoding system, language aptitude, superior intelligence, practice, a good educational background or a great desire and motivation to learn how to communicate effectively.

To express a complicated idea or to respond to a complex question (example: "What are your thoughts about God?") will require relatively sophisticated language skills. A person who struggles with such a question would not necessarily have a language disability. His "computer" may be simply overtaxed by such a demanding question.

People who in general have difficulty communicating may have a chronic problem finding the precise word to express themselves. They may talk haltingly or intersperse "you know" repeatedly in a conversation. This habit can also be acquired by hearing others model such speech patterns. Indeed, the words "you know" have become pandemic in Americans' speech today. Such words serve two functions: they act as transitions between thoughts, and they represent an awkward attempt on the part of the speaker to convince himself that he is understood.

51

Minor communication deficiencies must be distinguished from language disorders. The person who has difficulty responding to simple questions (example: "What time is it?") will most likely have a language disorder, assuming he knows what time it is but cannot express what he knows. He may be unable to retrieve the words he needs to express what he knows, or he may be unable to articulate clearly. In both instances, specialized language or speech therapy would be advisable.

Language is a means of bridging the universe within us with the universe outside us. Those who are unable to establish this bridge will probably experience a profound sense of isolation.

Children who have difficulty decoding and encoding sensory stimuli are particularly high risk candidates for feeling isolated. Because they are unable to respond efficiently to the world around them, to express themselves and to make their needs known, learning disabled and language disabled children frequently experience a profound sense of frustration.

The first symptoms of a language disorder will often appear as developmental delays in the acquisition of language. The typical progression from cooing to babbling to speaking isolated words may not occur, or, as was the case with Andrew, the progression may be interrupted. In kindergarten the child with a language disability may not be able to say the names of the colors, the days of the week or the months of the year. He may also not know how to count or know the words to the songs that the children sing in class.

There is a wide spectrum of specific symptoms that might indicate the presence of a language disability. A child with such a disability may manifest many symptoms, or he may manifest only a few. The symptoms may be severe or they may be subtle. The following checklist is intended to help you determine whether your child should be evaluated by a qualified speech and language therapist. The symptoms on the list include both decoding and encoding deficits that are characteristic of a possible language disability. In the event that you note sufficient "yes" answers to warrant concern, you should contact a qualified speech and language therapist who will be able to evaluate the information and suggest an appropriate course of action.

SYMPTOMS OF LANGUAGE DISORDERS [14]

	YES	NO
AUDITORY PROCESSING DEFICITS		
Difficulty paying attention to auditory stimuli	☐	☐
Difficulty discriminating sound versus no sound	☐	☐
Difficulty locating where sound is coming from	☐	☐
Difficulty discriminating different sounds	☐	☐
Difficulty distinguishing primary sounds from background sounds	☐	☐
Difficulty associating sounds with the source of the sounds	☐	☐
Difficulty filtering out extraneous sounds	☐	☐
Difficulty sequencing ideas	☐	☐
Oral reversals (example: emeny instead of enemy)	☐	☐
Circumlocutions (imprecise, roundabout communication. For example: "that place down there where they sell the thingamajig")	☐	☐
LINGUISTIC PROCESSING DEFICITS:		
Poor Grammar	☐	☐
Wrong verb tenses	☐	☐
Assigns only broad meanings to words	☐	☐
Does not perceive subtle meanings or differences between words	☐	☐
Difficulty understanding spatial prepositions (beneath/beside)	☐	☐
Difficulty understanding words denoting time and space (before/here)	☐	☐
Difficulty understanding comparative adjectives and superlatives (bigger/biggest, far/near, rough/smooth, fast/slow)	☐	☐
COGNITIVE (THINKING) PROCESSING DEFICITS:		
Difficulty following oral directions	☐	☐
Difficulty expressing thoughts and information	☐	☐
Difficulty classifying ("What are dogs, lions and horses?")	☐	☐
Difficulty putting events in sequence or order	☐	☐
Difficulty making comparisons	☐	☐

14. You will probably need to consult your child's classroom teacher to complete this checklist.

	YES	NO
Difficulty understanding or expressing the moral of a story	☐	☐
Difficulty predicting the outcome of a story or event	☐	☐
Difficulty differentiating between fact and fiction	☐	☐
Difficulty remembering and expressing facts	☐	☐

EVALUATION DEFICITS

	YES	NO
Difficulty drawing conclusions ("Why did she need her mittens?")	☐	☐
Difficulty relating to cause and effect (Hot fudge is made from a. ice cream b. chocolate c. dessert)	☐	☐

SOCIAL PROBLEMS

	YES	NO
Difficulty understanding subtle verbal and non-verbal cues	☐	☐
Excessive talking	☐	☐
Talking at inappropriate times	☐	☐

WRITTEN LANGUAGE PROBLEMS [15]

	YES	NO
Difficulty expressing in written words what is known (dysgraphia)	☐	☐
Difficulty copying letters, numbers or words	☐	☐
Difficulty writing spontaneously or from dictation	☐	☐
Difficulty drawing (but no problems copying)	☐	☐
Difficulty organizing thoughts for writing	☐	☐
Difficulty writing with good syntax (but no difficulty with spoken grammar)	☐	☐

APHASIA/DYSPHASIA [16]

	YES	NO
Difficulty making facial motor movements to produce sound [17]	☐	☐
Difficulty imitating sounds	☐	☐
Difficulty remembering words (can repeat them)	☐	☐
Difficulty formulating sentences (but can use single words)	☐	☐

---

15. See subsequent section in this chapter, "Written Language Arts Problems."

16. See note on page 49 for a discussion of the differences between aphasia (complete loss of language) and dysphasia (partial language deficiency). Note that motoric symptoms that are characteristic of aphasic and dysphasic children are similar to those that are characteristic of minimal brain damage.

17. This condition is called dyspraxia. (See Glossary of Educational Terms)

	YES	NO
Difficulty naming common things (example: triangle, radio)	☐	☐
Difficulty recalling a specific word	☐	☐
Substitutions (rattle for beetle)	☐	☐
Distorted body image (as reflected in drawings)	☐	☐
Difficulty copying designs	☐	☐
Difficulty with directional concepts (right/left/ up/beside)	☐	☐
Poor attention span	☐	☐
Poor coordination	☐	☐
Clumsiness	☐	☐
Hyperactivity	☐	☐
Emotional disturbances	☐	☐
Difficulty recognizing common objects by touch	☐	☐

Highly effective teaching techniques have been developed to help children with language disabilities. The earlier a child's problem is diagnosed, the sooner the remedial therapy can begin. The sooner the language therapy begins, the lower the risk that the language disabled child will experience demoralizing frustration and possible emotional damage.

If you feel that your child may have a language disability, and if language therapy is not available through your school district, consult your pediatrician. Request that he or she refer you to a private language clinic or to a university associated speech center which offers diagnostic and clinical services.

Speech Disorders

Speech patterns which interfere with communication and detract from what is being said, or speech patterns which cause self-consciousness or apprehension may signal a speech disorder. Although such a disorder would fall under the general heading of a language disorder, speech disorders have distinct characteristics and causes.

Unlike a language disorder in which the brain has difficulty associating thoughts with the words that are used to express those thoughts, speech disorders involve a physiological deficit which interferes with the production of sound. A speech disorder may also be the result of an inability to use efficiently the muscles or organs that produce sound. Some children may have both a language disorder *and* a speech disorder.

Although most children with speech disorders are physically normal, they often experience motor coordination problems, developmental delays and behavior problems. Approximately 15% of children with speech disorders actually have physical abnormalities. The genetic or organic factors which cause speech problems include:

1. Cleft palate
2. Physiological deficiencies in the mouth or jaw
3. Muscular paralysis of the larynx
4. Loss of larynx
5. Brain damage
6. Nasal obstruction
7. Hearing loss

One of the most common types of speech disorders involves difficulty with articulation. Typically, a child with articulation deficits will have problems enunciating or pronouncing words properly. As a consequence, the child's communication may be difficult to understand. He may omit sounds. For example, the child may say "at" when he intends to say "cat." Or the child may substitute one sound for another in the word he wants to say (example: "pag" for "bag"). [18] Frequently, children with speech disorders will distort words (example: "furog" for "frog") or distort sounds such as the "r" and the "l" sounds. [19] Other symptoms of a speech disorder involve lisping, stuttering, stammering and cluttering.

Stuttering, stammering and cluttering are the result of disturbances in speech rhythm. The causes of such a condition may involve genetic, physiological, or emotional factors. There are many theories about the source of such problems. Research seems to indicate a higher incidence of central nervous system disorders in children who stutter. The problem appears to be more common when a child is born prematurely or when there are multiple births. [20]

The ability to articulate sounds is acquired sequentially. A young child will typically say "wawa" instead of "water" because most three-year-olds have not yet acquired the ability to pronounce the "t" sound. As the child matures, his articulation skills improve.

When a child's articulation does not appear to be improving as he matures, he may require speech therapy. Minor articulation problems will often disappear of their own accord by age eight or nine. If the child's articulation problems persist beyond that age, the child will need special help. Here is a chart of the approximate developmental stages at which children acquire specific articulation skills.

18. Word substitution as opposed to sound substitution is considered to be a language disorder.
19. This symptom is called lalling although this term is somewhat outdated.
20. Attributing causes to stuttering is somewhat controversial and some authorities contend that there are no clearly defined causes.

Articulation Skills

Age	Sounds
3 years 5 months	b, p, m, w, h
4 years 5 months	t, d, g, k, ng, y
5 years 5 months	f, u, s, z
6 years 5 months	sh, l, th

Don't be concerned if your four year-old has difficulty pronouncing the "l" sound. Your child should not be expected either physiologically or developmentally to pronounce such a sound properly. A six year-old child, however, who cannot pronounce the sound "b" may be manifesting a potential speech disorder. If either you or your child's preschool or kindergarten teacher suspect that there may be a speech problem, you should consult your family pediatrician or request a speech evaluation by the school district.

Delayed speech in a child may also indicate a language or speech disorder. Children should be talking by two to three years of age and parents whose children are not speaking by this age should consult their pediatrician.

Delayed speech may be attributable to any of the following causal factors:

1. Deafness
2. Developmental aphasia
3. Mental deficiencies
4. Cerebral palsy
5. Mental illness
6. Personality disorders
7. Lack of motivation

Another type of speech problem involves an actual disorder in voice production. Such disorders are characterized by deviations in loudness, pitch, duration, flexibility and quality of sounds. The specific symptoms include: harshness, hoarseness, nasality and "breathiness."

Speech disorders can be a serious source of embarrassment for a child. The ability to communicate effectively is one of the primary criteria by which children and adults are judged, and the importance of acquiring language skills cannot be underestimated. Any investment you make in remedial language or speech therapy is a wise investment. The emotional implications of an untreated language or speech disorder can be disastrous, and repairing a child's self-esteem once serious emotional damage has occurred can be far more costly and time-consuming than early diagnosis and treatment.

Written Language Arts Problems

To express with words what is inside one's head a person must first be able to decipher what is outside in his environment. Our eyes, ears and sensory receptors function like the lens of a camera or the microphone of a tape recorder. They are conduits from the external world to the internal world. The center of this internal world is our brain.

The brain can process the data from the external world instantaneously. Within a microsecond, the brain can discriminate, associate, analyze, integrate, organize and interpret a continuous barrage of sensory stimuli in the form of words, visual symbols and sensations. Within another microsecond, it can produce words and symbols which express its response to this data.

When a child is unable to decode data or "link" it with corresponding words and symbols, his communication is impeded. Imagine, for example, a poet who is unable to perceive the relationship between the petals, the stem, the color and the shape of a rose. It would be impossible for such a poet to communicate the image of a rose.

The words that a poet or a child in fourth grade uses to encode his perceptions will represent the end product of the decoding/encoding process. A child's perceptual processing and written encoding skills should improve if he is given adequate opportunity to practice his writing and speaking skills and if he receives feedback and guidance on how to perfect those skills.

School is intended to provide the student with the practice, guidance and feedback he needs to refine and perfect both his written and spoken communication skills. As a child progresses in school, his sentences will become more and more sophisticated. Simple sentences which communicate isolated ideas, facts or feelings (example: "Yesterday, Mom and I went to the park.") will evolve into more complex sentences. Ultimately he will be able to create paragraphs which express more complicated ideas, facts and feelings. With further guidance, feedback, criticism, practice and effort, these paragraphs will evolve into essays and reports which testify to the student's ever-expanding intellectual and educational development.

Certain children possess a greater aptitude for written expression than other children. Researchers have actually pinpointed specific areas of the brain as being responsible for language encoding (or output). Perhaps the organic composition of these encoding areas of the brain determines a person's capacity for language development and a person's language aptitude.

Students with good language arts aptitude will generally master the mechanics of written expression with greater facility than their classmates. Their essays and reports will be better organized and more creative. Their grammar will be more accurate and their syntax (sentence structure) more precise and esthetically pleasing.

Writing ability, like athletic ability, may be a genetic gift, but the craft of writing is a skill which is developed primarily through practice. Even children with good language aptitude will require guidance and feedback from their teachers during the formative years of their education. Like a talented ballerina or a basketball player, the child with "natural" writing ability needs to be coached, encouraged and critiqued.

Children who do not possess a "natural" aptitude for expressing themselves in writing especially need coaching. Unfortunately, it appears that American elementary and secondary students are being given less and less opportunity to practice written expression and to receive meaningful criticism. The tradition of the "weekly essay" has been abandoned in many school districts. Many teachers simply do not want to be burdened with the responsibility of grading them. Often the teachers themselves cannot write effectively. As a consequence, it is not uncommon for fifth and sixth graders in some school districts to write no book reports or essays during an entire academic year!

Writing skills are acquired sequentially. Each time a teacher assigns a writing project, he or she provides the student with an opportunity to improve his writing skills. Each time the teacher corrects a child's syntactical and grammatical mistakes, he or she creates an opportunity for the student to learn how to eliminate these mistakes. Extensive practice and meaningful criticism are essential to the mastery of any skill, and especially to the mastery of language arts skills.

Basic written communications skills can be developed in all but the most handicapped of students. A child does not need to possess a superior language aptitude in order to learn how to express himself in writing. The following are components that produce children who can write well:

1. Good teaching and a good language arts program.
2. An emphasis on writing skills in the curriculum.
3. Practice (regularly assigned essays, book reports and term papers).
4. Meaningful criticism with an emphasis on teaching self-editing skills.
5. Parental support of the student and the teacher (this means making sure the writing assignments are completed, handed in and corrected).

Many students with a language arts problem do not have a language disability. Their language arts problems are the result of their not receiving the benefits of the five components listed above.

Ideally, a child who is deficient in language arts should be identified as early as possible. The first symptoms will begin to manifest themselves as early as second or third grade. Poor punctuation, sentence fragments, incomprehensible sentences and poor grammar are the danger signals of a potential problem which may begin to hinder the child in fourth and fifth grade.

A checklist follows which may aid you in determining whether your child has a language arts problem. The checklist is intended primarily for students in the fourth grade and above, and some of the categories listed are not applicable to children in the first three or four grades of elementary school. If you suspect that your child has a language arts deficiency, ask your child's teacher to help you complete the checklist. The teacher will know which skills your child should have mastered at his grade level in school. A pattern of relevant "no" answers probably indicates a language arts deficiency.

The skills listed on the checklist can be developed, refined and perfected only when the child is provided with sufficient opportunity to practice, edit and rewrite. It is absurd to expect students to master any craft or art without adequate training.

LANGUAGE ARTS CHECKLIST

	YES	NO
Uses capital letters when appropriate	☐	☐
Uses correct punctuation	☐	☐
Sentence formation		
Avoids sentence fragments (sentences do not contain subject and verb)	☐	☐
Avoids run-on sentences (too many ideas included in sentences)	☐	☐
Uses proper subject/verb agreement (example: "the boy goes," not "the boy go")	☐	☐
Topic sentences express main idea of paragraph or essay	☐	☐
Paragraphs are well organized	☐	☐
Knows when to start new paragraph	☐	☐
Ideas are presented sequentially	☐	☐
Can summarize in writing what has been read	☐	☐
Spelling is essentially correct		
Can identify parts of speech	☐	☐
Can express ideas within a reasonable time-frame	☐	☐
Can edit own work and find most grammatical and syntactical errors	☐	☐
Essays and reports are written neatly and legibly	☐	☐

MENTAL RETARDATION

In most school districts in the United States, two primary criteria are used to identify a child as being mentally retarded: [21] 1) the child's level of intellectual functioning is determined to be below 70 on an I.Q. scale; and 2) the child's behavior is determined to be nonadaptive.

Mental retardation will generally affect a child in four overlapping areas of his life: education, health, emotions and social interaction. A pattern of specific deficiencies is associated with mental retardation. These deficiencies, which will vary depending upon the degree of retardation, will affect a child's ability to concentrate, organize, remember, use language and develop socially acceptable behavior.

In some instances, the first indications of mental retardation are recognizable during infancy and early childhood. The symptoms include:

21. Some school districts are now using the term "mentally delayed" instead of mentally retarded.

61

1. Impaired sensory-motor development (the normal progression from crawling to walking to running is delayed or not achieved).
2. Impaired communication skills.
3. Delayed acquisition of self-help skills (feeding, toilet training, etc.).
4. Inadequate development of socialization skills.

Many of these symptoms may also be indicative of possible brain damage, environmental deprivation, possible perceptual dysfunction and language disorders. If you perceive these symptoms in your child, discuss your concerns with your family pediatrician. He or she will be able to evaluate the specific symptoms and perform the required diagnostic tests.

Certain behavior symptoms which are characteristic of mental retardation may manifest themselves during childhood or during early adolescence. These symptoms include:

1. Difficulty applying academic skills to daily life situations (example: figuring out proper change in a store).
2. Difficulty applying appropriate reasoning and judgment to solving problems (example: "What do we have to do to get there on time?").
3. Difficulty acquiring acceptable social skills.

Children who are retarded will often experience more anxiety than other children. [22] Because they have greater difficulty acquiring academic skills and grasping concepts, retarded children often learn to anticipate failure, especially when the tasks and projects are challenging. As a possible defense mechanism the retarded child may acquire a rigid set of behaviors which mimic or imitate the behaviors of others who are not retarded. For instance, a retarded child may look to other children for cues as to what is right or wrong because he does not trust himself to make certain types of social decisions.

Because of articulation problems, limited vocabulary, poor auditory and visual processing skills and poor grammar, many retarded children have a difficult time with language. These language deficiencies make their social adjustment all the more difficult. Retarded children will generally respond positively to rewards, however, and will often work hard to achieve praise, money or comfort.

22. These general characteristics do not apply to all retarded children. See discussion of Down's Syndrome and PKU on page 64.

The degree to which a child is considered retarded is based primarily upon I.Q. In most states three common educational classifications are used to distinguish the different levels of retardation: E.M.R. (educably mentally retarded), T.M.R. (trainably mentally retarded) and P.M.R. (profoundly mentally retarded).

Children are classified E.M.R. when their I.Q. range is 55 to 70 (in some states, 50-75). E.M.R. students are capable of mastering basic academic skills such as reading, writing and math. In most cases, children who are classified E.M.R. can become economically and socially self-sufficient. When E.M.R. students graduate or leave school, few appear to be retarded. In most cases, children who are classified as E.M.R. become economically and socially self-sufficient. When they complete their education and have mastered basic survival and academic skills, they are generally able to hold jobs, marry and become responsible parents and citizens.

Children who are classified T.M.R. have I.Q. scores that are in the 25-55 range. The T.M.R. students will be able to read very basic words and will be able to master basic number concepts. Few T.M.R. adults, however, ever become totally self-sufficient. Most will require varying degrees of supervision and financial support.

Children who are classified as P.M.R. have I.Q. scores of under 25. From an educational standpoint, the primary objective is to help these children acquire basic self-help skills. Unfortunately, some of the more severely retarded do not achieve this objective. Those classified as P.M.R. will require continued care and supervision as adults and will not be able to function without supervision and financial support.

The point at which a definitive diagnosis of mental retardation can be made will vary depending upon the nature of a child's retardation. Children who are diagnosed as E.M.R. are seldom identified as being retarded until they start school. Because their appearance and social behaviors are normal, these children are usually referred for testing to the school psychologist only when it becomes apparent that they are having difficulty mastering the academic material that is being presented to the class.

It is not uncommon for the marginally retarded child to be retained in the early grades of elementary school, especially when there are no special programs available or when the child's mental retardation has not been accurately diagnosed. Most school districts, however, have special programs for the E.M.R. student in which the curriculum and the pace at which academic material is presented are less demanding than in the regular school program.

Diagnosis of the T.M.R. and the P.M.R. child often occurs at an earlier age than the E.M.R. child because of the more profound nature of their symptoms. In general, the pediatrician will recognize and identify the physical symptoms and the developmental deficits.

Several medical conditions and genetic factors will alert physicians to the possibility of retardation. These conditions and factors include gross developmental delays involving atypical patterns of sitting, crawling, walking, speech, toilet training, socialization skills, common sense, and fine and gross motor coordination. Other characteristics include facial disproportions, abnormalities of the eyes and ears, skin conditions, and abnormalities of the fingers.

The causes of mental retardation are diverse. The factors responsible may involve complications during pregnancy or labor, a history of retardation, exposure to disease, accidents or infections. Genetic factors may also be responsible. Down's Syndrome, which affects approximately 10% of the moderately to severely retarded children, is the result of a chromosomal defect. The condition occurs more commonly when women conceive after the age of thirty-five. [23] The overall incidence of Down's Syndrome is 1 child per 600 live births.

Specific types of retardation will result in distinct physical and personality traits. The physical characteristics of Down's Syndrome include flattened facial features, small nose with low bridge, upward slanting eyes (the result of epicanthic folds of skin), colored spots in iris of eyes, flattened back skull, small ears, small mouth, furrowed tongue surface and fine, thin, straight hair. In general, those affected by Down's Syndrome are basically happy and good-natured and appear to have less severe emotional disturbances than other T.M.R. and P.M.R. children.

PKU (Phenylketonuria) is also a genetically based condition which results in an enzyme deficiency. The physical and personality characteristics of children with PKU are quite distinct from those with Down's Syndrome. PKU characteristics include fair skin, blond hair, blue eyes, eczema, undeveloped tooth enamel and seizures. Fifty percent of the children afflicted with PKU have microcephaly (small heads). Unlike children who have Down's Syndrome, children affected by PKU tend to be unhappy and unfriendly. The behavioral symptoms include emotional instability, aggressiveness, temper tantrums and schizophrenic outbursts.

A large percentage of mentally retarded children can be educated and many can learn to become self-sufficient and productive members of society. Even the more severely retarded child can often be trained to contribute to his own welfare and to function with a degree of independence. With love, parental support and good teaching, many retarded children and adults can learn to maximize their potential and enjoy many of life's rewards.

23. Recent research suggests that the father's age may also be a factor in the incidence of Down's syndrome.

CULTURAL DEPRIVATION & LANGUAGE DEFICIENCIES

A Classroom Where Children Learn To Be Retarded

The high school classroom was set up like a club house. There was a comfortable sofa, a stereo, big pillows on the floor and posters on the walls. The students sat around listening to music or chatting with their friends. The teacher sat at her desk reading a magazine. It was, as she later indicated, "socializing time" for the students.

The class was comprised of E. M. R. junior and senior students. All of the students had been tested and had been found to be retarded. The teacher informed me that the class was designed to prepare them for the "outside world." The curriculum was intended to teach the students basic survival skills so that they could find employment.

The occupational and vocational training consisted for the most part of the teacher helping the students fill out application forms for jobs and driver's licenses. From time to time I observed that the students would wander back to their desks and practice filling out sample job application forms. Most of their time, however, was spent talking, listening to music or flirting.

The students in the class ate their lunch before the other students in the school. After the "regular" students ate their lunch, most of the boys in the E. M. R. class functioned as janitors for the rest of the school, cleaning up the lunch area and emptying the trash cans. They were paid for performing this service.

It was apparent that most of the students in the class were functionally illiterate. Out of fourteen students in the room, only five spoke English as their native language, and eighty percent represented minorities.

As I chatted with several of these young adults, I was surprised to discover that many were quite articulate, especially when they were talking with me or with their friends in their native language. Each of them had accepted the "fact" that he or she was retarded. Having accepted this "fact," the students were now being groomed for their respective roles in life. Intuitively, I sensed that many of these students were far more capable than their teacher or they themselves believed. If this was true, then I was observing a tragic waste of human potential.

65

Language And Cultural Factors

Our educational system is oriented toward students who are able to understand spoken and written English and who are able to communicate fluently in this language. Those who design curricula and educational objectives generally assume that the students will be proficient in English. [24]

Children who do not speak English at home or children who come from other cultures and who are thrust into the American educational system are frequently at a severe disadvantage. Because these children are expected to function in a classroom where English is the vehicle for communication, many language deficient or culturally disadvantaged children experience severe academic problems. The challenge of trying to understand a teacher who is explaining something in a language which is not your own or trying to understand a textbook in a "foreign" language can be awesome and demoralizing.

It is reasonable to assume that the child has some sort of learning disability when he is unable to process sensory information in the form of spoken language or written language. This assumption is not valid in the case of children with a language deficiency. Although it is very possible that such children may also have learning disabilities or language disabilities (as distinguished from language deficiencies), the primary difficulty that they have with language may be traced to their not having had adequate practice speaking, reading and writing English.

Accurately identifying the needs of a child with language deficiencies can be very difficult. This difficulty is often compounded because children who have language deficiencies in English may also have language deficiencies in their native language, especially if they speak a dialect or if they speak their native language only in limited contexts. Were such children tested in their native language, there is a good chance that they would manifest language deficiencies and even illiteracy in that language.

Subcultures which de-emphasize education or which place little value on academic achievement tend to produce children with academic problems. This de-emphasis on the value of education makes distinguishing between academic problems which are the result of specific learning disabilities and those which are the result of cultural or language influences very difficult. Does the distractible ghetto student, for example, who is chronically inattentive to detail and who is a poor reader have perceptual processing deficits, or are his academic difficulties the result of disinterest, poor teaching or lack of parental encouragement? This question must be answered if the child is to receive meaningful assistance.

24. Most school districts do provide special programs for children with language deficiencies. The ultimate goal of such programs is to integrate the student into the standard curriculum.

Diagnostic testing must take into consideration the total child, and especially his home environment. [25] Using the scores on aptitude, diagnostic and achievement tests as the exclusive criteria for determining a learning assistance strategy is a disservice to children who are language deficient or culturally disadvantaged. There is no magic formula for helping these children, but to disregard the causal factors increases the risk of an inadequate diagnosis and a subsequently inadequate education.

PERCEPTUAL DSYFUNCTION

Kristin: Struggling To Catch A Speeding Train

The little girl's parents were upset and confused. They had just learned that their five year old daughter would not be permitted to enter the academic kindergarten at the private school where she was currently attending preschool. The kindergarten teachers had decided that the child was not developmentally ready to participate in their highly academic program. [26]

The policy of this particular private school was to screen all "candidates" for kindergarten to determine the level of their learning readiness skills. The program was highly accelerated, and five year olds were expected to be able to read at the upper first grade level by the time they completed kindergarten. The teacher had become highly proficient at screening out those children who would not be able to handle the program. The parents of children not accepted had the option of reapplying the following year if they so desired. In the interim they could either enroll their child in a less demanding kindergarten program or have their child repeat the school's developmental preschool program.

Kristin's scores on her school's screening test were very low and confirmed the preschool teacher's observation that Kristin was socially and developmentally immature and deficient in both gross-motor and fine-motor skills. Kristin also had an especially difficult time participating in group activities. She demanded the constant attention of the teacher and was highly distractible and inattentive.

Kristins' parents were shocked that she was not being permitted to enter the academic kindergarten. Their oldest child had gone through the very same program three years previously and was currently doing very well in the second grade. Without realizing it, Kristen's parents were

25. Many achievement and diagnostic tests are themselves culturally-biased. In some instances, the tests may ask questions which might penalize children who are not exposed to certain experiences in their culture. In other instances, the use of English on the test will penalize language deficient children.

26. Although intense, academic preschool programs may be beneficial for certain children, other perfectly normal children may not be developmentally ready to handle such programs and may experience profound feelings of inadequacy as a consequence.

expecting her to equal her brother's accomplishments. Kristin's father, a very successful attorney, appeared to be particularly offended by this rejection of his daughter.

Kristin's parents had adamantly refused to accept the results of the kindergarten screening test administered by the school, and the headmaster referred the family to our center for an independent evaluation. After testing Kristin and reviewing the preschool teacher's evaluation form, [27] I concluded that the school was correct in their assessment. Kristin was not developmentally ready to adjust to an accelerated academic kindergarten program.

The tests that I administered revealed significant deficiencies in perceptual processing skills. Kristin's coordination, memory skills, discrimination skills and spatial skills were at approximately one year below the norm for her chronological age. Her draw-a-person was especially immature for a five year-old. Although she could identify colors and primary body parts (example: show me your knee), she could not identify secondary body parts (example: show me your jaw), and could neither recite the alphabet nor identify written letters. She could count to ten, but she could not recognize any written numbers.

Many of the learning readiness skills that Kristin lacked had been taught to her in the preschool program. Apparently, Kristin had never mastered these skills or she had forgotten them. Without these readiness skills, Kristin would have difficulty succeeding in a program oriented toward highly efficient learners.

During the diagnostic conference and evaluation, I observed that Kristin was very emotionally dependent upon her mother. She constantly looked to her mother for reassurance and repeatedly complained that she was getting tired. It was an effort to get her to concentrate on any task for more than a few seconds.

When I shared with Kristin's parents the results of my evaluation, I sensed that they were finally willing to accept the facts. I explained that Kristin had perceptual processing and perceptual motor deficits. She needed time to allow her perceptual skills to develop, and she also needed specialized learning assistance. The prognosis for her ultimately overcoming her perceptual problems was excellent, but she was not yet capable of handling a rigorous and demanding kindergarten program.

After the results of the diagnostic evaluations were explained, Kristin's parents agreed to place her in our developmental perceptual training program. Her parents also concurred that Kristin would be better off in a nonacademic public school kindergarten program. They agreed to stop comparing her to her older brother.

---

27.   You can find a copy of the teacher evaluation form which we use at our center in Chapter 5 in the section entitled "Teacher Feedback."

Children do not all develop at the same rate. In some instances, their perceptual development is blocked for reasons that are not totally understood. Fortunately, perceptual processing deficits can be identified even in preschool, and there are proven methods of remediation which can spare children from the demoralizing effects of repeated frustration and school failure.

Kristin fortunately received the specialized help she required, and her learning readiness skills improved dramatically. She was also placed in a less pressurized kindergarten. As she learned to read, she became less and less emotionally dependent on her mother. Within twelve months of beginning her remedial program, Kristin was functioning as a normal first grader.

The Facts About Perceptual Dysfunction

A very important distinction must be made between a perceptual (or sensory) *impairment* in which there is a measurable defect in one or more sensory receptors (such as the eyes or the ears), and a perceptual *dysfunction*. A perceptual dysfunction occurs when the brain receives the essential sensory data but is unable to decode this data properly. Such decoding deficiencies are generally the result of specific deficits involving orientation, discrimination, memory, association and/or concentration.

It is not totally clear why children develop perceptual dysfunctions, and why some children learn how to compensate for their perceptual processing deficits more successfully than other children. Many very successful people have struggled with and prevailed over their perceptual learning problems. The list includes Albert Einstein, General George Patton, Thomas Edison, and Nelson Rockefeller.

At one time or another we have all been the victims of a temporary perceptual dysfunction. Most of us have had the experience of being given directions when we were sleepy or distracted. Although under normal conditions we probably would be able to follow or remember them, we find ourselves asking that they be repeated or written down.

For instance, let's assume that you live in San Francisco and attend a party in Los Angeles. You decide to drive home to San Francisco after the party. You may have to ask someone at the party how to find the appropriate freeway. Because it is late and you are tired, you may have difficulty following the instructions. You attempt to compensate for your temporary auditory processing deficits by writing down the instructions. As you drive along, you see a sign saying San Francisco. You turn onto the freeway, but after a few miles you discover that the sign had actually said San Fernando, not San Francisco. Because you are fatigued, your brain has inefficiently

69

processed both the auditory information and the visual information. Your difficulty remembering the directions indicates a temporary auditory memory deficit and your difficulty in discriminating the letters reflects a temporary visual discrimination deficit.

Under most circumstances, the human brain functions like a marvelously complex and efficient computer. This "computer" is continuously taking in sensory information in the form of sensations (touch or smell), visual or auditory symbols (written or spoken language), and data (information/thoughts/ideas). The "computer" then instantaneously processes the information. Input (spoken or written language) will elicit output (spoken or written responses).

Turn right at this corner.
Please print.
The discount is 10%.
Answer the odd numbered questions.
List the dates chronologically.
How do you spell "thought"?

Human beings tend to take their "computer" for granted. When we get cold, we simply button up our coat. When we receive change at a supermarket, we simply do a quick subtraction to verify that the register is correct. It is only when we are sleepy or distracted and when our "computer" doesn't function efficiently that we truly appreciate our brain's marvelous capabilities.

In most instances our brain can process information with remarkable speed. Certain types of sensory input can elicit output in milliseconds. The instruction "turn right" will trigger in most people an immediate association with the right side of their body and with the meaning of the word "turn." A simple diagram describing the process would be:

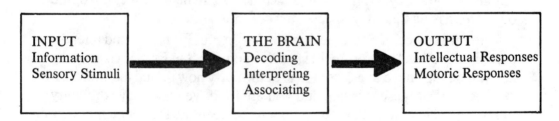

INPUT
Information
Sensory Stimuli

THE BRAIN
Decoding
Interpreting
Associating

OUTPUT
Intellectual Responses
Motoric Responses

In addition to producing output, the brain also functions to monitor this output. When your brain recognizes that it has made a mistake, such as having you turn left when you were asked to turn right, it can immediately correct the mistake (assuming of course that your brain knows the difference between right and left!)

The human "computer" does have limitations. Imagine being given directions by someone with a very pronounced accent or in a technical language that you have not been trained to understand. Your "computer" will probably not be able to process this information efficiently because it has not been programmed to do so.

A child in school must be able to process a wide spectrum of sensory data: symbols (example: "b" or "+"); directions (example: "Open your science book to the exercises at the end of Chapter Six"); memory skills (example: "When adding mixed fractions you must first find the common denominator"); discrimination skills (example: "The first word on the spelling test is 'standing' "); association skills (example: "If 'thin' is the antonym for 'fat,' 'tall' is the antonym for what?"); and organizational skills (example: "Plot all of the information you derive on either chart #1 or chart #2"). To process this data, a child must be able to decode the essential information. The symbol for the letter "b" is written in a code that children are expected to learn. Learning to read is simply learning the accepted written code for spoken language. Reading is the process of "breaking" the code, or decoding.

The child who does not have an organic neurological disorder and is not retarded or emotionally disturbed, but who cannot decode sensory information, probably has a perceptual dysfunction. The child's perceptual processing deficits may affect his capacity to decode, interpret, or associate the information coming to him from his environment in the form of sensory stimuli. Although the particular symptoms and causes of the dysfunction will vary from child to child, significant perceptual processing deficits almost invariably result in learning problems.

Perhaps one of the most common symptoms of a perceptual dysfunction is an inability to pay attention. When a student has difficulty orienting toward and focusing on the sensory data he is receiving, his process of decoding this data must be inefficient.

On the next page you will find a checklist to help you determine if your child is manifesting any of the common symptoms of a perceptual dysfunction. The list is not intended to be a definitive indication of the presence or absence of a perceptual learning disability. Rather, it is intended to help you decide whether a diagnostic evaluation is advisable. Although I have divided the symptoms into three major categories, many of the symptoms could have been placed under more than one category.

COMMON SYMPTOMS OF
A PERCEPTUAL DYSFUNCTION

BEHAVIOR	YES	NO
Short Attention Span	☐	☐
Difficulty Following Directions	☐	☐
Overactive	☐	☐
Impulsive	☐	☐
Fidgety	☐	☐
Distractible	☐	☐
Accident-prone	☐	☐
Forgetful	☐	☐
Daydreams	☐	☐
Slow in Completing Tasks	☐	☐
Excitable	☐	☐
Unpredictable	☐	☐

NEUROLOGICAL		
Gross-Motor Coordination Deficits (sports, etc.)	☐	☐
Fine-Motor Coordination Deficits (drawing/ handwriting, etc.)	☐	☐
Clumsy	☐	☐
Awkward	☐	☐
Poor Balance	☐	☐
Right/Left Confusion	☐	☐

ACADEMIC		
Poor Reading Comprehension	☐	☐
Difficulty with Phonics	☐	☐
Letter and Number Reversals	☐	☐
Inaccurate Reading	☐	☐
Poor Handwriting	☐	☐
Inaccurate Copying (from blackboard or at desk)	☐	☐
Difficulty with Math Computational Skills (addition, etc.)	☐	☐
Difficulty Understanding Math Concepts	☐	☐
Difficulty Working Independently	☐	☐
Sloppy Work Habits	☐	☐
Difficulty with Spelling	☐	☐
Difficulty with Language Arts Skills (essays/ syntax, etc.)	☐	☐
Poor Organizational Skills	☐	☐
Poor Planning Skills	☐	☐
Incomplete Projects	☐	☐
Difficulty Following Verbal and Written Instructions	☐	☐
Chronic Procrastination	☐	☐
Disturbs Other Students	☐	☐

Seldom do children have all or even most of the symptoms listed above. It is also important to note that some of the symptoms may also be indicative of other types of learning problems. A significant pattern of "yes" responses would suggest the possibility of a perceptual dysfunction, however, and a diagnostic evaluation by a qualified professional would be advisable.

There are certain behavior characteristics which are common by-products of a perceptual dysfunction. These include:

1. "Immature" behavior
2. A dislike for reading
3. A negative attitude toward school
4. Impatience
5. A low tolerance for frustration
6. An unwillingness to do homework
7. A difficulty accepting responsibility
8. Resistance to accepting help
9. Difficulty keeping up with the class
10. Little self-confidence
11. Extreme sensitivity to failure

As with any type of problem, the degree of a child's perceptual dysfunction can range from extremely severe to moderate to subtle. Severe perceptual dysfunctions make the mastery of academic skills very difficult. In some instances even relatively subtle perceptual processing deficits can significantly impede learning.

Severe perceptual learning disabilities will generally require intensive academic therapy and learning assistance. Ideally, this assistance should consist of more than simple tutoring. Learning assistance which does not address the source of the learning problem increases the probability that the problem will persist or recur. [28]

Fortunately, there are many methods that have proven successful in treating perceptual dysfunction. The nature of the child's problem, the type of training the teacher has received, and the teaching philosophy of the school district, tutor or the private learning center will determine the specific method that is employed.

---

28. Tutoring is an excellent resource in helping a child "catch up." A child who has missed school because of illness or a child who is having difficulty with Spanish will undoubtedly benefit from tutoring. A learning disabled child, however, will require specialized remedial methods designed specifically to help the child overcome the learning disability.

Whatever the remediation method, it is important that parents recognize that a child's perceptual learning problems may not initially respond to remediation, especially if the problems are severe or if they involve chronic distractibility and inattentiveness. Even moderate and subtle perceptual dysfunctions may be difficult to resolve. Parents should allow adequate time before making any decisions about the efficacy of the remediation strategy. Alternative strategies should be explored if no in-roads into correcting the learning problem are observed within a one-year period. Although the learning problem may not necessarily be resolved in one year, parents should be able to see progress. The decision to consider alternative approaches should not be made unilaterally, but rather in consultation with those who have been providing the learning assistance.

The time required to remediate perceptual learning disabilities can range from forty hours of intensive clinical remediation to twelve years of ongoing classroom learning assistance. The amount of time required will depend on the nature and severity of the student's perceptual dysfunction and the efficacy of the remediation methods that are used. Some perceptual dysfunctions may never be totally remediated. Training a child to compensate successfully for his dysfunction may be all that can reasonably be achieved in instances where the perceptual problems are very severe.

An example of successful compensation would be when a student uses his finger as he reads to help him "track" words more accurately. The child has instinctively realized that his eyes are not moving efficiently from left to right as they scan words in a line of print, and he has intuitively learned how to compensate for his deficiency. [29]

Visual tracking deficits are the result of erratic movement of the eyes as they "track" words horizontally across the page. The common consequence of a visual tracking deficiency is inaccurate reading, mispronounced words, dropped syllables, dropped word endings and skipped lines. The tracking problem will frequently cause children to reverse individual letters ("b"/"d"), reverse groups of letters ("saw" may be seen as "was"), or substitute words (the word "introduction" may be substituted for the word "institution").

The ideal objective in helping a child who reads inaccurately is to correct the child's visual tracking deficiencies completely. Attaining this goal is unlikely unless the child receives highly specialized assistance and perceptual training. In the interim, the child's index finger can serve a very practical and utilitarian function. It can act as a "brake" or "governor" and permits the child to control his visual-motor muscles. Using his finger the child can at least get through his reading assignments. The alternative is demoralizing failure.

29. Some classroom teachers discourage their students from using their index finger or some other device to help them read. I feel strongly that these teachers are making a mistake. As the child's visual-motor muscles become stronger as a result of practice and specialized learning assistance, the child's need to use the fine-motor muscles of the hand to supplement the visual-motor muscles will decrease. If you prohibit the child from helping himself, you run the risk that the child will become demoralized and develop profoundly negative associations with reading.

Perceptual problems are in many respects enigmatic. Determining the source of these problems is often difficult. We do know that perceptual problems can affect several members of the same family. Frequently, a grandfather, an uncle, a father, a mother or a cousin may have experienced the same learning problems as the child. At our center we often work with several children from the same family. Our clinical experience tends to confirm that a genetic factor is involved in perceptual learning problems. Other factors may also be responsible for severe perceptual dysfunction. These include trauma during childbirth, prenatal injury, or injury during childhood.

It is important to note that most children with subtle to moderate perceptual dysfunction do not have brain damage. Although they may have some of the "soft" signs of a neurological dysfunction (example: poor balance or poor coordination), seldom do E.E.G. examinations reveal indications of organic brain damage. It is also important to differentiate the terms Minimal Brain Dysfunction (M.B.D.), which is another term for perceptual dysfunction, and Minimal Brain Damage, which is used to describe a condition where actual organic brain damage can be determined. Unfortunately, these terms are often used synonymously, even by professionals.

Although there is a vital distinction between a perceptual dysfunction and brain damage, there are many common denominators. Many of the behavioral, academic and motoric characteristics are similar, but generally the symptoms manifested by the child with organic brain damage will be more severe. The major common characteristic of both a perceptual dysfunction and organic brain damage is neurological inefficiency (sensory processing deficits). Extensive evidence documents the success that has been achieved in treating children with perceptual dysfunction and with organic brain damage. With appropriate therapy, many of these children can be trained to process sensory information more efficiently. During the last twelve years, I have observed thousands of children at our center learn to overcome or to compensate for perceptual processing deficits. Other institutions throughout the United States have had similar successes using a wide range of teaching and learning strategies.

SPECIFIC LEARNING PROBLEMS

Brent: A Bright Child Who Couldn't Learn To Read

When I said hello to Brent, he refused to respond or even to acknowledge me. I could sense his anger and frustration. The child was clearly demoralized.

For approximately four months we had been attempting to teach this cherubic seven and a half-year-old to read. After more than twenty hours of intensive clinical learning and remedial reading assistance, he was still unable to identify any of the basic letters or sounds with any consistency. Brent would seem to master the sound of a letter and then one minute later he would be unable to remember either the sound or the letter. In desperation, our staff had employed several different teaching techniques but with no success. Brent seemed incapable of recognizing letters and of associating the sounds of letters with their written symbols.

I assigned Brent to our most senior teacher. This teacher had had extensive experience helping severely learning disabled and reading disabled students. Despite her many talents and her seemingly inexhaustible patience, I had begun to sense her mounting exasperation as she worked with Brent.

Although I had become very concerned about Brent's lack of progress, I was far more concerned about his growing unhappiness and frustration. Not only did I feel our teaching strategy was not working, but I sensed that our intense desire to teach him to read was doing more harm than good.

I called Brent's mother and suggested a comprehensive diagnostic work-up by a pediatrician who specialized in treating children with learning disabilities. I also called all the staff members who were working with Brent into my office for a conference. Together we reviewed the methods we had used and designed a new teaching strategy. A staff member volunteered to implement the new program, and the responsibility for teaching Brent to read was turned over to her.

In the interim, the pediatrician reported no indications of a neurological disorder. He suggested that medication, specifically amphetamines, might help Brent to concentrate and to read. Brent's parents, who had serious misgivings about using amphetamines, rejected this recommendation.

With great patience the new teacher began making modest inroads into Brent's reading problems. The progress was erratic, however, and periodically Brent would seem to forget much of what he had been taught. As Brent and his teacher learned how to rebound from these periodic setbacks, his anxiety decreased. The setbacks became less frequent, and Brent's self-concept also began to improve.

It has been one year since Brent was first enrolled at our center. He is now able to read at a basic primer level. Although Brent's gains are modest, they represent a prodigious effort on everyone's part.

Brent is currently working with a highly talented reading specialist whom we hired specifically to help Brent and several other of our severely reading disabled children. She reports that Brent's reading problems are among the most significant that she has encountered in her many years of teaching reading disabled children. Nevertheless, he continues to make progress.

Brent's reading problems are the direct result of profound perceptual processing deficits. His visual memory skills and auditory memory skills are extremely deficient, as are his sound/letter/word retrieval and associative skills. [30] Despite these profound perceptual processing deficits, Brent's I.Q. is in the superior range.

At the last conference, we recommended that Brent's parents consider a recently developed, experimental drug protocol. Clinical experience with this relatively harmless drug appears to indicate positive results when it is used to treat dyslexic children, but to date no conclusive research has been done to validate the protocol. The theory behind the treatment program is that dyslexic children are actually suffering from a mild form of disequilibrium, and that small doses of a motion sickness drug can correct this equilibrium problem and eliminate symptoms of dyslexia in the process. The jury is still out as far as Brent is concerned. His parents are receptive to the use of medication, and the next step is up to the physician. In the meantime, we are continuing to provide both perceptual training and reading help.

Reading Problems

Most children learn to read regardless of the reading system that is used to teach them. In many respects, the phenomenon of planned obsolescence would appear to be as integral to the textbook publishing industry as it is to the automobile industry. Just when a school district or a state commits to a particular approach, the publishing companies change direction and develop a new series or a new approach. The new reading series now becomes the "definitive" approach, and the publishers pull out all the stops to persuade the school district or the state to purchase this new "definitive" program.

A good teacher can teach most children to read using a 1950's primer. [31] Publishers will contend that they have been forced to develop innovative reading systems because of deficiencies in teachers' skills. They argue that the systems guarantee that children will learn to read even if the teacher lacks good teaching skills. Unfortunately, reading skills are never-

30. See Glossary of Educational Terms for a definition of these terms.
31. I do not dispute that modern reading materials are generally more relevant to a child and that high-interest material encourages the child to read. A good teacher, however, can teach using just about any material. The key is the teacher and his or her skills and enthusiasm.

theless deteriorating throughout the country. The explanation for this phenomenon is complex, and the fault cannot be attributed exclusively to teachers, the educational system or publishers of reading programs.

Perhaps one of the most significant contributing factors in the deterioration of American students' reading skills is that our culture is continuously changing, and the cultural support systems which historically encouraged reading, studying and academic excellence have also changed. The family of the 1980's is quite different from the family of the 1940's. Single parent families, television, computer games, less rigorous standards of discipline, and less rigorous educational standards have in many instances replaced the traditional two parent family, radio (which encouraged children to create their own fantasies instead of having them cast in Hollywood), the homework ethic, discipline and demanding standards of educational excellence.

During the formative years, children are sufficiently adaptable to be able to ingest and utilize just about any program that is designed to teach them to decipher the printed word. A phonics approach may prove to be very successful with certain children, and a sight word approach may prove to be somewhat more effective with others. Most children can respond positively to either method.

Children who are adequately taught but who still have difficulty learning to read are atypical. For whatever reason or reasons their "computer" is not efficiently deciphering or decoding the symbols in which written language is represented.

There are many specific deficiencies which can result in reading problems. The most common of these are listed below. To evaluate your own child's reading skills, you will most likely need to consult your child's classroom teacher.

COMMON CAUSAL FACTORS OF READING PROBLEMS [32]

	YES	NO
VISUAL IMPAIRMENT (inability to see with acuity)	☐	☐
VISUAL TRACKING DEFICITS (inability to see words, phrases and sentences accurately because the eyes are not moving efficiently across the printed line. Typical symptoms: word substitutions, omitted syllables and words, word additions, word inversions and losing one's place when reading).	☐	☐
VISUAL DISCRIMINATION DEFICITS (inability to distinguish certain letters from other letters. Example: "b"/"d").	☐	☐

---

32.   Your child's classroom teacher may not be able to evaluate your child in all of the areas covered by this checklist. You may need to consult a reading specialist.

	YES	NO
VISUAL MEMORY DEFICITS (inability to remember the visual shape of letters and words, and inability to associate these shapes with letters, sounds and words)	☐	☐
VISUAL AND/OR AUDITORY ASSOCIATION DEFICITS (inability to associate the sound or the visual configuration or the meaning of the word with what is seen or heard).	☐	☐
PHONICS AND/OR BLENDING DEFICITS (inability to sound out words. This particular problem is usually the result of causal factors included in this list).	☐	☐
AUDITORY IMPAIRMENT (inability to hear certain sounds, especially in the high frequency range, can make the initial mastery of reading difficult for primary age children).	☐	☐
AUDITORY DISCRIMINATION DEFICITS (inability to hear the difference between sounds such as the short "i" and the short "e" sound. The ability to distinguish the sounds letters make is the starting point in the process of teaching the primary school child to read. Discrimination skills are the key to decoding words).	☐	☐
AUDITORY MEMORY DEFICITS (inability to remember the sounds that letters make or to remember how groups of letters are pronounced).	☐	☐
"PART-WHOLE" PERCEPTUAL DEFICITS (inability to perceive relationships between individual sounds and whole words, or between words that are read and their meaning when used in sentences or paragraphs. Example: a child who can sound out a common word and yet not be able to tell you what the word means. Such "part-whole" difficulties usually manifest themselves in reading comprehension problems).	☐	☐
RETRIEVAL DEFICITS (inability to recall or associate information or skills that have previously been learned or mastered).	☐	☐
VOCABULARY DEFICITS (inability to recall the meaning of words or to associate the meaning of a word that had previously been mastered).	☐	☐
CONCENTRATION DEFICITS (inability to pay attention or to focus when reading).		
EMOTIONAL PROBLEMS (distractibility or negative attitude which is the result of personal or family disharmony).	☐	☐

The ultimate objective of the process of learning to read is to acquire the ability to comprehend what is being communicated through the medium of written symbols or words. There are three basic levels of comprehension:

LEVEL 1 — **Recall of Facts (literal)**

> Example: Jaimie opened the door, opened her umbrella and walked down the path.
>
> Question: Can you name three things Jaimie did?

A child who can read this material and who has difficulty answering questions which require remembering factual information may have one or more of the following reading deficiencies:

1. Visual memory deficits
2. Part-whole perceptual deficits (can read words but does not associate the meaning with words)
3. Intelligence limitations
4. Concentration deficits

LEVEL 2 — **Inferential (perceiving cause and effect)**

> Example: Jaimie opened the door, opened her umbrella and walked down the path.
> Question: What kind of day was it?

A child who is able to read the sentence in the example above but is unable to draw conclusions based on the content of the sentence is manifesting difficulty with inferential reasoning ability. Such difficulty signals a lack of comprehension and a lack of ability to generalize about what has been read. Inferential questions are intended to probe a student's capacity to respond to information which is implied but not directly stated. Inferential comprehension demands a personal response as opposed to a simple regurgitation of facts.

LEVEL 3 — Applicative (critical processing of information)

> Example: Jaimie opened the door, opened her umbrella and walked down the path.
>
> Question: What would you have done if you were with Jaimie as she began to walk down the path?

To respond to a question which requires applicative skills, a child must be able to evaluate information and offer a response which would be appropriate to the context. The ability to analyze, infer and draw conclusions from data represents the highest level of comprehension. The quality of the child's ability to respond will directly reflect such factors as educational training, cultural background and intelligence.

The capacity to comprehend can be developed. Indeed, the primary objective of education is to train children to think. With practice, children can learn techniques for recalling information, making inferences and drawing conclusions from stated information.

Extremely intelligent children frequently have an inherent ability to analyze, infer and apply information. But even the extremely intelligent child who possesses a natural ability to draw inferences can further develop this ability with practice and training.

The first step in the development of comprehension skills is the acquisition of basic reading skills. The ability to decode words and read them, however, does not guarantee comprehension. A child must be able to understand the explicit and implicit meaning of words if he is to be able to comprehend what he is reading.

The capacity to associate words with their meanings is the cornerstone of vocabulary and comprehension skills. The words "umbrella" or "path" used in the examples cited previously will elicit in most children an immediate mental image. These children will associate these words with their past experiences.

Words such as "umbrella" or "path" are very basic words in a child's vocabulary. They represent objects which are concrete. Other words, such as "allegiance" or "abolish," represent ideas which are less concrete and more abstract. Understanding such words requires higher level memory and association skills.

Abstract words such as "allegiance" are particularly difficult to understand for children with comprehension problems. Indeed, the definitions of such words are themselves abstractions. For example, the synonym for the word "allegiance" is the word "loyalty." Since both "loyalty" and "allegiance" are abstract concepts, children who have difficulty operating on a conceptual level would probably be confused by these words.

There are excellent teaching methods and materials which can help children to deal more successfully with abstract words and concepts. These resources are available to all learning assistance specialists. The ability to deal with abstractions can be developed in many children. The use of an elementary or intermediate level dictionary can be an invaluable resource in helping children understand the meanings of words.

Many children with reading comprehension problems also have difficulty understanding and remembering the meaning of words which are not abstract. Frequently they will read a word which they do not recognize and then make no attempt to find out what the word means, even though this word may be essential to their comprehending the material. It should come as no surprise that these children are often confused about what they are reading.

In order to provide meaningful assistance, the specific deficits which are interfering with a child's reading comprehension must be pinpointed by means of testing. [33] These specific deficits include an inability to recall facts, make inferences, or apply information. An individualized remediation strategy can be developed through testing. If the child's deficiencies are primarily perceptual (example: poor visual tracking), the remediation protocol should be designed to provide training that will either correct this deficiency or at least teach the child how to compensate for it successfully.

When a child's problem does not involve the actual process of deciphering words but, rather, is conceptual and involves recall, inferential or applicative skills, the child should receive remedial assistance in these areas. Such assistance will help the child organize and direct his analytical thinking skills. Children can be taught how to read a chapter or a book so that they can perceive relationships and retain information. Children can also be taught to look for key words and ideas in a paragraph. Some children acquire the ability to perceive these relationships and retain information naturally and require little or no training. Other children who do not have this "natural" facility can acquire it in much the same way that, with practice and desire, a "nonnatural" athlete can become very competent at a particular sport.

The primary emphasis in the early stages of a child's elementary school education is upon basic decoding skills ("word attack," blending, sight word recognition, phonics and tracking) and information recall. Some children perform well at this stage of learning to read but begin to falter in

33. A test which simply provides the child's grade level or percentile score may not be particularly useful in helping to design a remediation strategy. Either the child's responses to a question missed must be analyzed or a different type of reading test administered. Ideally, such a test should define the specific deficit areas.

fourth, fifth or sixth grade when higher level inferential and applicative skills are emphasized. Such children may need specialized remedial support until they can master the required skills. If the child's comprehension problem is due to limited intelligence, then it is likely that the child will require prolonged learning support.

Spelling Problems

Three very essential perceptual processing skills are prerequisites to being able to spell with proficiency. The first skill involves auditory discrimination. A child must be able to distinguish auditorily the different sounds that letters make. This ability to distinguish sounds is especially critical when the word being spelled is phonetic. [34] A child who cannot discriminate properly between such words as "pen" and "pin" will probably have difficulty spelling many of the words which make up the English language.

One of the essential components in spelling proficiency is the ability to remember auditorily. The sound "ou" in the word "round" can be made only by two letter combinations: "ow" and "ou." A child who is asked to spell this word would have to remember the two combinations of letters which produce the sound and that the "ow" combination is seldom found in the middle of a word (exception: "crowd").

Children with a facility for spelling probably will not be consciously aware of phonetic rules. Their brain or mental computer will instantaneously retrieve the correct letter combination to produce the word "round." For such children, the word/sound/auditory discrimination/auditory memory/retrieval/association process occurs with little or no effort.

Visual memory is another essential component in the equation that produces good spelling skills. This is especially true with words which are nonphonetic. The many words in the English language which are either nonphonetic or exceptions to the general rules of spelling make visual memory the single most important perceptual processing skill involved in spelling. The word "respondent," for example, might just as easily be spelled with an "ant" in the last syllable instead of an "ent." The endings "ant" and "ent" are often pronounced the same way, which makes it difficult to determine from the pronunciation of the word that it requires an "ent" to be spelled properly. Nor is there a spelling rule which would indicate that "ent" is the correct spelling. The only way to learn how to spell such a word is simply by memorizing how it is spelled.

34. "Phonetic" refers to words which follow prescribed rules of pronunciation and spelling.

There are several other important factors which can affect a person's spelling ability. These factors include:

1. Attention to detail
2. Concentration
3. Desire
4. Pronunciation
5. Practice

Spelling words correctly requires attention to detail. Only one letter need be incorrect in even the most complicated of words for a teacher to circle the word in red ink. No rewards are given on spelling tests for words which are "almost correct."

Certain personality types appear to have a greater facility for acquiring good spelling skills. Precision and attention to detail are the primary characteristics of such personalities.

Desire is another key factor in the acquisition of good spelling skills. Students who intend not to make spelling mistakes generally make fewer mistakes. Such students will look words up in a dictionary if they have doubts about the proper spelling, and they will also edit their essays and reports more carefully.

Frequently, children will spell words incorrectly because they are pronouncing them incorrectly. The word "prerogative" is often spelled "perrogative" because that is how many people pronounce it. Parents who perceive that their child is pronouncing words incorrectly should selectively try to correct their child's pronunciation. Exercise caution, though. Parents who correct their child repeatedly can elicit resentment and inhibit parent-child communication.

Even students with poor visual memory skills can improve their spelling with practice. Although children with poor visual memory skills may need additional exposure to a particularly difficult word before they master it, all children can become better spellers with sufficient effort and practice.

Some students can discipline themselves to do well on the weekly spelling test, but their spelling may be atrocious on essays and reports. In order to spell words properly in an essay, a student must look very critically at what he is writing with the intention of finding and correcting mistakes. The student must have self-discipline and must be able to force himself to look up words when he senses a word "doesn't look right."

Although spelling skills can be developed and children can be taught phonetic rules and spelling rules, spelling is learned primarily through practice and memorization. There are specific techniques and programs available to resource specialists that help children with spelling problems. There are also many fun games that families can play together which can help children become better spellers. Parents of children with profound spelling problems should consult the resource specialist at their child's school for suggestions.

Math Problems

A child who is struggling with math may have a deficiency in either conceptual skills (understanding how numbers function) or computational skills (doing mathematical operations). Many children with severe math problems will have deficiencies in both areas.

The successful resolution of a child's math problems requires that his specific deficiencies be identified accurately. To assign a child additional problems or to drill him in multiplication tables when he is confused is of little value. A child who has difficulty adding numbers with decimals may not know how to add, or he may not understand decimals. If he is confused about the concepts, then the first step in his remedial process is to explain the concepts involving the particular mathematical operation. If the child has difficulty with computational skills he may simply need more practice adding. If he is inattentive or sloppy, then additional practice or an incentive program for neatness may be appropriate.

Most children are capable of grasping basic arithmetic. When shown how to add or subtract, they will generally catch on quickly to the operations involved. Most children can also master more complicated operations such as multiplication and division with relative ease. These operations involve a large amount of rote memory. Even those children who are considered to be of below average intelligence can learn to do math by rote.

Children who experience problems understanding how numbers relate to each other frequently have difficulty mastering operational or computational skills. Such difficulties may indicate deficient perceptual processing ability. Efficient auditory and visual memory, visual discrimination and tracking are as essential to the development of math skills as they are to the development of reading skills.

The first step in the effective remediation of a math problem is identification. Diagnostic math tests can quickly reveal whether a child's problem is conceptual or computational and can pinpoint the specific conceptual or computational deficits. For example, a child may be confused about fractions because he doesn't understand the part/whole concepts involved in the mathematical operation. Once this conceptual difficulty is identified, teachers can then use specific remedial methods with the child which will help him master the necessary concepts. [35]

If a child's problem is computational, he can do specific exercises and practice problems which reinforce accuracy and develop operational skills. Guided practice and basic repetition can be a very important remedial tool, provided the child first understands the concepts involved in the mathematical operations he is practicing.

When a student's computational deficits are due to inattentiveness, he may respond to a behavior modification program. Such a program could be designed to reward the child for accuracy. The child's parents or teachers could set up a system, for example, in which the child receives points for each problem he does correctly, accurately and/or legibly. Money or a prize or award can be used as the incentive. Parents or teachers could also use negative reinforcement (example: "These problems need to be redone so that they are more legible.") as an integral part of the system. [36]

Handwriting Problems

In order to write legibly and accurately, a person must be able to control the fine-motor muscles of the hand. A child acquires the ability to control these muscles in stages during the course of his development.

Most three year-olds will naturally gravitate to crayons and chalk. At first their ability to grasp the crayon will be awkward. With practice their ability to control their fingers will improve, but at the early stages of development their drawings will appear disjointed and bear little resemblance to reality.

As the child matures and has more practice manipulating objects, his fine-motor proficiency will increase. He will learn how to cut with scissors and he will begin to be able to draw things which can be identified by others.

In kindergarten the child will be taught how to form letters and numbers. At first, forming these letters and numbers will require great effort. The child's hand and fingers must learn how to obey the commands of his brain.

35.   The use of manipulatives (units such as pennies, cubes or popsicle sticks which are used to represent the relationship that exists between numbers) can be an invaluable resource for helping children who are "stuck" and do not understand the basic concepts of arithmetic.

36.   See Chapter Five: "Monitoring Your Child's Performance" for a discussion of the use of rewards as incentives for children.

The kindergartener's ability to control the fine-motor muscles of his fingers will generally improve as a function of practice and maturity. Through a process of trial and error, the child will begin to perceive spatial relationships more accurately. As he perceives these relationships and as his fine-motor control improves, he will begin the process of learning how to scale down his letters and numbers so that they fit into the prescribed space.

While most children will learn how to form their letters and numbers, other children will have difficulty acquiring spatial judgment and developing fine-motor proficiency. Their letters will appear misshapen, disproportionate, and illegible. Although they may practice just as much as the other children do, they will achieve only marginal improvement.

Potential handwriting problems will generally begin to manifest themselves in kindergarten or first grade. Parents and teachers are more likely to recognize blatant fine-motor problems and begin remedial assistance. In some instances, handwriting problems do not become a source of concern until third or fourth grade.

Parents and teachers often associate the handwriting difficulties of older children with inattentiveness, impulsiveness, or sloppy work habits. These factors can definitely contribute to the problem, but the source of illegible writing may be fine-motor deficiencies or spatial judgment deficits which were not properly identified in kindergarten or first grade.

To be effective, the remediation strategy for poor handwriting must address the causal factors. Resource teachers can assign specific fine-motor activities which are designed to develop better coordination skills if poor handwriting is the result of fine-motor coordination deficits. If the child has difficulty with spatial judgment (i.e., difficulty distinguishing size, shape and relative positioning), he can be given specific training activities to improve these perceptual processing skills. [37]

Handwriting problems which are the result of inattentiveness, impulsiveness or sloppiness can also be corrected, assuming that the student is willing to work at overcoming the problem and assuming that the teacher communicates clearly that students are expected to write legibly.

Many older students with handwriting problems are defensive about their "sloppy" writing. This defensiveness is the result of having been nagged and lectured for years about how impossible it is to read what they have written. Habits tend to become entrenched. Teenagers can be as resistant to giving up "bad" habits as their adult counterparts are.

The process of helping a student improve his handwriting is akin to the process of helping a person improve his tennis game. If you wanted to improve your tennis game, you would probably seek out a coach or tennis

37.   Spatial orientation or figure-ground deficits (see Glossary of Educational Terms) can often be identified by a test called the Bender-Gestalt. See Testing Appendix.

pro. The coach would analyze your tennis game to identify its weaknesses. He or she would then recommend a specific set of exercises designed to correct the identified deficits. The exercises might focus on particular components of your swing or follow-through if you were having difficulty with that aspect of your game.

The same principles apply to improving a child's handwriting. Precise identification of the deficits will suggest the specific exercises. There are no magic "bullets," however, which will help a child to write more legibly. The retraining process will require effort, practice and a willingness to improve.

ATYPICAL LEARNING PROBLEMS

Selby: A Star In A Family Of Superstars

It didn't take very long for me to recognize that the ten year-old was very bright and very perceptive. His father explained that he had been referred to our center by the principal at his son's private school. Selby, a sixth grader, was struggling in school despite the fact that he was intelligent and came from a highly academic family.

Selby's mother was an artist. His father was a surgeon and taught at a medical school. Selby's father also had the distinction of having won a gold medal in the Olympics.

Selby was experiencing increasingly more difficulty keeping up with his class and understanding the material that was being presented in school. His reading comprehension scores had been declining each year, and Selby was now testing approximately six months below grade level. The curriculum at his school was oriented approximately three years above grade level, and Selby was rapidly becoming discouraged.

Selby did not begin talking until he was four and a half years old. At first his parents suspected that he might be deaf, but a hearing test confirmed that Selby could hear. Dysphasia was considered as a possible explanation, but Selby responded so quickly to language therapy that the therapist doubted that the child was truly dysphasic. Neither the physicians nor the speech and hearing center could pinpoint the cause of Selby's problem.

Selby's language problems were quickly corrected. Within eight months of beginning his therapy, Selby was talking normally. The speech therapists and the physicians at the medical school dismissed him with a "clean bill of health."

During the first three years of elementary school, Selby proved to be an excellent student. He was one of the best readers in his class. His math skills were also excellent. Quick and eager to learn, Selby enjoyed school and was proud of his academic accomplishments.

Selby's parents began to perceive a deterioration in his performance and attitude when he entered fourth grade. Academic work was no longer easy for him. He was frequently confused by the material in school and completing his homework assignments had become a monumental struggle. Although he worked diligently at his homework, Selby's efforts were becoming less efficient. Because of the difficulties he was experiencing, Selby had become more and more dependent upon his mother to help him.

Selby's older brother, Jeff, was an excellent student whose I.Q. was 170. Everyone in the family was keenly aware that when Jeff had been Selby's age, his performance in school had been significantly better. In addition to his academic talents, Jeff was also an excellent diver, and appeared destined to make the Olympic Diving Team. Selby was also a good athlete, but his brother was a superb athlete.

Selby's parents were divorced. They said that Selby had handled their divorce relatively well. The parents were now good friends, and Selby saw his dad regularly. While their parents were going through the divorce, both children had seen a family therapist for a short while. She informed the parents that the children were dealing with the divorce well and that they did not require ongoing therapy.

On the surface, Selby did not appear to be envious or resentful of his very exceptional brother. In fact, Selby gave the appearance of being proud of his brother's accomplishments. Their parents felt that their sons were not in competition with one another, and they seemed to have a good relationship.

Although Selby's parents claimed that they did not compare their children, it was clear that they were proud of their older child's academic success and disappointed by their younger son's lack of academic accomplishments. Selby had been born into a family of superstars. In his own right Selby was also an exceptional child, but he did not perhaps have the same particular abilities that the other members of his family possessed.

My diagnostic tests did not conclusively indicate a learning disability. They did show some subtle auditory processing deficits and subtle visual memory deficits. An item analysis of Selby's reading test revealed that he was having problems with inferential and applicative reading comprehension skills. [36] Although there were some learning deficits, I could not make a definitive diagnosis of a learning disability if I relied exclusively on the

36. See pages 80-81 for a discussion of the different levels of reading comprehension.

standard diagnostic criteria. A meaningful diagnosis would have to take into consideration not only Selby's learning deficits but also the pressure he was experiencing at home and the accelerated curriculum of his school.

I suspected that there were emotional components involved in Selby's learning problems, despite the therapist's assessment (which I received secondhand). I also suspected that the divorce had affected Selby emotionally, and I inferred from certain statements made by the parents that there was more competition between Selby and his brother than the family was acknowledging. Selby realized that his brother was excelling and that he was not. Selby could not help but be aware of his parents' value system with its strong emphasis on educational achievement.

Although by most traditional diagnostic standards Selby did not have a learning disability, his learning deficits combined with his emotional stress made him a candidate for learning assistance. I recommended a three hour per week program which would focus upon improving Selby's reading skills and correcting his subtle perceptual processing deficits. Rebuilding Selby's confidence in his own abilities would also be a key component in the remediation strategy.

I urged Selby's parents do two things: 1) to be patient for six months, and 2) to stop making comparisons between their two children. I explained to the parents that although Selby would continue have problems in school for a while, I was certain that his reading skills would improve dramatically as he began to respond to the learning assistance. Once Selby began to succeed in school, his potential achievement would be limited only by his own expectations of himself. My prognosis proved accurate. Selby is now an *A* student.

Unusual Learning Problems

Identifying the specific factors which are responsible for the learning problem can be very challenging when a child's learning problems are subtle or atypical. A child who is testing above grade level in reading, for example, may have difficulty reading aloud or understanding his textbooks. Another child who has a very high I.Q. may, nevertheless, be doing *C* work in school. The child may not have any conclusively identifiable learning deficiencies, but his teachers and parents recognize that the quality of his classwork is below the level of his ability.

Children with nonspecific learning disabilities are frequently enigmatic to their parents, their teachers and even school psychologists and learning disabilities specialists. Although everyone may recognize that these children are not learning effectively, no one is quite sure why they are stuck. Their learning deficits do not conform to the standard pattern.

A child with nonspecific learning disabilities may perform well in some subjects and terribly in others. He may do well in math and poorly in reading one year, and do just the opposite the following year. Another child may pay attention in class when certain subjects are being taught and be totally distracted when other subjects are being taught. He may do excellent work for one teacher and be completely unresponsive and irresponsible for another teacher. Or he may do good work for a period of time, and then appear to give up and do nothing.

Children with subtle, unusual or enigmatic learning problems may never be tested for a learning disability. If they are tested, a precise diagnosis may not be possible because the symptoms of their problems are difficult to define. [37]

One of the unfortunate consequences of the atypical or nonspecific learning disability is that the child, his parents and his teachers may erroneously conclude that the student is only capable of marginal, erratic performance. Such expectations have a disturbing tendency to become self-fulfilling. Some children with atypical problems will figure out how to resolve their own learning problems without learning assistance, but many of these children will unfortunately continue to perform marginally.

There is nothing intrinsically wrong with doing *C* work if that is the best work a student is capable of doing. There is something wrong, however, when a child wastes his potential or becomes convinced — erroneously — that he is incapable of doing good work.

One of education's most important functions is creating an opportunity for children to become excited about learning. This desire is the key emotion which will motivate a child to acquire not only these basic skills but also the more advanced technical and thinking skills that form the foundation of a career.

Learning is an innate human desire. Most children want to learn, but some children have atypical learning needs and require an atypical learning strategy. To describe such children as being underachievers, "immature," or poorly motivated neither pinpoints why these children are having difficulty learning, nor does it suggest any specific approach to helping them actualize their potential.

Identifying a nonspecific learning disability involves an unavoidable element of subjectivity. A school pyschologist who is locked into relying exclusively on objective standardized tests may reject the possiblity that a child has a learning problem because the problem does not conform to the standard criteria. Some children who do not deviate significantly from the standardized norms will have difficulty learning. This difficulty may have nothing to do with I.Q. or low motivation. Understanding why a child is functioning poorly in school requires more than just administering a test

39. See Glossary of Testing Terms and Testing Appendix.

and grading it. The child's home environment, school environment, learning strengths and deficits, perceptual skills, and emotional responses are all factors which must be examined and considered.

A child's performance in school must be assessed not only in relationship to the national norms but also in relationship to his potential and the school he is attending. Other factors which must be considered include the expectations of the child's parents and of the child himself.

If parents feel that their child is not performing commensurate with his ability, they should request that their child be diagnostically tested at his school. If their child does not qualify for testing because he is not significantly below grade level, the parents must then decide whether or not they want to have him tested privately.

A child with atypical learning problems may simply need to be taught *how* to concentrate, *how* to organize his ideas and time, *how* to study, *how* to prepare for exams and *how* to write a report or an essay. These objectives can be achieved by means of a wide spectrum of creative teaching techniques, incentives, and parental and teacher support and encouragement.

The sad reality is that most school districts are primarily concerned with providing help for children with specific identifiable learning problems. Although an excellent argument can be made for giving the needs of the severely and moderately learning disabled child top priority, an equally good argument can be made for providing meaningful learning assistance for children with nonspecific, atypical learning disabilities. The child with an atypical learning disability who is unable to achieve his potential represents a loss of human potential that is no less significant than the lost potential of a child with a severe, identifiable learning problem. Any waste of human potential is tragic, whatever the reason, and the primary responsibility of parents and educators is to do everything in their power to prevent this tragedy from happening.

CHAPTER FOUR _____

Emotional Problems & Learning Disabilities

STEVE: NO ONE WAS LISTENING

One Friday afternoon a student who had been in my class for approximately six weeks handed in his weekly quiz, picked up his books and left the room. At the time, I was a graduate student at a major university and was teaching part-time.

The student's name was Steve, and I noticed as I glanced at his paper that he had drawn a chain of little circles through all his answers. Although I could still read the answers with some effort, I was annoyed that Steve had chosen to cross them out. Feeling that as a new teacher I had to establish and clearly define my standards and requirements for my students, I decided to give Steve an *F* on the quiz. On the top of his paper I wrote: "Why did you cross out your answers?" When I returned his quiz the following Monday afternoon, I asked Steve the same question. He smiled, shrugged and responded, "I don't know."

After leaving my class that Monday, Steve went to his English class where he received an *F* on a report he had handed in the previous week. After English class, he went to the gym where he informed the freshman basketball coach that he had decided to quit the team. From there he returned home, went to his father's dresser, took out his father's revolver, pressed the barrel to his temple and, while his three year-old sister watched, pulled the trigger.

When I learned of Steve's suicide the next day, I was devastated. I had hardly known the boy, and frankly, he was not one of my favorite students. He seldom contributed in class and he didn't seem particularly interested in what I was teaching. Shocked and profoundly saddened, I began to examine my own role in what had happened.

The previous week I had attended a lecture in an educational psychology course which dealt with behavior modification. The essence of this educational philosophy is that children should be rewarded when they fulfill the requirements (positive reinforcement) and punished when they don't (negative reinforcement). I felt that I had followed these precepts exactly. What had gone wrong?

The next day I approached the professor after class. "What would you have done if one of your high school students had drawn a chain of circles through all of his answers on a quiz?" I asked. He responded, "I would have recognized that there was something troubling the student, and I would have talked with him to find out what it was." I was crushed. I wanted him to tell me that I had handled things properly and that I shouldn't feel badly. But obviously I had not handled things properly, and Steve was dead.

The reasons for Steve's suicide became apparent as I pieced the story together. Steve's father was a successful physician who had very high expectations for his son. He wanted him to be the best at everything he did. He expected Steve to make the basketball team and to be an *A* student. Steve must have decided that he couldn't or didn't want to fulfill these expectations, and he began to sabotage himself in school. Although his decision to fail expressed a rejection of his father's values, it also expressed his own sense of hopelessness and worthlessness. When Steve finally realized that failing and quitting did not enable him to escape his tension and depression, he probably could see no other alternative but to commit suicide. This anguished and senseless act of self-destruction was the only way that Steve could express his pain, his futility, and his anger.

Steve may have had a learning disability, but there had been no prior evidence that his academic difficulties were the result of any specific, identifiable learning deficits. Steve's academic problems resulted from profound emotional conflicts. For whatever reason, Steve was unwilling or unable to permit himself to succeed. A child who feels unworthy of success, cannot allow himself to reach for or accept success.

The child who resides beneath a mask of indifference, smugness, toughness, arrogance or shyness is often a very fragile and very frightened person who feels compelled to hide his innermost emotions from others and from himself. To help such a child, parents and teachers must look beneath the facade. If they perceive fear, unhappiness and insecurity, then their immediate priority is to do whatever they can to help the child resolve these potentially devastating emotional conflicts. The alternative is to do nothing in the vain hope that the problems will go away. Unfortunately, fear, unhappiness and insecurity seldom go away of their own accord.

Children learn very early in their lives to disown their negative feelings because they sense that these feelings are unnatural and therefore "bad." They learn that only "bad" children hate or hurt their parents and that "good" children are loving, responsible and respectful. A child who senses that his own innermost feelings are mean and angry may conclude that he is a "bad" or a "mean" person. In order to cope with his "meanness," the child may attempt to disown his feelings or pretend they don't exist. He may decide to punish himself for his emotions by choosing to fail or to misbehave or to have accidents. Or the child may choose to act out and to press his parents' and his teachers' "hot buttons," knowing that in so doing he will upset them and will probably be punished. By structuring his own punishment the child may be unconsciously atoning for his self-perceived "badness." Suicide is the ultimate expression of all a child's disowned emotions: the pain, the futility, the anger, the sense of worthlessness. Tragically, the child committing this last desperate act is convinced that he has no alternative.

RECOGNIZING AN EMOTIONAL PROBLEM

Emotional problems can be as academically incapacitating for a child as any specific learning disability. The learning disabled child can often be identified and treated either at his own school or within his school district, but identification and treatment of a child's emotional problems generally require resources that most school districts do not possess. [1] Children with emotional problems will often manifest many of the same learning deficits as do children with learning disabilities. The result can be misdiagnosis and improper treatment of the child's primary problem.

Children, like adults, tend to hide their weaknesses, vulnerabilities and insecurities, not only from others, but also from themselves. They may camouflage fear with toughness or self-doubt with cockiness. They may pretend to be happy when really they are unhappy. They may feign indifference when actually their feelings are very intense.

Unfortunately, a child's emotional problems may not become apparent to parents and the teachers until much emotional damage has been done. Emotionally distressed children will often unconsciously repress their feelings and their problems. To protect themselves, they will develop coping mechanisms and defense mechanisms which may be very difficult to penetrate. Often these children are frightened by their emotions and choose not to deal with them. They may deny the existence of these feelings to themselves and to others, hoping that somehow the bad feelings will go away. The smiling, seemingly happy-go-lucky child may actually be a seething cauldron inside. What the child presents to the world is a misleading facade, and the child's parents and teachers may have no idea of the conflicting emotions which are torturing the child. Ironically, the child himself probably has no idea how unhappy and angry he is inside.

There is a direct relationship between learning problems and emotional problems. Although a learning problem can cause emotional problems, the converse is also true. The child who is intent on sabotaging himself, or the child who is indifferent or chronically angry or withdrawn, is seldom capable of learning efficiently. Internal discord will make it impossible for the child to fulfill his learning potential.

---

1. Many California high schools, for example, have recently been forced to eliminate their school counselors because of severe budget problems.

Children with emotional problems are often caught up in a complex and desperate struggle with themselves and with their parents. Sometimes this struggle is quite obvious, and other times not. When a child purposefully chooses to fail, he is making a statement about how he feels about himself. His behavior and his performance are a reflection of the disharmony he feels within himself.

Had a school psychologist seen Steve (the student in the preceding anecdote), he or she probably would have diagnosed Steve as an underachiever who lacked motivation. Perhaps the school psychologist might have been able to identify certain specific learning deficits. Had a clinical psychologist or psychiatrist seen Steve, he or she probably would have diagnosed Steve as an alienated, disturbed child who desperately needed counseling. It is probable that both the school psychologist and the clinical psychologist would have recognized Steve's extreme emotional turmoil. Tragically, no one, including myself, had been perceptive enough to refer Steve for a psychological evaluation.

The learning deficiencies of an emotionally disturbed child can seldom be remediated by a tutor or a learning disabilities specialist working independently. In order to progress academically, such a child will need the support of a therapist or counselor. Unless someone helps the child sort out and deal with the conflicting emotions which are responsible for his unhappiness, the unhappiness can overwhelm him and make it impossible for him to function in school.

DISTINGUISHING BETWEEN AN EMOTIONAL PROBLEM AND A LEARNING PROBLEM

The line delineating an emotionally-based learning problem from a non-emotionally-based learning problem is not always clear. There are many behavioral characteristics which are common to both types of problems. They include disruptive behavior, indifference, hostility, daydreaming, sloppy work, incomplete assignments, an inability to pay attention and an inability to follow instructions. Because few parents are trained to distinguish between a "simple" learning problem and a more complex emotionally-based problem, parents may need to seek professional advice.

Unfortunately, the advice from professionals is sometimes conflicting. The family pediatrician may recommend medication such as Ritalin to calm down the child. The classroom teacher may recommend retention. The psychologist or psychiatrist may recommend individual therapy. The family counselor may recommend family therapy. And the private learning disabilities therapist may recommend perceptual training. When faced with a myriad of conflicting recommendations and diagnoses, you have no choice but to rely on your intuition. You must trust the advice which "feels" right and be guided accordingly. In the final analysis, you must follow the counsel of the professional who has the most credibility in your eyes. It may be necessary to consult several professionals in order to find two who confirm each other's diagnosis and recommendations. Such a process can, of course, be expensive and time-consuming. But dealing with the consequences of doing nothing or making the wrong decision can be far more expensive and time-consuming.

A child who has a poor self-concept because he is not succeeding academically probably does not require psychotherapy or counseling. If the child's poor self-image is the direct result of school failure and frustration, his self-concept should improve as his learning problems are remediated. Once he becomes convinced that he can succeed in school, his positive feelings about himself and his abilities should increase commensurately. The longer the child is forced to suffer with his learning disability, however, the more difficult it becomes to repair the emotional damage. Without help, the child's self-concept will continue to deteriorate. Learning assistance which is implemented during the first critical years of elementary school significantly reduces the danger of self-concept damage.

The child with a positive self-image has acquired a powerful emotional resource. When parents and teachers purposefully create a context in which a child can learn to enjoy and appreciate his uniqueness as a human being, they are practicing affirmative parenting and affirmative teaching. Affirmative parenting and teaching are two of the most critical components in the process of rebuilding the self-esteem of the learning disabled child.

Unlike the child with minor emotional problems who will generally respond positively to learning assistance, the child with a serious emotional problem will probably require psychotherapy before he will be able to respond positively to a learning assistance program. Although it may be possible to coordinate counseling and learning assistance, it is often necessary to make inroads first into the emotional problems before real progress can be made toward resolving the learning problems.

A child who represses his negative feelings is unconsciously attempting to deny the existence of these emotions. By forcing his feelings into compartments within his mind and by locking the door to the compartments, the child can create the illusion of being okay emotionally. Ultimately, the doors to the compartments must be unlocked and the repressed feelings must be freed before the child can begin to function effectively.

DOUG: THE VICTIM OF A MESSY DIVORCE

A cute little boy of seven with a mischievous smile and sparkling eyes entered my office with his mother and father. His name was Doug, and he was in the second grade. His family had been referred to me by the headmaster of his private school [2] because Doug was struggling to keep up with his class.

The initial diagnostic evaluation revealed certain specific learning deficits. These included poor fine-motor coordination (symptom: sloppy and illegible penmanship); poor concentration (symptoms: inattentiveness and daydreaming); poor visual tracking (symptoms: inaccurate oral reading); and poor reading comprehension. It was as if the symptoms of Doug's learning disability had been taken directly from a learning disabilities textbook.

Despite his learning problems, Doug appeared to be well-adjusted and happy. His parents, however, were genuinely concerned about their son's lack of progress in school, and they were very anxious to have me work with him. Their concern was shared by the headmaster and Doug's teacher. Both expressed serious reservations about Doug's ability to handle the curriculum of the school.

Doug's parents reported that there were no significant family or medical problems. After testing Doug and evaluating the background information provided by his teacher and parents, I concluded that he had a moderate learning disability. Although the learning disability was not severe, it was serious enough to require immediate attention, especially since Doug was attending a demanding private school with very high academic standards.

Having identified Doug's learning needs, I proposed a learning assistance strategy to his parents. The program would involve intensive perceptual training activities to correct the child's specific perceptual processing difficulties and exercises to develop fine-motor control and visual-motor skills. In addition, I suggested a comprehensive phonics and reading comprehension program. Doug's parents readily accepted the proposal and after just six two-hour sessions we all could see a noticeable improvement in the child's learning skills. Doug seemed pleased with the progress he was making. His classroom teacher was equally pleased.

Suddenly, Doug's performance in school began to deteriorate. He forgot skills he had mastered. He could no longer pay attention or follow instructions. Once again, his handwriting became sloppy. When he experienced the slightest frustration, he would become resistant and would cry.

2. It may appear from the anecdotes that *all* our students attend private school, but this is not the case. Approximately 25% of the children we work with are enrolled in private schools. In many cases, private schools do not offer specialized learning assistance and consequently, refer children to outside agencies.

It was clear that Doug was experiencing serious emotional turmoil. Although I had worked with many learning disabled children who had temporarily regressed or reached a plateau during the remedial process, I sensed that there was something more profoundly amiss with Doug.

When I conferred with Doug's parents, I discovered that they had decided to divorce. The divorce proceedings were bitter, and the parents were very angry with one another. In a misguided attempt to be "fair," the parents had given Doug the option of deciding with which parent he was going to live! How could a seven year-old child not be distracted in school when he was being asked to make such a monumental decision?

Doug's parents had placed him in a double bind. If he loved both his parents, he could not help but feel anything but overwhelming guilt when forced to choose between them.

A basic learning disability had become an emotional problem. Doug was unwittingly torn apart emotionally. Unless his emotional stress was resolved, his academic progress would be uncertain. Family counseling was critical, not to save the marriage, but to save the child.

There *is* a reciprocal relationship between a child's emotions and his academic performance. One affects the other and vice versa. Recognizing and identifying a child's emotional problems can sometimes pose a very real challenge, not only to parents, but also to teachers, pediatricians and even psychiatrists and psychologists. The symptoms of the problem may be misleading because a child may unconsciously camouflage his feelings. When the child's behavior patterns are chronic or extreme, diagnosis is generally less difficult.

SCOTT: TERRIFIED BY ANYTHING NEW

The woman on the phone sounded very distressed. She requested that I test her eight year-old son Scott for a learning disability. I explained that my procedure is to spend approximately two hours and thirty minutes with the child and his parents during the initial diagnostic screening and conference.

On the day scheduled for our appointment, the mother came into my office and informed me that Scott refused to get out of the car. She explained that her son was often frightened by anything new, and this refusal was a typical reaction. I went out to the car to talk to the child. When he saw me coming, he got out of the car, picked up a big rock and climbed on the roof of the car. I could see the terror reflected in his eyes, and I realized that talking with him now would be fruitless. The child's mother and I went back into my office. I suggested that she not leave, but, rather, that she observe one of our classes and pay no attention to her son. We left the door to the observation room open.

99

After about twenty-five minutes, Scott got down from the top of the car. From a vantage point far from the door, he could see his mother in the observation room. Slowly, he began to move closer and closer to the door. He seemed curious about what his mother was doing in there. Finally, Scott came right up to the doorway and asked her what she was doing. She replied that she was watching some children in a class who were being helped with their reading and spelling. The boy began watching too. After about ten minutes, I asked him if he would be willing to come into my office with his mother so that I could test him and find out if he needed help in reading too. He agreed.

When I tested Scott, I found that he had a learning problem. It was equally clear that he also had serious emotional problems.

Scott urgently needed psychotherapy. When I discussed this need with Scott's mother, she refused to consider my recommendation. She would only consider learning therapy.

I agreed to work with Scott in the hope that ultimately I would establish enough credibility with the parents to convince them of the absolute necessity of taking the child to a psychiatrist or clinical psychologist. I had no illusions about being able to correct Scott's emotional problems. The child's problems were profound, and I was only equipped to deal with one aspect of a multi-faceted situation. In the end, the parents did agree to seek the therapy Scott desperately needed.

COMMON SYMPTOMS OF AN EMOTIONAL PROBLEM

A child's behavior is the barometer of his emotions. The symptoms of an emotional problem are diverse and will vary from child to child. The signals of a child's internal discord or unhappiness can be very blatant or very subtle. One child may act out his anger in the form of hostility or sarcasm. He may become a chronic bully or prankster. He may express his anger by fighting or by attempting to control others. His aggressive behavior and hostility mirror his inner turmoil. Another child may react in the opposite manner and become shy or withdrawn. Unlike the blatantly angry child, the shy child tends to repress his feelings. For example, he may be unable to relate to the other children and may have no friends. Another child may telegraph his internal conflict by means of bizarre or inappropriate behavior. He may act especially silly or be fascinated by fire.

The symptoms of emotional problems will vary in form and expression. Although most parents sense intuitively when their child's behavior is chronically inappropriate, they often do not act on their intuition. Rather than seek professional help, they allow the situation to persist, in the vain hope that the problem will correct itself.

The following checklist is intended to help parents recognize some of the symptoms which are characteristic of emotional problems. It is not intended to be a definitive guide. Its purpose is to help you decide if a professional evaluation of your child is advisable.

PROFILE OF EMOTIONAL PROBLEMS

	YES	NO
DISORGANIZED THINKING		
Lack of Orientation (time, place, people)	☐	☐
Delusions (persecution, grandeur)	☐	☐
Sensory Distortion (auditory and/or visual hallucinations)	☐	☐
NONADAPTIVE BEHAVIORS		
Withdrawal (seclusiveness, detachment, excessive sensitivity, inability to form friendships)	☐	☐
Tantrums	☐	☐
Superstitious Activity (motor rituals which must be performed before doing a task)	☐	☐
Extreme Mood Changes	☐	☐
Excessive Fantasizing	☐	☐
Phobic Reactions (fear of people or germs)	☐	☐
Fixations (excessive and exclusive interest in something)	☐	☐
Suicidal Tendencies	☐	☐
PHYSICAL DYSFUNCTIONS		
Bed Wetting (in older children)	☐	☐
Incontinence (in older children)	☐	☐
Repeated Stomachaches (also possibly a symptom of a physical problem)	☐	☐
Sleep Disturbances	☐	☐

As you interpret your responses to the preceding checklist, it is important to distinguish between an occasional episode with sleep disturbance, for example, and a chronic condition. A child may at times fantasize or have a temper tantrum without being emotionally disturbed. Recurring symptoms, however, should be a source of concern and warrant professional consultation.

There are other behavioral characteristics which might also indicate that your child is in conflict with himself, his family or his environment. Although the symptoms do not necessarily indicate an emotional problem, these behaviors, if they are recurring and excessive, should signal parents that they need to monitor their child closely. The behavioral characteristics include:

1. Explosive anger or hostility
2. Excessive fearfulness
3. Chronic bullying
4. Chronic lying
5. Depression
6. Excessive anxiety
7. Chronic control of self or of other people
8. Chronic stealing
9. Self-defeating behavior

Generally a child in distress will reveal his internal discord through his behavior. Once alerted to characteristic behaviors of emotional distress, parents can decide when and if professional intervention is appropriate.

SELECTING A THERAPIST OR COUNSELOR

In the event that you conclude your child would benefit from counseling or, at least, a diagnostic evaluation by a therapist, you are faced with the often difficult process of selecting the appropriate person to treat your child. There are many different types of therapists and there are many different techniques for dealing with emotional problems. Although any of the different techniques can be successful if the person using them is well-trained and skillful, a particular method may be more effective with one child or family than with another child or family.

Few parents have the background to evaluate objectively the relative merits of different therapy techniques. Because a family in distress is emotionally vulnerable, they may have difficulty trusting their instincts about a therapist's abilities. Trusting your intuition in this assessment process is not only valid, but essential! A therapist may be highly trained and impressively educated, but his success will be significantly reduced if you or your child cannot relate to him or her.

Perhaps the safest way to select a therapist is to rely on the recommendation of someone you respect. The primary sources of referral would be your child's pediatrician, your family doctor or a friend. Other sources include your minister, the school psychologist, your child's teacher or the local mental health association. [3]

3. Your local mental health association will probably be able to provide you with information about the fees of the therapists or agencies to which they refer you. Don't hesitate to ask the therapist about his fees when you call for an appointment. The association should be able to recommend alternative counseling resources if the fees are a problem.

For a therapist to be effective, he or she must have your child's and your family's trust and support. The entire family must be willing to make a commitment to the process of therapy. Patience is also essential, for emotional problems are seldom resolved quickly. A child's or a family's problems develop over the course of many years. To expect the dynamics of that problem to be realigned in one or two sessions with a therapist is unrealistic.

CONFRONTING A PROBLEM
VS. RUNNING AWAY FROM IT

The emotionally disturbed child has acquired a distorted sense of himself and his world. The distortions will manifest themselves in different forms but usually the element of fear is often a common denominator. The reasons why children become fearful are varied. Sometimes conditions in the child's environment are responsible. The causal factor that would be the most obvious source of emotional problems is the psychological or physical abuse of a child by his parents. There are, of course, many other less blatant causal factors. Some parents have a difficult time expressing their love, and as a consequence, their child may conclude that he doesn't deserve to be loved. He may become frightened by the resentment and the angry feelings he has toward his parents. Because of these unpleasant emotions he senses deep within him, he may acquire a profound sense of guilt.

Understanding why a child has developed distortions in his perception of himself and his world is more difficult when a child's environment does not appear to be creating emotional distress. The child's parents may be doing everything in their power to love and support the child. They may be demonstrative in expressing their affection. They may actively encourage communication within the family. They may be scrupulously fair in showing their love to each of their children. They may acknowledge each of their children's unique qualities and encourage each child to express and develop these qualities. In short, they may be doing everything that "ideal" parents should do in raising their children. Their child may develop emotional problems despite this seemingly near-perfect job of parenting. For reasons that are sometimes inexplicable, children who appear to have excellent parents can sometimes be troubled and insecure, while children with less than ideal parents can sometimes emerge from childhood emotionally unscathed.

The objective in confronting an emotional problem is not to blame, but, rather, to create a context in which the problem can be resolved. Certain types of emotional problems do not appear to be caused by environmental or family factors. Autism and some forms of schizophrenia are examples of severe personality disorders which may be the result of genetic or biological factors.

Parenting is a continual test of one's resources. At one time or another, every parent loses his or her patience or overreacts. No parent is perfect, and there isn't a parent alive who hasn't regretted something he or she has said or done to his or her child. Although all parents inevitably make mistakes in raising their children, parents' minor errors in judgment do not generally cause emotional problems.

A child's emotional problems will inevitably become the entire family's emotional problem. The acting out behavior of a child who is experiencing emotional turmoil can create a great deal of family stress. This stress may, in turn, fuel more emotional turmoil in the child and more inappropriate behavior. A potentially vicious cycle is created.

Depending upon the nature of the child's emotional problem, it may be advisable for the child to participate exclusively in individual therapy or counseling, or it may be more appropriate for the entire family to become involved from the onset in the counseling process. The therapist should be able to recommend the appropriate course of action.

The prospect of counseling or psychotherapy can be very threatening to a child. If the child is frightened by feelings he has suppressed, he may resist therapy because he senses that he will ultimately have to deal with emotions that he would prefer not to examine. To confront such emotions requires great courage. The natural instinct is to run away and the child may need much support, patience and understanding from his family during the process of therapy.

Children receiving therapy or counseling may insist that everything is okay and that they no longer need to continue. It is essential that parents consult the therapist before deciding unilaterally that it is time to discontinue therapy. To permit the child to discontinue before he works through his problems could be a terrible mistake. By manipulating his parents into permitting him to discontinue the therapy, the child is most likely engineering another failure for himself.

A child's therapy sessions are subject to the same conventions of confidentiality that safeguard an adult's therapy session. A therapist would most likely be willing to discuss with parents a child's progress and, perhaps, some of the general subjects that are being examined. He or she would *not* be willing to reveal information that the child provided in confidence. To do so would jeopardize the patient-therapist relationship which must be built upon trust. An exception would be made if the child's life or someone else's life were in jeopardy.

Parents may also have misgivings about seeking counseling or therapy. They may fear that the therapist will hold them responsible for their child's emotional problems. Because they are fearful of discovering something unpleasant or of being accused of being inadequate, these parents may resist having to explore their own relationships and their own innermost feelings. Parents who have unresolved or unacknowledged marital problems or who have disowned feelings of anger that they themselves would prefer not to confront, might be threatened by counseling or therapy.

Therapy encourages people to look at what is going on in their personal lives and in their collective family life. Its purpose is to reveal alternative strategies for dealing with problems and to unlock psychological doors which may have slammed closed because of fear and misunderstanding. As repressed feelings are expressed and examined, there may well be intermittent pain and joy. The process can lead to a liberation from the irrational fears which can poison the emotions of everyone in the family if the participants persevere.

The child with an emotional problem or a learning problem can feel terribly isolated. It is likely that he will sense that he is different from his brothers and sisters and the other children in his class. If his coping mechanisms and his defense mechanisms [4] involve socially non-adaptive behavior, they will tend to accentuate and call attention to the differences.

The atypical child will have atypical needs. He will most likely require more patience, more assurance and, perhaps, more firmness than other, less troubled children. Defining and responding appropriately to the special needs of the atypical child will demand parenting skills above and beyond the ordinary.

Parents are fallible, and even the best of parents may be occasionally unaware of, or unresponsive to their children's problems. They may also not feel equipped to handle their child's emotional problem. For parents to admit their limitations and seek outside professional help is not a sign of weakness, but rather an indication of their love, wisdom and strength.

4.   See Chapter Six for a more comprehensive discussion of defense mechanisms.

CHAPTER FIVE_____

Communicating With Your Child's Teacher

CHRISTINE: LEARNING THE RULES OF THE GAME

The woman sitting across from me watched intently as I tested her daughter. Her child was a fourth grader, and she was a fifth grade teacher.

She explained that Christine attended a school in a different district from the one in which she taught. During the last three months, she had been receiving notes from her child's teacher complaining about Christine's distractibility and unacceptable behavior in class. Although Christine's scores on standardized reading and math tests were several months above grade level, her performance in class was poor.

Christine was refusing to do her homework and had developed an intense dislike for school and the teacher. Her mother reported that she had observed a significant deterioration in both the quality of Christine's work and her attitude. She had become quite alarmed.

Christine's mother had initiated several parent-teacher conferences, but the conferences had consisted mainly of the teacher cataloguing all of Christine's many shortcomings as a student. The teacher was exasperated and made little attempt to hide her frustration. She admitted that she simply couldn't motivate Christine or get her to behave in class. Inasmuch as she was responsible for thirty other children who were eager to learn, she felt it would be unfair if she devoted 50% of her time to supervising Christine and neglected her other students.

As a classroom teacher herself, Christine's mother had sat "on the other side of the table" during countless parent-teacher conferences. On those occasions parents were soliciting information from her about their children. Now she was the concerned parent who was desperately trying to find a solution to her own child's learning problems. Christine's mother was perplexed and frustrated. Her daughter's teacher had apparently all but given up on trying to help Christine.

Christine's mother showed me the Teacher Evaluation Form [1] that the classroom teacher had completed. On it the teacher had indicated that Christine's primary difficulties were in the areas of behavior and attitude. Her work was seldom completed on time and was usually sloppy and illegible. The teacher also reported that Christine was impulsive, hard to discipline, and resistant to help. She also disturbed the other children in the class.

1.   See section entitled "Teacher Feedback" in this chapter for a facsimile of this form.

As I tested Christine, I could sense her resistance and anger. She had built up a set of psychological defense mechanisms to protect herself from feeling inadequate. She was particulary sensitive about making mistakes on the tests I was administering and became very easily discouraged. Whether her anger, resistance and sensitivity were primarily the result of her lack of academic success, or whether these behaviors were symptomatic of a more profound emotional problem, was not yet clear.

I concurred with the classroom teacher that Christine's academic skills were at or above grade level. Although Christine had a difficult time focusing and paying attention for more than a couple of minutes at a time, she was able to concentrate for much longer periods of time when we were discussing subjects which interested her.

The strained relationship that had developed between the teacher and Christine seriously concerned me. If we were to be successful in helping the child, Christine, her parents, *and* the teacher would all have to participate in making the learning assistance program work.

Transferring Christine to another class was one possible solution to the problem, but I had misgivings about such a move. There was a danger that Christine might conclude that her mom would always be willing to rescue her everytime she experienced difficulty. I felt that it would be preferable if Christine and her teacher could resolve their conflicts. If they could, Christine would have learned the important lesson that sometimes in life a person has to accommodate herself to someone she doesn't particularly like.

I was prepared to recommend that Christine be transferred to another teacher if the relationship between Christine and her teacher could not be salvaged. Five more months of negative feedback and conflict could have a seriously demoralizing effect on the child. Christine could well develop a potentially irreversible aversion to school.

I proposed an individualized remedial program for Christine that would emphasize specialized activities designed to train children to concentrate. I also suggested that a behavior modification system be used at home and in school. The system would require the cooperation of the classroom teacher, and I suggested that a conference be held at Christine's school so that we could discuss the proposed strategy with the teacher. The meeting would also afford me an opportunity to observe Christine in class.

I explained to Christine's mother that we would monitor her daughter closely. If we saw no improvement in her daughter's attitude and performance in school within three months I would refer Christine for a psychological evaluation to determine if her resistance and distractibility were symptomatic of an underlying emotional problem.

My staff would focus on improving Christine's concentration skills, and they would also help her with her schoolwork so that she could begin to experience some academic success. We proposed to set up a system of incentives to encourage her to complete and do her assignments accurately and legibly. We also included a system of negative consequences to discourage irresponsibility. [2]

It proved unnecessary to refer Christine for psychological testing. Christine responded very positively to the program at our clinic and to the behavior modification system that we established for her at home and in school. Christine's schoolwork began to show dramatic improvement, and she became quite excited about the gains she was making.

At first, the teacher was cautious about participating in the learning assistance strategy, but once she began to see Christine's improvement she actually became very enthusiastic. Each day she completed a simple progress report that required approximately one minute to fill out. [3] This report, which she sent home with Christine daily to be initialed by her mother, provided both Christine and her mother with important input about her performance and effort.

Christine learned that she had choices. She could *choose* to concentrate, or she could choose not to. She could also *choose* to do good work or poor work.

During the period of transition from irresponsibility to responsibility, Christine needed emotional and academic support. Once she learned how to concentrate, her self-confidence grew and she began to feel better about herself. Christine chose to succeed. Her attitude and her work improved dramatically. Ironically, Christine and her teacher ultimately resolved their conflict and became very fond of each other.

THE CLASSROOM TEACHER:
A VITAL ROLE IN THE DRAMA

Perhaps the most important learning of all occurs during the first formative years of a child's life. During these critical four years a child acquires a sense of his own power to influence the world around him. He can smile, cry, pout, be good or be bad. Almost every action he makes will elicit a reaction.

A child also learns the limitations of his power during the first four years of his life. He learns that there are standards of behavior to which he must conform. For instance, he learns that he cannot hit other children

2. This system of positive incentives and negative consequences is discussed in the subsequent section of this chapter entitled "Monitoring Your Child's Performance".
3. A facsimile of this daily progress report can be found in the subsequent section of this chapter entitled "Monitoring Your Child's Performance".

indiscriminately, and he learns that he must obey his parents whether he wants to or not. As he gets older, more and more rules and regulations are imposed on him. The child realizes that when he breaks the rules, he will probably be punished. Children who don't recognize this fact of life often will have difficulty later with authority and with conforming to the codes and strictures of society.

During this critical developmental period, a child's sense of self is in flux. Sometimes he is omnipotent. As a two year-old, he need but say the word "dada" for his parents and grandparents to go into ecstacy. On other occasions, he is forced to confront his powerlessness and his dependency on his parents. When it is bedtime, he has little choice but to go to bed. Although he may cry and make a fuss, he will be required to go to bed.

When a child of five is deposited in his kindergarten classroom on the first day of school, he quickly comprehends that the teacher is an extension of his parents. His parents have passed their power and authority to the teacher, who now has the authority to give and rescind permission, to praise and to punish. For five hours a day the teacher will continue the process of preparing the child to succeed in a competitive world where he will be acknowledged and rewarded on the basis of his skills, intelligence, attitude, responsibleness, competence and ambition.

School is the first real arena where a child will be tested by others and by himself. If the child is socially and academically successful in this arena, his self-confidence and his self-esteem will grow. If he is socially and academically unsuccessful, his self-confidence and his self-esteem will probably diminish.

Although a child's sense of his own capabilities and potential may change, his sense of identity is formed during the first six years of his life. By the age of seven, the child may have already unconsciously decided whether he will be a leader, a follower, an independent or an iconoclast. At this age, there is also a good chance that the child may have decided whether he is an achiever or a non-achiever. Some children by the age of seven have even unconsciously determined whether they are to be winners or losers in life. Children and adults can alter their self-concept, but such an alteration is not achieved easily.

The role of the teacher during the formative years of a child's life cannot be overemphasized. In conjunction with the child's parents, the elementary school teacher will help shape the child's thoughts and by word and deed will reinforce the rules, ethics and values of society. He or she will not only inculcate skills, data and information, but will also continually provide the child with feedback about his abilities, performance and potential. By means of praise and criticism the teacher will encourage the child's effort, discourage his irresponsibility and nurture his potential.

110

If the teacher is wrong in his or her assessment of a child's ability and potential, or if the teacher is indifferent, insensitive, prejudiced, incompetent or simply burned-out, the consequences for the child can be tragic.

The respective responsibilities of a child's parents and a child's teachers are awesome. Together they can help shape the course of a child's life.

HELEN: HER STUDENTS' PARENTS SERVED NOTICE

When I was a graduate student, I had a close friend who was teaching mathematics two periods a day in a junior high school as a requirement for her master's degree. Helen taught one class of eighth grade trigonometry and one class of ninth grade algebra. The school at which she taught was located near the university, and the majority of her students' parents were associated with the university. Many had visited her class and had introduced themselves to her.

The school where I was teaching was located some distance from the university. Most of my students came from a middle class background. Unlike Helen, I found that I seldom had any interaction with my students' parents unless I initiated the meeting.

In October both Helen's school and my school had open school night. One hundred percent of her students' parents attended. Only fifteen percent of my students' parents showed up at my classroom.

Among the parents of Helen's students attending were two Nobel Prize winners and many professors who taught at the university. The parents all listened respectfully as Helen carefully explained her objectives, her teaching methods, and the criteria she would use to evaluate the students and their progress.

The parents began to ask questions after Helen had completed her presentation. The questions were extremely perceptive and raised many issues that Helen had not considered. All of the parents were concerned about what their children were being taught and how they were being taught. Although none of the parents criticized or challenged her, they did serve Helen notice that they would be monitoring her performance as a teacher very closely. The parents were not about to lower their expectations because Helen was only an intern teacher. They fully expected their children to master certain skills by the end of the academic year. And although they communicated to Helen that they supported her, these parents also made it clear that they would hold her accountable for achieving her stated objectives.

111

The parents of my students did not express any concerns about my educational objectives for their children or about my teaching methods. They appeared to trust me implicitly and to be somewhat in awe of my position as a teacher. Their primary concern seemed to be getting home as quickly as possible.

When Helen and I compared our experiences with our first open school night, she was both apprehensive and excited about the challenge of fulfilling the expectations of her students' parents. I, on the other hand, felt somewhat complacent. That year Helen worked much harder than I did preparing for her classes. And she also did a much better job.

PARENTAL INVOLVEMENT

The issue of parental involvement in education is a controversial one. Although some school districts and some teachers encourage parental participation in the education process, other districts and teachers do not.

Parent participation in such organizations as the local P.T.A. is generally encouraged, but such participation may be limited to sponsoring paper drives, helping out on the playground, or chaperoning field trips. If parents were to attempt to become involved in formulating teaching philosophies, establishing academic priorities, or determining teachers' qualifications, they would likely encounter active opposition.

Most teachers resent parents "meddling" in their affairs for much the same reasons that physicians resent non-professionals "meddling" in the affairs of the local community hospital. Professionals tend to establish territoriality. Sometimes they develop an inflated sense of their expertise, autonomy, and prerogatives. Teachers are no exception. Most would not accept a parent telling them how they should teach, grade papers, or run the classroom.

Parental involvement is not a license of parents to interfere in the operation of the classroom or the school. Few parents possess the objectivity or the professional expertise to formulate educational philosophy or to critique the teacher. But this lack of objectivity or expertise does not necessarily negate the value of a parent's insights or intuition.

A parent does not have to be an educator or a Nobel Prize winner to sense intuitively that a teacher or a school is not fulfilling his or her child's academic needs. Parents who are concerned, reasonable, and when necessary, persistent, should have the right to express their concerns. They should also be able to expect that the school and teachers will consider and examine these concerns seriously, even if the parents' perceptions turn out to be inaccurate or their concerns excessive or unwarranted. Parents who are unreasonable, accusatory, hostile, or arrogant should anticipate justifiable opposition from both teachers and administrators.

Parental involvement and participation in a child's education serves notice on schools and teachers that not only are the children being held accountable for their performance, but, so too are the teachers and the administrators. Ideally, teachers, parents and administrators will be allies in the process of providing children with the best possible education. They all have in common the same basic objective: to help children become productive, self-sufficient, competent and confident. To achieve this objective each group needs the support of the others.

TEACHER FEEDBACK

The parents of children with learning problems have a critical need for information about how their child is functioning in the classroom. Without this information it is impossible for parents to participate intelligently in the process of helping their child overcome his learning problems.

General, nebulous descriptions of a child's classroom performance are of little help in designing a meaningful learning assistance strategy or an effective behavior modification program. Examples of such descriptions might include:

"He's not keeping up."
"He's reading below grade level."
"He's immature."
"He is creating a disturbance in class."
"He's having trouble with his math."

All of these statements may indeed be very accurate, but they are not very precise. Were these statements made to me, I would respond:

"How is he not keeping up with the class?"
"What specific reading deficits does he have?"
"In what way is he immature?"
"What does he do that creates a disturbance in the class?"
"Is he having difficulty with concepts or with mathematical operations?"

The more precise and specific the teacher feedback, the more guidance and direction that feedback will provide the designers of a remediation strategy.

As a learning disabilities specialist, my need for precise information is understandably greater than that of a typical parent of a learning disabled child. But parents also need to know as much as they can about their child's problem if they are to be able to evaluate their options intelligently when seeking a resolution to the child's learning problems.

113

A child who has a reading problem, for instance, may need a reading tutor, or he may benefit from a more comprehensive learning assistance program. If his reading problem is caused by a perceptual dysfunction, his parents will need as much information as possible as they wrestle with such decisions as whether their child requires placement in a full time E.H. (educationally handicapped) class or whether he simply needs an hour of assistance each day from the reading resource specialist.

Although the school may recommend a particular program to the child's parents, the parents may have reservations or concerns about the appropriateness of the program. Without meaningful input from the classroom teacher, evaluating the options becomes impossible. Parents have no choice but to accept the school's recommendation at face value or to reject the recommendation and run the risk of making decisions that may be flawed because they are based on inadequate information.

It's true that a little knowledge can be dangerous. But no knowledge can be disastrous. The more parents know about their child's learning problems, the more they are able to contribute to the remediation process. This parental support is essential to the successful remediation of a learning problem.

On the following page is a copy of the **Teacher Evaluation Form** that we use at our center. The form is sent to the classroom teacher of each child that we evaluate. A second form is sent to the resource specialist if the child is in a special program. The feedback we receive is an important and integral component of our diagnostic and remediation procedure. It provides us with information about how a child is functioning in the classroom. This information is correlated with the results of the diagnostic tests we administer and with the information parents provide us about their perceptions of their child.

The primary function of the **Teacher Evaluation Form** is to provide us with important information about a child's academic strengths and weaknesses. The form also helps classroom teachers focus on the student's specific deficits. Teachers who might otherwise tend to describe a child's learning difficulties in terms of immaturity can use this form to help them identify the child's learning deficits in precise terms. The advantage of discussing the child's learning problems in terms of specific deficits is that definite goals can be established for helping the child, and specific strategies can be employed for achieving those goals.

TEACHER EVALUATION FORM

Please Note: You may not be able to evaluate this student in all of the categories listed below because of the child's age or because of limited involvement on your part with the student in specific areas.

Key: — 0=Never / 1=Rarely / 2=Sometimes / 3=Often / 4=Always

Please Indicate the Appropriate Number in Space Provided

Overactive	_____	Difficulty With Spelling	_____
Appears Clumsy	_____	Reverses Letters And	
Fidgety	_____	Numbers	_____
Unpredictable	_____	Difficulty Tracking	
Impatient	_____	Words	_____
Sensitive	_____	Difficulty With Phonics	_____
Social Problems	_____	Difficulty With Word-	
Daydreams	_____	Attack Skills	_____
Excitable	_____	Difficulty With	
Easily Distracted	_____	Blending Skills	_____
Easily Frustrated	_____	Difficulty With	
Appears Immature	_____	Memory Skills	_____
Disturbs Others	_____	Poor Reading	
Resistant To Help	_____	Comprehension	_____
Impulsive	_____	Difficulty Verbalizing	_____
Poor Self-Concept	_____	Inaccurate Copying	
Difficulty Working		From Blackboard	_____
Independently	_____	Inaccurate Copying	
Difficulty Concentrating	_____	At Desk	_____
Short Attention Span	_____	Omits Syllables	
Hard To Discipline	_____	And Word Endings	_____
Leaves Projects		Difficulty Following	
Incomplete	_____	Written Directions	_____
Accident-Prone	_____	Difficulty Following Oral	
Unhappy	_____	Directions	_____
Sloppy Work Habits	_____	Difficulty With Written	
Difficulty Keeping Up		Language Arts Skills	_____
With Class	_____	Difficulty With Sight	
Slow Completing Work	_____	Word Recognition	_____
Right-Left Confusion	_____	Difficulty Accepting	
Poor Sense Of Balance	_____	Responsibility	_____
Difficulty With Coor-		Difficulty Organizing	
dination (Gross-Motor)	_____	And Planning Projects	_____
Difficulty With Hand-		Difficulty With Math	
writing (Fine-Motor)	_____	Skills	_____

COMMENTS: (Please include any pertinent information regarding your student's learning problems that has not been covered in the preceding list.)

Once the child's problems have been identified, it is possible to design a behavior modification strategy for the highly distractible child or to implement an incentive program for the child who does not complete his assignments on time. If the form reveals that the child has difficulty with coordination, for example, parents and teachers may decide to enroll the child in an adaptive P.E. program or in a karate class to help him improve his coordination.

If the **Teacher Evaluation Form** indicates that your child is having difficulty copying from the blackboard, his vision should be tested. The school nurse, a pediatrician, an optometrist or an opthamologist can perform the test. Such a test might reveal a visual problem that could be corrected with glasses. If the test indicates no impairment, the next logical step would be a diagnostic evaluation of your child for a visual dysfunction. Perhaps your child simply needs to be placed closer to the blackboard in order to be able to copy more accurately.

When trying to interpret the teacher's responses on the checklist, you should focus primarily on those deficit areas that he or she has rated with 3's or 4's. Almost every child will daydream "sometimes." There is however, a justifiable source for concern when the problem is chronic and the teacher indicates that the child "often" or "always" daydreams.

A pattern of 3's and 4's is a clear indication of an actual or a potential learning problem. You or your child's teacher will want to bring such a pattern to the attention of the school psychologist. If the psychologist concurs that the pattern might indicate a learning problem, then subsequent diagnostic testing would be in order. You may need to become assertive or you may be forced to seek a diagnostic evaluation from outside sources if this testing is not available, or is denied.

PARENT-TEACHER CONFERENCES

Communication between parents and classroom teachers is particularly important when a child has a learning problem. Parents first need to know what their child's specific deficits are, and then they need to know whether their child is making progress.

Parents who are able to ask the appropriate questions and who are able to interpret and evaluate the teacher's responses will be able to participate more effectively and more intelligently in the remediation process. **The Teacher Evaluation Form** is designed to help parents acquire the specific information they need to identify their child's problem. By periodically resubmitting the checklist to the teacher, parents can also use the form to monitor their child's learning progress.

Parents who know or suspect that their child has a learning problem are well advised to request that their child's teacher complete the checklist prior to their scheduled conference. They will want to review the form before the meeting. The conference should focus on specific deficit areas, and should offer an opportunity to explore possible remediation strategies.

I suggest that the teacher complete a second Teacher Evaluation Form before the next parent-teacher conference. This procedure will allow parents and teachers to compare the initial and subsequent evaluations and to determine if the child's work has improved. If the parent sees that there has been little or no improvement, the parent can use the information contained on both forms to provide documentation that will support a request for a diagnostic work-up by the school psychologist.

Parents should be realistic in their expectations of the classroom teacher. Children who have significant learning deficits will require specialized assistance, and it is unlikely that a classroom teacher with thirty children in his or her class will be able to provide this necessary specialized assistance.

Teachers are, above all, human beings, and most human beings have a tendency to become defensive when someone else becomes offensive. Communication is seldom successful in an adversarial situation. Under such circumstances defending one's position becomes paramount. Most teachers are far more cooperative when they are treated with respect and when they feel that their efforts are supported.

It may be necessary for parents to communicate frankly their concern about their child's lack of academic progress. To blame the teacher for this lack of progress would not only be a tactical mistake but may also be unfair. Parents who express their concerns and then ask the teacher: "What can we do to solve this problem?" are far more likely to gain the teacher's active participation in the resolution of the child's learning problems.

JARGON

Parents who either elect to become involved in their child's education or who are forced to do so by circumstances will have to communicate with educators. Communicating with educators often involves dealing with educational jargon.

Educational jargon, and specifically learning disabilities jargon, serves an important function. It facilitates the identification and the description of learning deficits and permits professionals to communicate specialized information quickly and easily.

Paradoxically, jargon can also impede communication, especially when professionals in a particular field use this highly specialized vocabulary with someone who is not familiar with it. Because jargon tends to exclude "outsiders" from understanding what is being said, it can easily become a barrier between professionals in a particular field and "laymen." This phenomenon is as true in the field of education as it is in the fields of medicine or electronics.

Jargon is also sometimes used to create an aura of professionalism. When it is used in this way, its function becomes distorted. A professional who uses technical words as a smokescreen is misusing them. Those that do use jargon in this manner may be insecure about their credibility or their authority. They realize that it is difficult for any layperson to question or challenge a professional whose language is so technical that it is incomprehensible.

In most instances, the dynamics of a learning disability can be explained with very little jargon. Although professionals may find it useful to be able to use one word to describe a complex process, they should be able to explain the problem in terms that any parent can understand.

A school psychologist, for example, may report that your child has a perceptual dysfunction involving deficits in auditory and visual discrimination. Because you may be embarrassed to reveal your "ignorance," you might be reluctant to ask for clarification. Were you willing to risk appearing "dumb" and were you to ask the school psychologist to explain what the terms mean, he or she would tell you that your child is having difficulty processing information that he sees and hears. Your child may not be able to hear the difference between the "i" sound in the word "pin" and the "e" sound in the word "pen." When reading he may confuse the "b" and the "d" letters.

It is also quite common for parents to be confused about the meaning of the scores that their child receives on standardized or specialized tests. For instance, if you were told that your child had difficulty on the I.T.P.A. in the area of grammatic closure, it would be reasonable for you to ask what the letters I.T.P.A. stand for and what the test is designed to measure. The psychologist could then explain that the Illinois Test of Psycholinguistic Abilities is a specialized test which measures the degree of perceptual processing efficiency a child has achieved.[4] Ideally, the psychologist would then give you several examples of correct and incorrect grammatic closure.

Example: The boy and his father go/*goes* to the store.
             She likes the girl what/*who* sings.

4.   See Testing Appendix for a description of this test.

118

Test scores can and should be presented to parents with a clear, written explanation of what the tests measure and what the scores mean. Unfortunately, this is not always the case.

If you find yourself confused by terminology or test scores, don't hesitate to request an explanation. And if later you feel that you need further clarification, you should feel totally justified in requesting it. Admitting that you don't understand the jargon is not an admission of ignorance. You have the right of access to any educational information which pertains to your child and you also have the right to insist that this information be explained in terms that you can understand.

I am aware that I too am guilty of having used jargon in this book. I have done so because I feel that these words and terms are ones that parents need to recognize and understand. All of the words I've used are defined either in context or in the glossaries at the end of the book. You will also find that certain words have been included in the glossaries which do not appear in the text of this book. These words are highly technical and will be used by some professional educators. In the Testing Appendix you will find a description of some of the diagnostic, aptitude and achievement tests commonly used with children.

EVALUATING PROFESSIONAL RECOMMENDATIONS

The results of the diagnostic testing must be analyzed, interpreted and correlated with the subjective impressions of the classroom teacher. The child's performance in class and his attitude and effort during the testing procedure are all critical components in the diagnostic equation. Once this data is analyzed, interpreted and correlated, a professional recommendation as to the appropriate Individual Educational Plan should result.

In California, parents are encouraged to participate in the I.E.P. meeting.[5] Typically, the school psychologist, the classroom teacher, the principal, the school nurse, the learning disabilities specialist, or resource specialist, and the child's parents will attend this conference. The parents also have the option of inviting a professional from outside the school district to represent them and to participate in designing the learning assistance program and to establish the objectives for the program. During this meeting, the child's learning needs will be assessed, a remedial strategy will be designed and specific goals will be designated.

The parents of the child who is being evaluated must decide whether to accept or reject the strategy and objectives. Making this decision can be a traumatizing experience, especially when parents feel that they don't fully understand the issues involved or that they don't have the knowledge or the experience to evaluate either the recommendations or the proposed remedial program adequately.

5.   The term that is used to describe this evaluation conference will vary from state to state and the structure of the meeting will also differ. The meeting described in this section represents the standard procedure in California.

119

Parents who are confused may be hesitant to ask "dumb" questions. They may feel that it would be presumptuous of them to question the recommendations of professionals and specialists. It is at this evaluation meeting, however, that any reservations, questions and disagreements should be expressed and examined. If the professional recommendations are inappropriate, inadequate, or poorly conceived, a whole year can be wasted before the parents and school personnel will have another opportunity to design a more suitable learning assistance strategy.

The following checklist is intended to help parents participate in the evaluation process with greater confidence. The list has been specifically designed to identify those areas which should be explored during the I.E.P. conference.

EDUCATIONAL PLAN PARENT CHECKLIST

	YES	NO
Teacher Evaluation Form has been completed?	☐	☐
I agree with the teacher's assessment of my child's classroom work.	☐	☐
I need to discuss certain areas of disagreement or confusion.	☐	☐
I have seen the results of the diagnostic tests which my child has taken.	☐	☐
I understand what the tests measure.	☐	☐
I understand the scores that my child achieved on the diagnostic tests.	☐	☐
I feel the scores are valid.	☐	☐
I have a clear understanding of the remedial programs which are available.	☐	☐
I concur with the conclusions that have been drawn in this meeting.	☐	☐
I feel that I must consult an outside authority before I agree to the recommendations that have been made today.	☐	☐

Any area of confusion or disagreement should be discussed during the I.E.P. meeting. If the answers or explanations provided by the professionals participating in the conference do not make sense to you or are in conflict with your own impressions, you have a right — and indeed an obligation to your child — to request that they clarify the issues to your satisfaction. If you do decide to follow the school's recommendations, you should allow the school a reasonable amount of time to demonstrate the efficacy of the learning assistance program.

I have found that the assessments and recommendations that result from I.E.P. conferences are generally on target and appropriate. Diagnostic testing protocols are, for the most part, reliable, and the majority of school psychologists I have dealt with are competent. If you conclude that the professional recommendations are valid, it is essential that you support the school personnel who will be implementing the remediation program.

If you conclude that the professional recommendations are not appropriate, your responsibility is to protect your child's educational interests as best you can. Questioning or vetoing a professional recommendation can be a very wrenching experience, especially when you have only your intuition to support you.

As a parent and a taxpayer, you have the right to expect adequate assessment and remediation of your child's problem. You also have the right to express your misgivings without fear of ridicule or negative repercussions for your child. When you feel intuitively apprehensive or when your reservations cannot be resolved to your satisfaction, you may need to turn to a professional from outside the district to help you assess the issues involved.

DEVELOPING REALISTIC EDUCATIONAL GOALS

Learning problems can seldom be resolved in a week or a month. The amount of time required to correct a learning problem will depend upon the severity of the problem, the age of the child, the skills of the teachers helping the child, the parents' support and the child's desire to overcome his problems.

Psychological factors, intelligence, environment and family dynamics will also play a significant role in the remediation process. Because there are so many factors involved, it may be difficult to predict how long it will take to remediate a child's learning problem.

Over the years I have seen four common remedial learning curves. Although these learning curves relate directly to our clinic's remedial programs, I suspect that they are fairly typical.

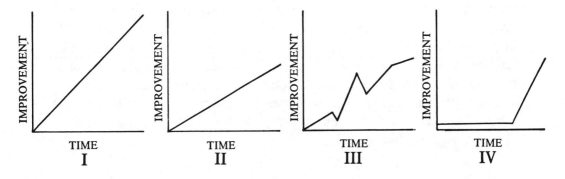

Learning curve #1 is, of course, the most gratifying for everyone concerned. The learning assistance strategy appears to function like a magic potion, and the learning disabled student begins to make dramatic improvement immediately. At our center we have found that perhaps 15% to 20% of the students respond in this way.

Learning curve #2 is more typical of the improvement that most learning disabled children make once they begin to receive remedial assistance. As the child responds to this assistance, his deficiencies will become less severe, and his enthusiasm for learning and his self-concept will improve commensurately. Although the improvement may be slow, the improvement will be steady. This learning curve makes it somewhat easier to predict when the child's learning problems should be resolved. Learning curve #2 represents the improvement that approximately 50% of the children at our center achieve.

The third learning curve shows a more erratic improvement in learning skills. Children whose remedial progress is characterized by learning curve #3 tend to manifest spurts of improvement followed by periodic regression or plateauing. A child with letter reversal problems, for instance, may eliminate his letter reversals for a period of time and then revert back to writing or reading words with the "b's" and "d's" reversed. Or a child may be less distractible for a month and then begin to manifest some of the same concentration problems that he had manifested previously. Our experience with thousands of learning disabled children has shown that most of the children who fall into category #3 will ultimately resolve their learning problems. Regression, however, can be very frustrating. During these periods the parents, the classroom teacher, the remedial specialists and the child himself simply have to grit their teeth and await the subsequent upturn. Approximately 20% of the children we work with are best described by learning curve #3.

Learning curve #4 is characteristic of approximately 10% of the children at our center. This learning curve is by far the most frustrating of all. Typically, a child in this category will show no improvement for months or even a year. Everyone involved can become quite demoralized and the child's parents can begin to question the efficacy of the learning assistance strategy. Although a reevaluation of any remedial program is advisable when a child shows little or no improvement, this reevaluation should be deferred until adequate time has been allowed for the program to demonstrate its effectiveness, or lack of effectiveness. Perseverence can lead to a breakthrough. Knowing when to persevere and when to "bail-out" of a learning assistance program can be very difficult. Parents must be guided by and must trust their intuition.

Resistant learning problems such as those described by learning curve #4 are discussed at staff meetings, and alternative remedial methods are explored. Teachers who have not worked with the child are encouraged to suggest ideas and share their insights. Such brainstorming often results in the infusion of new and creative techniques for dealing with the problem. This input can frequently help the teacher get the child "unstuck." In some instances the child may be assigned to another teacher if it is the consensus that another teacher has skills which might prove advantageous.

It is important that parents realize that their child may not respond in accordance with their preferred remediation timetable. The learning therapist may need to try several different remedial approaches before determining the appropriate protocol.

There is no way to determine with any certainty into which of the four learning curves a child's remedial progress will fall. Years of clinical experience and many incorrect predictions have made me conservative about making predictions. Sometimes children with severe problems will respond very quickly and positively to the remedial program. And sometimes children with relatively moderate or subtle problems will have a difficult time resolving them.

Educational goals for the learning disabled child must be reasonable and must take into consideration different response patterns. The goals should be reviewed periodically. If the educational strategy appears to be bogging down, alternative approaches should be considered. Parents and teachers must allow adequate time for the program to demonstrate whether or not it is effective.

I have often observed that something magical happens to children described by learning curve #4 just about the time that everyone is despairing most. For reasons that are difficult to explain, a sudden and dramatic breakthrough will occur and "the pieces will begin to fall into place." Predicting when this magic will happen is impossible. As a learning therapist, I have learned to trust my own intuition while wrestling with the decision to persist with a particular learning assistance strategy or to change course and implement a new strategy.

EVAN: FINDING AN ANTIDOTE
FOR CHRONIC DISTRACTIBILITY

After testing Evan, I knew that he was a good reader and was equally competent in math. The report from his classroom teacher indicated, however, that Evan was doing terribly in school. His work was disorganized and inaccurate. His handwriting was sloppy and illegible. Assignments were seldom completed and were rarely handed in on time. With justification, his teacher was quite concerned, and so was his mother. In fact, she was desperate.

123

Evan's mother had tried tutoring, counseling, and finally punishment in an attempt to help Evan improve his work in school. Nothing had helped, and now, despite the fact that he was testing more than a year above grade level, the school was recommending that her son be retained.

Evan could not focus on any material in which he was not interested for more than a minute at a time. He constantly gazed out the window. He would invariably lose his place when it was his turn to read aloud.

Evan had become the class clown. He made faces and strange noises and was a constant distraction for the other students in the classroom. Alternating between his private world of daydreams and his chosen role as a disruptive clown, Evan was becoming increasingly difficult to manage and to educate. I feared that he would ultimately become a school drop-out unless his behavior changed.

I recommended a perceptual training and behavior modification program. An additional half hour each week was to be devoted to an experimental Yoga/meditation program that had been recently added to our curriculum. I felt that the program would help Evan learn to gain greater control over his actions. The instructor would teach Evan to recognize when he was becoming distracted, when he was drifting off into his daydreams, and when he was behaving inappropriately.

We also encouraged Evan to keep a diary in which he could record his experiences each day and his impression of what had happened in school and at home. This technique was intended to help Evan become more centered and more aware of himself and his behavior.

After observing Evan at his school, I realized that his classroom teacher needed to monitor him more closely. Evan required immediate feedback from her so that he would know when he was misbehaving or becoming distracted. Unfortunately, the teacher seldom got up from her desk which she had placed at the back of the class. This sedentary teaching style made it difficult for her to provide Evan with the externally-imposed structure that he needed.

When I conferred with the teacher, I suggested a behavior modification system which would provide Evan with the feedback he required. The system would consist of the teacher's putting a wide piece of masking tape on the upper right hand corner of Evan's desk. On the masking tape she would mark off two columns. At the top of one column she would draw a happy face and at the top of the other, a sad face. Each time Evan misbehaved or was distracted, the teacher would place a check in the sad face column. When Evan was attending to his work, or simply behaving appropriately, the teacher would place a check in the happy face column.

To make the system work, the teacher would have to be willing to move around the classroom. [6] I wasn't sure that she would agree to this idea. Much to my pleasure, she readily agreed to the suggestion and did not seem at all defensive about having an outside consultant come into her classroom and make suggestions.

We discussed rewarding Evan for the number of checks he received in the happy face column and perhaps taking away privileges if he collected more than a certain number of check marks in the sad face column, but we decided against this approach. My intuition told me that simply acknowledging Evan's good behavior would be all that was necessary. Evan had experienced three years of negative acknowledgment, and I was fairly certain that the opportunity to receive some positive recognition would be sufficient motivation.

The classroom teacher also agreed to whisper to Evan an agreed-upon cue word to alert him when he was becoming particularly distracted. If the behavior modification system proved successful, it would help Evan internalize the external control so that he would ultimately be able to recognize for himself when he was not focused. The system also required that Evan receive lavish praise when he did something well or had a good day.

Slowly, Evan began to enjoy the positive recognition he was getting, and his attention span and behavior in class began to improve dramatically. In fact, many of the other children in his class requested that they too have the masking tape on their desk. The strategy worked and Evan began to participate actively in his own education.

MONITORING YOUR CHILD'S PERFORMANCE

Some children with learning problems compensate for their deficits by becoming very conscientious. Despite their learning deficits, they give 100% and spend long hours doing their homework and studying. In some instances, this determination is sufficient to permit them to overcome or, at least, to compensate for their learning deficiencies. Such children may require little or no learning assistance.

One of the common characteristics of children who have learning problems is an inability to control and monitor themselves. This absence of self-regulation may manifest itself in distractibility, sloppiness, inattentiveness and irresponsibility. Because school is a continual struggle, many children with learning problems give up and stop trying. [7] The temptation to give up, or to develop defenses, is very strong when life is reduced to a constant, difficult battle that offers little prospect of success.

6. A teacher could also monitor a child using this system from her desk by directing the child to put the checks on the masking tape in the appropriate column.
7. See Chapter Six for a more complete discussion of defense mechanisms and compensatory mechanisms.

The ways in which children give up the struggle will vary. A child may drift off into daydreams, or he may stop trying to complete assignments. Some children will choose misbehavior. By getting attention in this way, they are attempting unconsciously to divert attention from their limitations. Although this type of behavior only calls attention to the very inadequacies the child is trying to camouflage, the child is too close to the problem to perceive this irony.

Parents who recognize that their child has developed behaviors which are counterproductive must carefully monitor their child's performance in school. If their child is exhibiting irresponsibility by not completing his assignments, parents need to be aware of this behavior. Before they can respond appropriately, they must first decide whether the child cannot do his assignments because of his learning problems or is not doing them because of laziness. In the first instance, learning assistance may be necessary. In the second instance, firm parenting may be required. If the behavior is chronically irresponsible or manipulative, professional counseling may be indicated. Less chronic patterns of counterproductive behavior may simply require consistent parental discipline.

Irresponsible behavior demands some form of intervention. The nature of this intervention will be determined by the nature of the child's behavior.

Before parents can become involved, however, they must have accurate and current information about how their child is functioning in school. Because children tend to assess and report facts selectively, parents cannot rely exclusively on their child for an assessment of his daily performance. They also cannot risk waiting until the child's report card comes home.

On the next page you will find two **Daily Performance Checklists** that we use with children at our center whose effort and performance in class is less than acceptable. The first checklist is intended for younger children in grades one and two. The second checklist is intended for children in grades three through eight.

When we identify a child who is irresponsible or distractible, we send the child's classroom teacher a letter explaining the rationale behind our behavior modification strategy and the **Daily Performance Checklist.** We ask that the teacher complete the checklist every day. The form should only take the teacher a minute to fill out, and it is the child's responsibility to hand it to the teacher at the end of each class day. [8]

8.   Although some teachers may resent this "extra" work it has been our experience that most teachers are very cooperative about completing the form.

DAILY PERFORMANCE CHECKLIST
(First And Second Grades)

1 = Poor   2 = Fair   3 = Good   4 = Excellent

	Mon.	Tues.	Wed.	Thurs.	Fri.
Reading Work					
Math Work					
Handwriting					
Listening in class					
Keeping up with class					
Effort					
Behavior					
Comments					
Parents' Initials					

DAILY PERFORMANCE CHECKLIST
(Third Grade and Above)

1 = Poor   2 = Fair   3 = Good   4 = Excellent

	Mon.	Tues.	Wed.	Thurs.	Fri.
Completes Assignments					
On Time					
Neatly					
Completes Homework					
On Time					
Neatly					
Independence					
Effort					
Attention					
Attitude					
Behavior					
Comments					
Parents' Initials					

The teacher has the option of eliminating any area that he or she feels is not relevant to the child and adding areas that he or she feels are more relevant. The child is responsible for showing the completed form to his parents each evening. Once the parents have seen the daily evaluation and discussed it with their child, they initial it and send it with their child to class the following day.

The **Daily Performance Checklist** is meant to provide the parents with important information about how their child is doing in school. The checklist is not intended for all children. It is primarily oriented toward the child who is not able to regulate himself and who is unaware of his behavior.

Parents who use the checklist will know immediately if a child is misbehaving in class, falling behind, or not completing his assignments. If retention is recommended at the end of the year, parents would have been alerted to the potential problem well in advance.

The information provided by the checklist will help parents determine if the learning assistance strategy is working or if the child needs additional remedial support. By interpreting the scores on the form, parents will be able to decide whether their child needs learning assistance, more discipline, or simply more structure at home.

In addition to providing feedback, the checklist can be an integral component in an incentive program designed to modify the child's counterproductive behaviors. I generally recommend to that they set up a point system which will encourage their child to achieve better performance.

You will notice that the maximum possible points that your child can achieve using the older students' checklist is 220 per week. We recommend that you begin with a reasonable minimum requirement. A good starting point is 135 points per week. This minimum requirement permits the child to have quite a few scores of "2" (fair) on the checklist. If the child's score for the week is below 135, you might establish a rule that he not be allowed to watch television on the weekend. [9] If the score during the first week exceeds 150, the child might be given a special reward or prize, such as a movie, a trip to the skating rink or a tangible reward such as a model airplane, a T-shirt, or a doll. Some parents elect to use only positive rewards. They may give their child a penny for each point he gets in lieu of an allowance. This money could also be saved in a jar for special occasions such as Christmas or a day at the amusement park.

An incentive system may be offensive to some parents because they feel that offering a child a reward or money is tantamount to a bribe. While an incentive for working hard could be considered a bribe, this same logic would make a paycheck also a bribe. Most people work for incentives. It is wonderful when children are motivated by pride and the intrinsic satisfaction of doing a good job, but when a child has a habit of underachieving, he

9. Other priveliges may be denied which you feel might have more impact upon your child.

may need an effective motivator. Many learning disabled children are not highly motivated and an incentive may be the catalyst that inspires the unmotivated child to become actively involved in his own education. Once a child begins to experience success, his growing sense of self-esteem and pride will encourage him to continue doing a good job.

As the child develops more self discipline, his minimum point requirement should be increased. Perhaps five points could be added each week until a reasonable minimum performance standard is established. The minimum performance criteria should be realistic. For some children a minimum requirement of 160 points may be ultimately appropriate. For others, 180 to 200 points might represent the ultimate minimum performance goal.

When you review the checklist with your child, you may become aware of certain specific problem areas. You will want to discuss these problems with both the classroom teacher and your child. Don't hesitate to ask your child what he thinks should be done to bring up the scores in a particular area. Kids like to be involved in the process of solving their own problems. You are acknowledging the value of your child's insights and his ability to contribute to the resolution of the learning problem.

WORKING AS A TEAM

The effectiveness of any diagnostic procedure or any learning assistance program hinges upon the expertise of the people charged with the responsibility of implementing the program. The prognosis for the child improves significantly when these people are committed, skilled and enthusiastic, and when they are given sufficient time to do their job.

The more insight that you have into your child's learning disabilities, the more capable you will be of discovering and utilizing the resources which exist within your community. Your ability to evaluate professional recommendations, to select appropriate programs, to monitor your child's progress and to support your child and his teachers may be the pivotal factor in determining whether or not your child's learning problems are ultimately remediated.

Your involvement can be perceived by the district and the school personnel as a nuisance, as a threat, or as a valued contribution. Your attitude will to a large extent determine how the school authorities react to your participation.

Most learning disabled children will need a great deal of emotional support during the remediation process. From time to time, even the best of remediation programs can bog down. Parents and teachers must be prepared to offer encouragement. A child who learns to rebound from an occasional setback is acquiring an essential survival skill. The acquisition of this skill is every bit as important as the acquisition of academic skills.

Parents also need encouragement and support. Without this support, the parents of a learning disabled child can easily become demoralized. This is especially true when a child's progress is slow or when a child becomes resistant. The potential impact that teachers can have on parents who are concerned, confused and discouraged cannot be overemphasized. Teachers who sensitize themselves to the anxieties of the parents of their students significantly improve the chances that the students will be able to resolve their learning problems.

Parents and teachers play a vital role in creating the proper alignment of educational and emotional support resources. A child's ultimate ability to conquer his learning problem will directly reflect the attitude, expectations and encouragement of his teachers and parents. When the support systems are positive, the probability of successful resolution of the learning problem increases dramatically.

CHAPTER SIX

Parenting the Learning Disabled Child

LISA: FIGHTING A LOSING BATTLE

Lisa's parents were adamant. They would not consider another school for their daughter as long as she could continue to fulfill the requirements of the school she was attending.

Lisa's parents, the classroom teacher, the school principal and I met in the principal's office to discuss our concerns. Lisa was a fourth grade student attending a very academically demanding private school. She was battling desperately to keep up with her class, and it was apparent that the struggle was taking a terrible toll on her.

Lisa had recently begun to develop a nervous tick. She was spending three hours each evening trying to complete her homework and the class-work that she hadn't been able to finish during the day. We could all see that she was becoming more and more demoralized as the year progressed.

Unfortunately, Lisa's parents could not or would not recognize Lisa's increasing level of anxiety. They were convinced she could succeed at the school. To resolve her chronic distractibility, they proposed asking the family physician to put her on medication. They were certain that she would be able to fulfill the school's requirements with medication and learning assistance at our center.

Lisa had initially been referred to our center for a diagnostic evaluation by her fourth grade teacher. She suspected Lisa had a learning disability. My tests confirmed her suspicions. Lisa's learning disability was fairly significant. Lisa was attending a school that was oriented toward highly efficient learners of well above average intelligence. In this environment there were few opportunities for her to experience success in school. Despite the hours she put into her schoolwork, she was falling further and further behind her classmates.

From the very beginning of my involvement with Lisa's family, I had serious reservations about the appropriateness of Lisa's attending the particular private school in which she was enrolled. A child of average intelligence with a moderate learning disability did not belong in an academically demanding school with a highly accelerated curriculum.

Lisa's profile of symptoms was typical of a learning disability. She was having problems following verbal and written instructions, and her handwriting, reading and language arts skills were considerably below the standards of the school. Her teacher indicated that she was having difficulty working independently and that she required continuous supervision. Lisa had tested near grade level on standardized tests, but the average student in her class was testing at least three years above grade level. The work at school was becoming increasingly more difficult, and the teacher could see that the pressure on Lisa was becoming more and more intense.

Lisa's parents insisted that her work be objectively evaluated by the school at the end of the academic year. In the interim, they wanted her to continue in an intensive learning assistance program at our center. Lisa's parents were insistant that she be permitted to return to the private school the following year if she succeeded in fulfilling the school's requirements. They refused to consider any other alternatives. They also refused to consider family counseling.

By the end of the school year, Lisa had achieved the school's minimum grade point average requirements. The school and I had grave reservations when she was promoted to fifth grade.

Lisa had unwittingly been forced to assume a role in her parents' emotional drama. This drama also involved Lisa's sister who had a serious physical handicap. The parents recognized this child's more severe limitations, and they considered Lisa's academic difficulties negligible in comparison. If was as if we were taking away the parents' only hope when we suggested at the conference that Lisa would probably not be able to succeed at her current school.

A child who is encouraged to overcome a problem or to succeed at something which is difficult is being encouraged to test himself and his resources as a human being. Confronting this challenge and prevailing over it can be an exhilarating and an important confidence-building experience.

A vital distinction must be made between encouraging a child to test his resources and encouraging a child to beat his head against a wall. When parents force a child to confront an unrealistic and unfair challenge, they run the risk of demoralizing the child and destroying his self-confidence. The task of rebuilding the self-confidence of a demoralized child can be awesome, and the battle is not always successful.

Parents who fail to recognize that they are subordinating their child's best interests to their own emotional needs create an environment in which their child can develop psychological problems. All children need to succeed and to feel good about themselves and their abilities. Such success is basic to a child's mental health. Lisa was being denied the opportunity to experience these feelings. School had become a never-ending struggle.

Lisa's parents had become confused about priorities. Her continued attendence at the private school had assumed symbolic importance. This ten year old had become the family flagship, but the flagship was listing. Unless the course was changed, the "ship" was in grave danger of sinking.

REASONABLE VERSUS UNREASONABLE EXPECTATIONS

All parents have expectations for their children. Most parents simply want their children to be happy, self-confident and self-sufficient. Some parents, however, have very specific expectations for their children. These parents may want their children to achieve in life what they themselves have achieved, or what they themselves have failed to achieve. A physician may want his son or daughter to also become a physician. Or if the parent is not a physician, he may want his son or daughter to become one because it was *his* frustrated ambition to have become one. The child is thus assigned a role in a script that has been consciously or unconsciously written for him by his parent or parents. The role assigned may satisfy the child's own needs, or it may not. If the role fits the child, the script can be a source of inspiration. If the role does not fit the child, the script can be a source of despair. Pivotal in whether or not such a role fits a child are such factors as aptitude, interest, temperament, personality, and desire.

As parents, your expectations for your child can have a profound effect not only on his performance in school, but also on his emotional well-being. When your expectations are reasonable and congruent with your child's abilities, you are helping your child to achieve his potential. When your expectations are unreasonable and excessive, you can create psychologically damaging anxiety.

A world famous violinist may attribute her success to her parents' insistence that she practice as a child. These expectations may well have shaped the course of her life. But had those expectations been at odds with the violinist's temperment or ability, the resulting pressure and anxiety could have been psychologically devastating.

Having too few expectations for your child can be as emotionally damaging as having too many. Parental expectations which are especially permissive encourage laziness and irresponsibility. For most children, academic success requires effort. Rarely are children willing to make this effort when they feel that their parents do not expect it of them.

By communicating to your child that you expect him to try his best, you are preparing him to face the realities of a competitive world where diligence, attention to detail and responsibility are generally recognized and rewarded. Encouraging your child to develop these qualities is quite distinct from insisting that he receive *A*'s. For some children a *B*, a *C*, or even a *D* may represent a major achievement. If you fail to acknowledge this achievement, you communicate to your child a lack of acceptance. This lack of parental acceptance can have a profound effect on his acceptance of himself. A child who lacks self-acceptance has no chance for developing self-confidence. A student who is driven to get an *A* simply to please his parents, may achieve this objective. But in the process of learning to please his parents he may have become so other-directed that he has lost his own identity.

It is reasonable for you to expect your child to bathe regularly. It is reasonable to expect that your child not cheat or lie, and you are being responsible parents when you vigorously discourage your child from doing so. [1] It is also reasonable to insist that your child call home if he is going to be late for dinner or late in returning from a party. Such clearly communicated expectations encourage your child to become responsible. But is it reasonable to expect that a child who doesn't particularly like football make the football team? Is it reasonable for you to insist that your child take piano lessons for five years when he has no musical aptitude or interest?

Unless parents periodically examine their expectations and motives, they run the risk of confusing their own emotional needs with those of their children. The result can be devastating psychological trauma for the child.

DEFENSE MECHANISMS

For no apparent reason the boy pushed the other fourth grader who was waiting in line in the cafeteria. It was clear that the first child was trying to goad the second into a fight. The other children barely took notice of the incident; they were accustomed to this behavior from John. He was the class bully and the class "tough guy." He was also the worst student in the class.

Human beings can be both vulnerable and uniquely indomitable. The nature and the degree of a person's vulnerability and indomitability will reflect a complex mix of psychological, environmental and genetic factors.

---

1.   Chronic cheating or stealing could be symptomatic of an emotional problem that may require professional counseling.

At a very early stage in their development, children acquire both a conscious and unconscious awareness of their strengths and weaknesses. In kindergarten and first grade they begin to perceive how they perform relative to the other children. During these hours that they spend interacting with their peers, they develop a sense of their intelligence, their athletic ability, their social popularity, and their academic potential.

If a child perceives a weakness or an inadequacy, he will probably try to protect himself from being vulnerable to this weakness. A child who realizes that he is unpopular may become shy or he may become a bully. A child who concludes that he is "dumb" may choose to become a clown.

Human beings are programmed with a powerful survival instinct. This instinct operates on an emotional as well as a physical level. It can be devastating for a child to recognize that he has inadequacies. A child who is forced to confront his apparent inability to read or play baseball or make friends is at risk emotionally. To protect himself psychologically, he may develop behaviors which help him to cope with his limitations. Unfortunately, these defense mechanisms are often counterproductive and tend to accentuate the very deficiencies that the child is trying to camouflage. For example, the child who perceives that he is unpopular and becomes the class troublemaker in order to get attention is probably not going to win many friends with his behavior. It is a sad irony that most children (and adults) do not recognize that their defense mechanisms are self-defeating.

Helping the learning disabled child let go of his defense mechanisms requires that parents and teachers establish a reasonable balance between demanding too much and demanding too little from the child. The child's defense mechanisms can make this challenge quite difficult.

Although your child's defense mechanisms may be fairly transparent to you and his teacher, they will not be transparent to your child. His behaviors and attitudes reflect his *unconscious* effort to protect himself from being vulnerable to failure, rejection, frustration and disillusionment.

Encouraging a child to give up behaviors which are working at cross-purposes with his happiness and success may elicit a lot of resistance on the part of the child, especially if the behaviors have become well-entrenched. It may be obvious to the child's parents and teachers that his behaviors are counterproductive, but the child's unconscious mind may perceive these behaviors as essential to his emotional survival.

The nature of a learning disabled child's defense mechanisms will vary. Some of the most typical behaviors and attitudes include:

1. Irresponsibility
2. Indifference
3. Excuses and rationalizations
4. Laziness
5. Procrastination

6. Playing the role of victim ("It's unfair!")
7. Resistance
8. Emotional outbursts
9. Untruthfulness

Parents and teachers who frontally "assault" a child in their attempt to force the child to give up his defense mechanisms should prepare themselves for defeat. The more they push, lecture and cajole, the more resistance they are likely to encounter. When parents and teachers insist that the child change his behavior without offering him a viable alternative, they create a "showdown" which they cannot possibly win.

Until such time as the child becomes convinced that he can survive without his defense mechanisms, he will hold onto them for dear life. In this respect a child is no different than an adult who smokes because he feels that smoking permits him to be more at ease socially. Smoking becomes a social crutch that is integrated into the person's perception of himself. He will not voluntarily give up this behavior until he becomes convinced that he can be socially competent and socially confident without the cigarettes.

Your desire that your child relinquish his learning disability related defense mechanisms must be tempered by the realities of his learning problems. If the child's problems are severe, his defense mechanisms will probably be complex and well-entrenched and the remediation process may be long and arduous.

During the remediation process there may be periods of great academic progress that are followed by periods of regression. One moment your child may appear to have mastered a math concept, and the next moment he may once again become confused. Or your child may seem to have overcome his letter reversal problems, and then six months later he may revert to making the same mistakes.

Before your child will be willing to let go of his counterproductive behavior, he must first become convinced that he can survive in school without it. A seemingly irreconcilable paradox is created: to overcome his learning problems, the child must be willing to give up his defense mechanisms. But to relinquish his defense mechanisms, the child must first be convinced that he can learn. Convincing the child that he can learn requires quality learning assistance, infinite patience, sensitivity, understanding, support and love.

Many learning disabled children are convinced that they are inadequate, and they tend to give up when the going gets rough. During the remediation process, the child with learning problems will inevitably encounter frustration and setbacks. Although the child may have made significant gains, his self-esteem may still be quite fragile. The memories of past failures and of deep frustration can be very vivid. Setbacks can cause the child to reexperience a demoralizing sense of futility.

136

The setback may occur when the child is trying to master a particularly difficult skill. For example, he may do poorly on a spelling test after he was absolutely convinced that he knew all of the words on the list backwards and forwards. Confronted once again with his apparent limitations, the child may choose to withdraw into a protective cocoon. He may remobilize all of his psychological defense mechanisms as he tries to insulate himself from the pain of feeling incompetent. He may convince himself that the learning assistance isn't working and is a waste of time and money. He may want to quit, and he may attempt to manipulate his parents into permitting him to do so.

As parents, your natural instinct is to protect your child from experiencing pain. Resisting your child's self-defeating manipulative behavior will demand a large amount of emotional fortitude. To permit your child to quit when he is frustrated by a challenge is to permit your child to fail. There is a cumulative effect to quitting. With practice, it becomes easier and easier. Although parents may delude themselves that they are helping their child by repeatedly coming to his rescue, they are actually undermining the child's already tenuous self-esteem.

When a child who is confronting a difficult challenge cries, he is giving vent to his sadness, anger and frustration. The child's emotional system is in effect flushing itself out so that the child can get on with the business of solving the problem. Crying is a safety valve that can serve to free a child from the debilitating effects of imploding emotions. Although witnessing a child cry can be a heart-wrenching experience, his crying may signal that the healing process has begun. A child who expresses the powerful emotions that he has unconsciously repressed may be trying to free himself from the control that those emotions exert upon him. [2]

Parents who acknowledge their child's emotions nonjudgmentally are telling their child that it's okay for him to feel sad or angry or frustrated. By giving your child permission to *feel* what he feels and to *express* what he feels, you affirm your acceptance of his right to have and to show emotions. This affirmation of your acceptance is essential to your child's mental health. If, however, your child begins to use anger and tears as a bludgeon to make you feel guilty or to manipulate you into doing what he wants, then you might consider encouraging him to blow off steam in the privacy of his room. Children learn quickly that temper tantrums are an effective weapon for getting what they want.

As parents you will share your child's pain and sadness when he experiences a defeat or a setback. Your child must, nevertheless, be made to understand that you cannot permit him to quit simply because he is sad or angry or frustrated. Your child will probably not understand why you are taking this position, and he may become angry with you for insisting that he

---

2. There are many reasons why children cry. When parents sense that their child's crying is the result of profound fear or sadness, they should alert themselves to the possibility of an emotional problem which may require professional treatment.

complete the remediation process. He may not appreciate until much later in his life that you cared enough about him to risk his wrath by demanding that he persevere and prevail over his problem.

Your child's catharsis of unhappiness and tears may actually signal a turning point in the process of overcoming his learning disability. I have frequently found this to be the case in my own clinical experience. Often the act of crying helps the child get in touch on a visceral level with his resistance, his fear, his anger and his feelings of inadequacy. The child may have finally arrived at the point where he is willing to take ownership of his learning problem. At this important juncture in the remediation process, it is especially important that he realizes that his parents and his teachers are there to provide him with encouragement, understanding, support, and love.

Your child must be helped to understand that during the remediation process it's okay if he fails an exam, but that it's not okay if he doesn't study or if he gives up after failing. [3] At this point neither the grade nor the grade level is of primary importance. What is important is that your child learn to persevere. When he stumbles or becomes discouraged, he will need your support. When he does well or makes a breakthrough, he will need your acknowledgement and your praise.

Once the learning disabled child begins to take an active role in the remediation process, as opposed to a passive role, he can make major gains. The child has realized that the tutoring is not something that is being done *to* him, but rather, it is something that is being done *for* him.

COMPENSATORY MECHANISMS

The children at the class picnic had finished their lunch. The boys went to the softball field to choose up sides for a game. Most of the girls went to the volleyball net and they, too, chose up sides. Tim picked up his book and wandered off. He told the teacher that he preferred to read, but he also knew that if he played softball or volleyball, he would be chosen last because no one really wanted him to play on his or her team.

A child who perceives a weakness or an inadequacy within himself has four basic options:

1. He can develop defense mechanisms.
2. He can accept his limitations.
3. He can attempt to overcome his limitations.
4. He can develop compensatory mechanisms.

---

3. Not studying or trying are defense mechanisms. Parents must exercise patience, sensitivity and firmness as they encourage their child to give up these defense mechanisms.

Seldom is the child's choice the result of a conscious, analytical process. Most children will respond in a way that is consistent with their attitude about themselves. If they feel insecure and unworthy, they will probably unconsciously choose defense mechanisms as a means of coping with their limitations. Their psychological posture will be to protect themselves from emotional pain at all cost.

A child who accepts his limitations may or may not have a realistic sense of his actual potential. If a child concludes in first grade that he cannot sing very well and decides to accept this fact, he may be simply acknowledging the truth. But if the child concludes that he cannot read very well and if he then decides never to read, his response to his problem would be self-defeating. The acceptance of certain limitations can be psychologically healthy. The converse is also true. An unwillingness to prevail over certain limitations can signal psychological problems. How the child chooses (and is guided) to respond to his limitations can have a profound impact on the future course of his life.

The child who attempts to overcome his limitations is expressing confidence and faith in himself. The child senses his own power to take charge of his life. Such children are often achievers, and, in some cases, overachievers. People with an extreme form of this personality trait are compelled to test themselves constantly. They grow up into men and women who climb mountains and sail around the world and build financial empires.

The child who learns how to compensate for an area of weakness by developing a potential area of strength is essentially choosing the arena in which he wants to compete. Unlike a defense mechanism, which is generally an unconscious reaction, the compensatory mechanism may reflect a conscious choice on the part of the child to emphasize his areas of strength as opposed to struggling in areas where he is weak. Compensatory mechanisms can serve a positive or a negative function, depending upon the reasons for the compensatory mechanism. For example, if a child recognizes that he is not a particularly good athlete, he may choose to pursue art or music, especially if he perceives that he has talent in these areas. But if a child has a learning problem and decides to focus exclusively on athletics, he may end up as an adult with severely limited skills. These limitations may create serious economic problems later in life if the child is unable to make a living from athletics.

CORY: REBELLING AGAINST
TOO MUCH PARENTAL INVOLVEMENT

The mother sitting across from me was desperate. Her lips trembled as she struggled to keep from crying. She was a single parent who had been divorced for three years. Her ex-husband lived in another state. Cory, her seven year old son, was bright, charming, and outgoing. But she was convinced that he was intentionally driving her crazy.

139

I had been working with Cory for approximately six months. The child's learning problems were fairly severe — perhaps a 6 on a scale from 1 (subtle) to 10 (severe). Cory's learning problems were compounded by the fact that he was extremely strong-willed, and he hadn't yet decided whether he was ready to begin the process of conquering his learning problems. He liked the attention he was getting from his classroom teacher, his tutor and his mother.

Cory's father was an engineer who saw his son only four weeks each year during the summer. He had remarried, and he and his second wife had another child. Although he was quite concerned about Cory and had written me several times to inquire about his son's progress, his relationship with his ex-wife was extremely strained.

Cory's mother had recently moved to northern California from Connecticut. In Connecticut, Cory had been diagnosed as learning disabled and had been placed in a special education program. Upon arriving in California, Cory's mother requested that he be given special learning assistance and Cory was currently spending one hour each day in his school's resource center. At the same time, he was attending our center two hours per week for intensive perceptual training and academic remediation.

Cory tended to be irresponsible in school, and both his classroom teacher and the resource specialist suggested that his mother become involved in making sure that he completed his assignments. They also suggested that she help him at home with his math, reading and spelling. She accepted their recommendations, and she began spending one hour each evening helping Cory with his schoolwork. Cory was resisting these efforts by refusing to cooperate. Only by threatening or punishing him could she get him to sit down and do his homework. She was exhausted when she came home from work, and she had begun to dread the prospect of this new nightly ritual of arguing, cajoling and threatening.

Cory's mother had unwittingly permitted herself to become locked into a power struggle with her son. The power struggle had become so serious that it was destroying their relationship. In desperation, the mother had begun to consider whether it might not be wise to send Cory back east to live with his father. She was convinced that he needed more discipline, and she knew that she could not possibly be more stern with her son than she was already.

I asked Cory's mother whether she had experienced serious discipline problems with Cory prior to becoming his "tutor." She indicated that she had not. I then asked her if she wanted to continue to tutor her son. She said "no." She felt, however, she had to continue if he was going to make progress in school. I then inquired whether Cory had shown any improvement since she had started helping him at home. She replied that he had not. He had actually regressed. At this point I gave her "permission" to discontinue tutoring Cory.

As a general rule, parents should not attempt to teach academic subjects to their own children. This general prohibition does not mean that parents should not occasionally review spelling words with a child or occasionally help him with a difficult math problem. Helping your child with his homework is distinct from attempting to become your child's tutor. Most children want their parents to be parents and their teachers to be teachers. Even if a parent is a teacher he or she generally should not attempt to teach his or her own child, especially if that child has a learning disability.

With reluctance, Cory's mother had agreed to become her son's tutor. It was unnecessary for her to do so. Cory was already receiving assistance in school and at our center. If he was being irresponsible in school, there were far better strategies for correcting the problem than the one proposed by the classroom teacher and the resource specialist.

I suggested to the mother that we design a system which would permit her to get a daily report from school that would indicate whether Cory was completing his assignments. If Cory felt that he could not do the work or was having difficulty with his assignments, his responsibility would be to inform the resource specialist or the tutor at our center. Otherwise he would be held responsible for completing his work. A system of rewards and consequences was also designed and carefully explained to Cory. [4] If Cory was irresponsible, he would lose privileges such as Saturday TV. His mother agreed to discontinue helping Cory with his homework unless he requested help.

Four weeks later a very different woman entered my office. She was smiling broadly and was eager to share with me the recent progress that Cory had made in school. All of the tension at home had disappeared. Cory was completing his homework and keeping up with his class. The classroom teacher reported that Cory's reading had improved. There were periodic lapses into irresponsibility, but Cory accepted the consequences, and knew that he would have to go without TV on Saturday mornings when the lapses occurred. But most important, Cory and his mother were getting along again. The staff at the center had also seen a dramatic improvement in Cory's reading. He now seemed ready to participate actively in the remediation process.

Many children resist and resent parental help or involvement in their schoolwork, especially when they are sensitive about their learning deficits. Parents tend to insist on "closure." [5] When they help their child with school work, they may become very intense in their desire that their child "get it." This intensity and desire for closure on the part of parents will often cause the child to experience anxiety and can make him resist the help. A child who acquires negative or painful associations with his parents'

4. See Chapter 5: "Monitoring Your Child's Performance" for a description of such a system of rewards and consequences.
5. See Glossary of Educational Terms.

attempts to help him may begin to develop a profound aversion to the subject matter. Ironically, this aversion is the very thing the parents were trying to avoid by providing help for the child.

When offered selectively, parental assistance with schoolwork can be beneficial. But parents who lose their patience or who "overexplain" or "overdrill" will usually cause their child to react negatively to them and to the material being taught.

I suggest that parents who do elect to help their child with his schoolwork consider the following:

1. Make the sessions short and to the point.
2. Don't expect or demand "closure." Some children need several assistance sessions before they master a skill. Other children will appear to master an operation or a skill and then forget it.
3. Discipline yourself to be patient.
4. Quit for the day when you perceive that you are becoming frustrated or impatient.
5. Don't "play" teacher with your child, even if you are one by profession. Children want their parents to be parents and their teachers to be teachers.
6. If you don't understand something, such as "12 to the base four," admit it, and tell your child that he'll have to get help from the teacher.
7. If you are not in the mood to help your child, or if you recognize that you have a tendency to lose your patience, discuss your feelings frankly with your child. Consider hiring a tutor or a qualified high school or college student.

While some children resent and resist their parents' efforts to help them, other children have a tendency to become overly dependent on such help. Such children create a symbiotic relationship with their parents and run the risk of becoming incapable of working independently.

Parents can unconsciously encourage a dependent relationship with their child. An extreme example of an excessive parent/child dependency is a situation in which parents actually do their child's math problems or reports under the guise of "helping." The parents may rationalize their actions by contending that their child could not possibly do the work on his own. Unwittingly, these parents are perpetuating their child's learning difficulties. If a child is so confused or so lacking in skills that he cannot do the work that is expected of him then he should not do the work until such time as he is taught the necessary skills. A child gets nothing out of having his parents do his work.

5. See Glossary of Educational Terms.

Parents may also choose to intervene because they are overly concerned about grades. This type of intervention distorts the basic objective of the educational process, which is to train the child to develop his own intellectual resources.

Parents who become excessively involved in their child's schoolwork because they perceive their child as an extension of themselves tend to assume ownership of their child's accomplishments and failures. A common example of this phenomenon is seen in the case of parents who identify so strongly with their children's athletic accomplishments that they cease being parents and become stern, demanding, and, often, relentless coaches.

Some parents of learning disabled children are forced — with great reluctance — into the role of tutor. These parents may discover that their child is hopelessly behind and that there is no meaningful learning assistance available. As a last resort, they become tutors because they conclude that the only way that their child can survive educationally is with their help. Although such crisis intervention may be necessary, it can place a serious strain on the parent/child relationship.

There are parents who can successfully tutor their children. My experiences over the last thirteen years have convinced me that most parents cannot, and should not, if there other alternatives available.

TAKING OWNERSHIP OF A LEARNING PROBLEM

Throughout this book I have encouraged you to become actively involved in your child's education, especially if you have a child who is not progressing in school. As adults, you have certain prerogatives in structuring solutions to your child's problems. Although you do have prerogatives, you must remember that the learning problem belongs to your *child* and *not* to you.

Parents who have taken ownership of their child's problem tell me that "We have a reading problem," or "We studied our spelling last night." By taking ownership of their child's learning problem, these parents are unintentionally creating a symbiotic emotional dependency. This dependency discourages their child from developing his own emotional and problem solving resources. There is a real danger that the child may become so dependent on the "we" relationship that in order to preserve the dependency, he will unconsciously defeat any attempt to help him overcome his problem. Children can become addicted to excessive nurturing.

143

Although you will probably be on the receiving end of the emotional fallout that results from your child's learning problem, all that you can provide him is the *means* by which he can solve his problem. You can not solve the problem for him. The unhappiness, frustration, anger, and despair that your child may experience as a consequence of his learning problem will require patience and sensitivity. The most beneficial way for you to express your love and support is to work continuously at keeping the channels of communication open between your child and you and your child's school. Together you can establish reasonable academic goals, and together you can design a strategy for involving your child in the process of attaining these goals.

The emotional fallout from your child's learning problem cannot be disregarded. If your child is frustrated in school and takes out his frustration on his little sister, you will want to be sympathetic and understanding. At the same time you cannot permit your child to continue teasing or hitting his sister. You may be able to solve the immediate problem by buying your child a punching bag on which he can safely vent his anger. But you will also need to *communicate clearly* to your child how you feel about what is going on and why his behavior is making you unhappy. You will need to encourage your child to communicate how he feels. If he continues to tease or to hit his sister, he may need to be punished until he learns that it's okay to hit the punching bag but not okay to hit his sister. The ultimate solution, of course, lies in helping your child resolve his learning problems so that he will be less frustrated and angry. In the interim, your child will need to know unequivocally that there are certain basic rules of behavior which must be obeyed.[6]

STRUCTURE AS THE CORNERSTONE OF RESPONSIBILITY

All children need structure in their lives. Bedtime, mealtime, chores, homework, playtime, school, church — these defined and structured periods provide a child with a sense of order, security and stability. Learning disabled children in particular have special need for structure both at home and in school. Because the learning disabled child frequently has a difficult time managing and controlling the variables in his life, he can easily become overwhelmed when faced with too many options and choices. Too many choices tend to accentuate the inattentiveness and disorganization which are characteristic of many learning disabled children.

6.   See Thomas Gordon's *Parent Effectiveness Training* for an excellent analysis of parent/child communication strategies and problem ownership/problem solving techniques.

By establishing structure in your child's environment and by creating a clearly defined framework of family values, rules and expectations, you are communicating to your child where you stand on such important issues as honesty, education, effort and commitment. Your attitudes and the structure you establish provide your child with a frame of reference which will help him to evaluate the many choices he must make each day. Should he take one more " at bat" and be late for dinner? Should he study for the quiz? Should he reread his essay one more time before handing it in? His criteria for making these decisions will reflect the structure that you have provided for him. In providing this structure, you are helping your child create a sense of identity.

When you insist that your child do his homework, you are establishing a framework of values and attitudes that are essential to the proper formation of character. A youngster who is not expected to conform and adjust to the values of his family will probably have a difficult time conforming and adjusting to the values of his society. By insisting that your child do his homework, you are encouraging the development of responsibility. You are impressing on your child in a very meaningful way that he had better not expect a free ride through life.

During the formative years, it is a primary parenting responsibility to provide structure in a child's life. This structure takes the form of rules, guidelines, values, priorities and expectations imposed by the family and by society. Toddlers are taught not to eat dirt. Three year olds are taught not to run into the street. Six year olds are taught to look both ways when they cross the street, and eight year olds are taught to call home if they decide to go to a friend's house after school.

Structure, in the form of these external controls, provides the foundation upon which children begin to build their own internal control system. A six year old learns it is against the rules to cheat, to steal or to bully. A sixteen year old learns that it is against the rules to take the family car without permission. The internalization of externally imposed control is essential to developing self-control and self-discipline. Without self-control, a child will have a difficult time learning to function in any context where he is required to regulate himself, be it in the classroom or on the playing field.

If, as a toddler, your child never learned to obey the rules, there's a good chance that he won't obey them as a teenager. If, as a child of six, he never learned that he was responsible for the consequences of his actions, there is a good chance that he will not feel responsible for those consequences as a teenager or as an adult. A fourteen year old who has not learned how to govern himself will probably have a difficult time doing so at twenty.

145

Many children with learning problems lack self-discipline. The inability to self-regulate may manifest itself in inattentiveness, disorganization or inconsistency. Because the learning disabled child tends not to pay attention to such details as neatness, deadlines, punctuation, following instructions, completing assignments and planning projects, he frequently requires more externally imposed structure than does the typical student. During the remediation process, a well-structured home and school environment provides the learning disabled child with an important support system. Learning disabled children in particular need to know precisely what is expected of them so that they can orient themselves toward an acceptable standard of behavior and performance.

By creating a structured environment for the learning disabled child in school and at home, parents and teachers establish a context which encourages the child to become responsible. By insisting that the child conform to an external standard of behavior and performance, in effect, parents are training their child to become conscious of himself, his actions, and the consequences of his actions. This consciousness is the essence of responsibility.

In most instances, the school performance of the learning disabled child will have to be more closely monitored than the school performance of the nonlearning disabled child. Until such time as the child is able to demonstrate that he has acquired sufficient internal control, he will require external control. He may need to have his academic assignments and objectives clearly defined. He may also need to have his parents or teachers tell him precisely where in his notebook his assignments are to be written, and he may need to agree upon a specific amount of time that he will spend doing his homework each evening. (This is assuming that he is assigned homework, which, unfortunately, is not always the case.)

Parents who establish a structured environment for their learning disabled child generally have fewer parenting problems than parents who do not. Creating a structured environment does not mean that parents of learning disabled children need to be dictatorial or autocratic. Excessive parental control can result in either emotional alienation or emotional dependency. By attempting to control every aspect of their child's life, authoritarian parents deny their child the opportunity to grow up and become an effective and functional adult.

Helping a child to avoid serious or life-threatening mistakes is a natural parental instinct. But when parents deny a child the opportunity to learn from his mistakes, they are denying him an invaluable educational experience. The balance between justifiable interference and forbearance is delicate.

Ideally, a child should participate in the process of establishing structure in the family. For instance, a child who wants to be on the Olympic swim team must be willing to get up each morning at 5:30 to practice. If being on the swim team is important to him, he will have to agree to the structure and the rules established by the coach. The rules might include not eating sweets and going to bed early. Because the child has made the choice to be on the team, he will probably be willing and eager to comply with the rules.

Younger learning disabled children especially need rules to help them learn to govern themselves. Rules are an integral part of structure. For example, if you unequivocally communicate to your child that you expect him to do one hour of homework each evening, then he will know your position on the issue of homework. Rather than dictate when he must do his homework, however, you might consider giving him some choices so that he can participate in establishing the rules and the structure. You might offer your child the option of doing his homework right after school, before dinner, or after dinner. The rule in the family is thus clearly established: a fourth grader should do one hour of homework. When to do the homework can be left up to the child. Handling the issue of homework this way helps your child recognize that you are committed to the rule. He will also recognize that he too has some options and some power within the guidelines you have established.

You should explain family rules so that your child understands the reasoning behind them. You should also encourage your child to express his feelings and objections. If he feels that an hour of homework is too much, your child deserves an explanation about why you feel that one hour is reasonable. The child must understand that as parents it is your responsibility to establish reasonable rules. He must also understand that, although he may not always agree with the rules, he will be expected to comply unless he can present compelling reasons for not complying.

Rules should be fair. If your child offers a reasonable, nonmanipulative argument for reevaluating an established rule, you owe it to your child to examine this argument objectively. Don't be afraid to back down when the child has logic on his side. An example of such logic might be a situation where your child can prove that the teacher doesn't assign an hour of homework. If the parents are still committed to having their child do one hour of homework an evening, they would either have to request that the teacher specifically assign an hour of homework or they themselves will have to create educational projects for their child. Another option is for the parents to change their rule about the amount of homework the child is required to do.

Reasonable rules provide an important sense of security for a child. Rules which are not clearly defined and not consistently applied cause children to become confused and insecure. This lack of definitiveness and consistency can create a myriad of emotional problems, particularly for a learning disabled child.

Whenever I have been forced to establish limits for a child at our center, I invariably perceive a sense of relief on the part of the child. Some children resist accepting these limits at first, but once they realize that I'm firm and that the rules are meant to be obeyed, they stop testing. On an unconscious level, most children want their parents and their teachers to define the rules and to tell them what they are and are not permitted to do. Hopefully, the child's parents and teachers will be the ones who define the rules, and not a judge in juvenile court.

Attempting to help your learning disabled child develop responsibility can be an awesome challenge. Your child's emotional defense mechanisms may take the form of chronic laziness, belligerence, indifference or resistance. The longer this counterproductive behavior persists, the more entrenched it will become. Although learning disabled children must put forth greater effort than other children, many learning disabled children are intent on putting forth less. A child must first be convinced that there is hope before he will be willing to give up his self-defeating behavior.

DEVELOPING RESPONSIBILITY

You play a pivotal role in the process of helping your child develop responsibility. Your prerogatives to monitor and to regulate your child's behavior and performance will become more limited as he matures. One of your primary obligations as a parent is to prepare your child to assume control of his own life. You cannot be with your ten year old as he rides his bicycle to the store. You can only trust that he will be careful and not take unnecessary risks. You cannot be with your fifteen year old when he takes his history exam. You can only trust that he was responsible enough to prepare adequately for the exam and that he will concentrate and do his best while taking it.

The process of transferring control to your child actually begins on the first day of kindergarten. It is there that your child learns that he will be held responsible by adults other than his parents for his actions and his performance. He will learn that he is expected to obey the teacher's rules, and he will learn that he alone will have to deal with the consequences of his actions. If he decides to put paste in someone's hair, he will learn that he will probably be punished. If he does something well, he will learn that he will probably be praised. Making this transition from answering exclusively to you for his actions to answering to strangers also is a very important step in your child's development.

148

The first manifestation of your child's physiological and emotional drive to become independent can be seen in the impelling need of a toddler to explore the nooks and crannies of the house. As your child grows older, he will concurrently crave independence and parental support. This paradox is an inherent component in the process of his emotional and physiological development. The dilemma you face as parents is knowing when to support and monitor your child and when to back off and permit him to make choices for which he must assume responsibility. One of the most challenging situations that parents confront occurs when they recognize that their child is making a poor decision and they realize that their child must be allowed to learn from this mistake. Making mistakes is an essential part of the process of growing up to be an independent and fully functional adult.

The way in which parents transfer control to their maturing child is critical. In transferring control, both the child's chronological age and his level of emotional maturity must be taken into consideration. What may be appropriate to permit certain fourteen year olds to decide may not be appropriate for other fourteen year olds. To the extent to which they are capable, *all* fourteen year olds should be encouraged to take responsibility for their lives and their actions.

By the time your child becomes a teenager, his capacity to function with relative independence should be fairly well established. Although he will still require your guidance and support, he should have by now acquired the ability to make responsible decisions and should have come to the realization that he will be held responsible for his decisions. The ongoing process of transferring control to an emerging adult should be in its final stages. For example, your teenager should know how much time he needs to allocate to studying and to doing homework. He should be forming a realistic sense of his own abilities, and he should be developing a sense of what is important to him and what his priorities are.

KEVIN: CHOOSING AMONG THREE OPTIONS

It was obvious that Kevin was upset with the teacher. The seventh grader had been given a specific language arts assignment to complete during his tutoring session. When I entered the classroom, the instructor was telling Kevin that he was not satisfied with the amount and the quality of the work that Kevin had done during the hour. Kevin responded that he had been thinking, and that was why he had written only six sentences during the entire period. The teacher was skeptical. He told Kevin that if he didn't increase his output during his next session, he would have to stay for an additional hour in order to complete the assignment. Kevin's facial expression clearly indicated that he felt that this decision was unfair. Kevin wanted the teacher to know that he felt victimized.

As the center director, it is my responsibility to monitor not only the children's progress, but also that of the teachers. I felt that it was appropriate that I intervene. I told Kevin that I thought the teacher was on target in pointing out that he had not done very much work during the hour. I pointed out that not only was the work incomplete, but it was also sloppy and almost illegible. I then explained to him that although I realized that he felt the teacher was being unfair by insisting that he do more work, the teacher was accountable to me for what was covered during the class.

The assignment that the instructor gave Kevin was fair, and Kevin had the skills to complete it within the allotted time. I concurred with the teacher's assessment that Kevin was choosing to procrastinate. According to Kevin's regular classroom teacher, this was precisely what he was also doing in school.

Kevin had learned that whenever he appeared upset, his parents and teachers would back off and accept a minimum amount of effort from him. This behavior worked very well, and Kevin had never been forced to confront his learning problem. By playing victim, he avoided having to work. There was a real danger that he might conclude that this script would serve him throughout his life and that he would never need to put forth more than minimum effort.

I sensed it was time to change the dynamics of Kevin's script. I gave him three choices: 1) he could decide to do more work in class; 2) he could decide to come for an additional hour at the center; or 3) he could take the class assignment home to complete. I asked him if he felt that these choices were fair, and he reluctantly agreed that they were. I told him to think carefully about his decision during the week and that we would know by the quality and the quantity of his work during the next session what he had decided. The following week Kevin completed his assignment — neatly and within the time allotted.

By giving Kevin three options, each with clearly defined consequences, I established guidelines and performance standards, and, at the same time, I gave Kevin some control over his life. Kevin was being permitted to choose from among three options. Each option involved consequences. The opportunity for Kevin to manipulate had been eliminated. He chose to participate in the remediation process, and he began to make some meaningful inroads into his language arts difficulties.

MANIPULATIVE BEHAVIOR

Learning disabled children can become especially adept at manipulation. By manipulating, they are able to avoid the pain of having to confront their limitations. A child with a learning disability who says or implies that he doesn't have any homework when he actually does may not want or be

150

able to cope with having to struggle with additional schoolwork at home. When he tells you he doesn't have any homework, he may be consciously lying, or he may also have convinced himself that he doesn't have homework because that is what he wants to believe.

To expect a child to relinquish his manipulative behavior without a struggle is unrealistic. The child must first become convinced that he can survive emotionally without the system of manipulative behaviors before he would be willing to surrender his coping system. If the learning disabled child realizes that he can manipulate himself out of having to deal with his learning problems, he may begin to use this behavior every time he encounters a difficulty. With practice such a child can become very skillful at using manipulation to control both his parents and his teachers. There is an excellent chance that the highly manipulative child will grow up to be a highly manipulative adult.

Manipulative behavior can serve as an essential survival mechanism for children who feel inadequate. Most children become manipulative because they become convinced that they have no other viable options. The behavior can take many forms. Some children develop their charm and use it very effectively to get what they want. Others may throw temper tantrums or become disruptive when they don't get their way. The spectrum of manipulative behavior ranges from outright lying, blaming, and rebelliousness on the active end of the spectrum to indifference, irresponsibility and laziness on the passive end. To the struggling child, manipulation may represent the path of least resistance through life.

There is a "payoff" for every manipulation. The range of "payoffs" can vary from being permitted to stay up past bedtime to getting Mom to react by pressing Mom's "hot button." When your child perceives you or his teacher as slot machines, there is a powerful incentive for him to keep on playing the game. He will learn that all he has to do is pull your handle enough times for you to give in or give up. Realizing this, he will continue to manipulate you. Slot machines can easily become addictive.

The key to convincing your child to give up his manipulative behavior is to convince him the behavior doesn't work. You can accomplish this goal by not permitting yourself to be manipulated. I know that you may be thinking right now: "Easier said than done!" Resisting manipulating behavior can be one of life's greatest challenges.

The first step in developing a strategy for dealing with manipulative behavior is to obtain accurate information. This will permit you to discern truth from fiction. Establishing direct communication with your child's teacher is essential. This communication will tell you how your child is doing and precisely what is expected of him. By communicating directly with the teacher, you reduce the chances of a "surprise" in May when you suddenly discover that the teacher is contemplating retaining your child.

Direct communication also alerts the teacher to the need for closely monitoring your child's performance in class. The teacher's feedback will also permit you to monitor your child's work at home more closely.

Manipulative behavior is often scripted. To resist this behavior, you must figure out the "script." For instance, if your child tells you that he failed an exam because the teacher was being unfair, you can respond in several different ways:

1. You can agree with your child.
2. You can tell your child that he is not being truthful.
3. You can discuss with your child why he feels that the teacher is being unfair.
4. You can set up a conference where your child can safely express his feelings directly to the teacher.

Response #1 probably means that you have been "bamboozled." Your child may be right and the teacher may in fact have been unfair. But you need more specific information before you can reasonably support your child's position. To respond with "carte blanche" support only encourages your child to make excuses whenever he encounters difficulty or frustration. Children can become very adept at manipulating their parents into providing support for their irresponsible behavior.

Response #2 is setting yourself up for an argument. Your child may react by assuming the role of victim: "You never believe me or take my side!" To reject your child's contention of unfairness without a dispassionate examination of the issues involved encourages mutual distrust and disrespect. As a result, your child may focus on his disillusionment with your lack of "loyalty" and not focus on confronting and resolving his learning problems. You, in turn, will have joined the teacher in being the "heavy."

Response #3 offers you and your child an opportunity to explore the issues involved in your child's reaction to failing the exam. Although your child may be attempting to absolve himself of any responsibility for doing poorly without justification, he deserves an opportunity to express his feelings. Parents can play a very important role in this situation by functioning as a sounding board. The way in which you elicit information is critical. If you respond to your child's feelings judgmentally, you will succeed only in "turning him off." Conversely, if you encourage your child to express his perceptions and if you use this discussion as an opportunity to clarify the issues involved, you can help your child to reexamine his position more objectively. The following represents one possible strategy:

Parent:	What did the teacher do that was unfair?
Child:	She gave us a math test and she didn't ask us the things we were supposed to study.
Parent:	What did you think you were supposed to study?
Child:	Fractions.
Parent:	What was on the test?
Child:	Word problems.
Parent:	Give me an example.
Child:	If ¼ of the class of 32 students went to the football game and ¼ of those students who went bought popcorn, how many had popcorn?
Parent:	Does that problem involve fractions?
Child:	Yeah, I guess so, but she didn't ask fair questions.
Parent:	Do the other students in the class also feel the test was unfair?
Child:	I guess some do.
Parent:	Could you have been confused about how to use fractions?
Child:	Maybe.
Parent:	Do you think it is possible that the teacher felt she was being fair?
Child:	Well, she might have, but I still don't think she was fair.
Parent:	Perhaps the teacher wasn't really trying to trick you. Perhaps she was just trying to find out if you really understood fractions. Think about it. In the morning if you are still convinced that you have been treated unfairly, you ought to discuss it with her.

By suggesting alternative ways for a child to look at the problem, you are helping your child to gain a different perspective on what may be a recurring behavior pattern: in this instance, that of blaming others for his failures. When you resist the temptation to be judgmental and refrain from trying to solve your child's problem for him, you are modeling problem solving techniques that can serve your child in good stead throughout his life.

If your child's typical reaction to failure is to blame his teacher, your refusal to "buy into" this behavior discourages your child from manipulating you. At first, your child may be frustrated by you changing the dynamics of the script and by you not responding in you typical fashion. Initially this new "tactic" may confuse or unsettle your child, but in the long run he will probably appreciate the new relationship that you have established with him.

Response #4 represents another option. By encouraging your child to communicate directly with the teacher, you are discouraging your child from attempting to manipulate you into supporting irresponsible behavior. If your child is absolutely convinced that his teacher has been unfair and if he can present plausible justification for his position, to attempt to convince him that he is wrong would be unjust. Your child deserves an opportunity to express his feelings to the teacher without fear of punishment.

For this method to be successful, it must give your child the oportunity to safely express how he feels. Most classroom teachers would probably be receptive to having a conference. Encouraging your child to communicate openly and frankly with an authority figure can be an invaluable learning experience for him.

By recommending a teacher-child dialogue, you are supporting both your child and his teacher. If your child's perceptions about the teacher are accurate, the teacher needs this input. If your child's perceptions are inaccurate, your child needs clarification. If your child is being manipulative, he needs to realize that this behavior will not work.

The transition from manipulative to authentic behavior can be painful for everyone. Children will relinquish their manipulative behavior reluctantly. The "letting go" process must proceed in stages. Understanding, sensitivity, firmness, support and love are essential to a successful transition. Equally important is the student's perception of himself. He will be far more willing to give up his manipulative behavior if he becomes convinced that he can succeed without having to resort to the behavior.

MARK: RUNNING AWAY FROM HIS ANGER

From my office window, I could see the thirteen year old storm out of his classroom. He went to the bench in front of the center to wait for his mother. I knew Mark needed some time to cool off, and I also knew that Mark needed to go back to class.

Later in my office Mark explained with barely contained fury that the teacher who was filling in for the regular teacher had corrected him repeatedly when he had actually been doing the activity correctly. Feeling himself become more and more upset, he decided to leave the classroom. He told me that he would never go back into that classroom again.

As we talked it became clear that whenever Mark became upset, he would remove himself from the situation that caused his upset. Mark could see nothing wrong with this behavior. He explained that when he became angry, he became *very* angry. At such times it was best for him to go off by himself.

I asked Mark if he would also choose to walk out if someday his future boss unjustly corrected him for a mistake that he felt he hadn't made. He replied emphatically that he would. I then asked him if he would do the same thing if his next boss did something that he felt was unjustified. This time he replied with more reluctance that he would still walk out. I inquired what he would say to the next employer who was thinking of hiring him. Would he tell him why he quit his last two jobs? Mark didn't respond.

During the next ten minutes, Mark and I talked about anger. I told him some of the things that made me angry, and he told me about the things that made him angry. We also discussed the choices a person has about how he will handle his anger. Finally, we discussed how Mark had chosen to handle his anger.

Mark and I made a deal. If he could figure out a way to hold on to his anger until after class, he could then tell any of the teachers on my staff precisely what his feelings were without fear of getting into trouble. Walking out or blowing up in class would violate the agreement, and he would have to attend a makeup session.

I then informed Mark that it was time to go back to class and that I would work with him for a while. When Mark realized that I was not giving him a choice in the matter, he agreed to accompany me back to the classroom. We began working together and I could see immediately why the teacher had been correcting him. He was doing the assigned activities incorrectly, primarily because he was impulsive and wasn't concentrating. With some prodding on my part, he began to attend to the task. When I left the classroom to return to my office, Mark was doing fine. In fact, he had one of his best days at the center. After class he came into my office with a big smile on his face. He wanted to tell me that he had jumped rope thirty-six times while blindfolded. The previous week this overweight, poorly-coordinated teenager hadn't been able to jump rope at all!

Mark hadn't been permitted to run away this time. He learned that he had choices about how to deal with his anger and that he would have to deal with the consequences of those choices. If he chose to get angry at the teacher during class, there would be a punishment in the form of a makeup class. The same punishment applied to leaving the classroom without permission.

Mark's fear of his own anger compelled him to try to direct all situations in which he might possibly lose control. He exerted control by running away whenever he experienced frustration. In so doing, he deluded himself into thinking that he was handling the problem. Mark needed to learn that he could manage his anger without having to run away. He also needed to learn that he couldn't use his anger as an excuse or justification for giving up.

I had no illusions about having resolved Mark's anger problem during our short session together. I knew that Mark would ultimately require professional help in examining and sorting out the feelings that were triggering his anger. The sooner he began the process of delving into the source of this anger, the sooner Mark would be able to relinquish his fear of his anger. In the interim, Mark would have to develop a more effective way of dealing with his upsets. I hope that in the future Mark will discover his fury is not nearly as devastating as he fears it is. When that day comes, he will finally be willing to stop running.

HANDLING FAILURE AND FRUSTRATION

Sensitivity to failure is a very human characteristic. Even the most emotionally healthy child can begin to doubt himself and his abilities when faced with a series of successive failures. Most children are, however, able to bounce back from these occasional setbacks if their self-esteem is basically intact and if they recognize that the setback is temporary.

The child with a history of failure often lacks the necessary emotional resources to rebound from defeat because his self-esteem is fragile and because he realizes that he will undoubtedly encounter further setbacks. A child's perspective is to a large extent determined by his experiences. If his experiences have been negative, his perspective will probably be negative. Although the child may actually be making progress, he may remain convinced that he is hopelessly inadequate. With each new defeat, real or imagined, his self-esteem becomes more tenuous and his psychological defense mechanisms more impenetrable.

Unlike the typical student, few learning disabled children are able to say: "Today was a terrible day. But tomorrow, things will be better." For the child with a learning problem, there's an excellent chance that tomorrow will be an equally terrible day, unless the child is fortunate enough to receive help.

The learning disabled youngster is the victim of a vicious cycle: because he has failed so often, he never develops a positive mental attitude. Without a positive mental attitude he cannot develop the necessary willpower and determination he needs to be able to succeed.

It is because of this vicious cycle that the child with a learning problem must be repeatedly assured of the resolve and the support of his parents and teachers. This resolve and support will serve in the interim as a temporary surrogate for the resiliency, willpower, confidence and positive mental attitude that the child himself has not yet developed.

A child who has learned how to rebound from failure has acquired an essential survival skill and emotional resource. Helping your child develop this resiliency in the face of defeat or frustration is a critically important parenting function. Unfortunately, there is no magic formula that parents can use for teaching their child to handle failure. Some children when faced with a setback may find that it helps to talk about their feelings with their parents. Other children may need time alone to sort things out. As a general rule, talking about feelings is preferable to repressing them.

Knowing how to communicate with a child is a high-level parenting skill. Some parents have a natural ability to listen to a child without passing judgment and without taking ownership of the child's problem. They sense when to give their child time to mull over his options. They possess the necessary patience and forbearance to permit their child to wrestle with his feelings. Intuitively, they sense when it is appropriate to make a suggestion and when it is appropriate not to. They sense when to commiserate with their child over a setback and when to resist their child's manipulative "victim" behavior.

Those parents who have doubts about their ability to respond appropriately or effectively to their child when he is frustrated and discouraged can learn to improve the quality of their responses. To do so, they must attempt to understand the dynamics of their child's emotions.

Disappointment is a natural consequence of failure. A child who responds to disappointment by becoming excessively angry, depressed or indifferent may be signalling that he has an underlying emotional problem. A child who goes berserk when he fails at something is telling his parents with his behavior that he needs help. The youngster who responds to failure by retreating into an impenetrable shell is also signaling his emotional distress.

A frustrated child is an angry child. Some children will permit their anger to explode and their disharmony will be very apparent. There is nothing inherently wrong with a child's feeling angry. When the anger appears to be excessive, or when the anger manifests itself in destructiveness or violence, there is reason for concern.

Some children will contain and repress their anger and, as a consequence, their feelings will implode. Depression is anger turned inward. The process can be represented as follows:

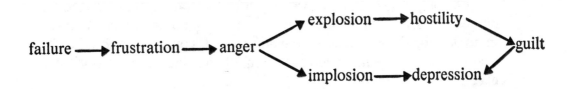

Anger and disappointment in the face of defeat are natural. When the explosion or implosion of emotions is extreme, intervention will be necessary. Better communication may be all that is required. Professional counseling may be necessary if the problems appear to be profound.

The ideal time for parents to intervene is when the child's frustration first begins to manifest itself. A simple observation or a simple question can open your child's emotional floodgates. You might say, for example: "Honey, I can really see that you're upset about not doing well on that spelling test." Or you might ask: "Would you like to talk about it?" By helping your child get in touch with his feelings and by creating a safe context in which he can express his feelings without fear of being judged, reprimanded, or told what to do, you activate a safety valve. The ultimate goal is to show your child how to activate that safety valve *himself* when he senses that he is becoming angry or depressed. Helping your child learn how to communicate his feelings and his perceptions provide him with a very powerful survival resource.

The key to communicating with your child about emotions is being able to listen. Were your child to say he's upset about the grade he received on a test and were you to reply: "Well, you're just going to have to study harder," your child may not want to share his feelings with you again. Your child did not ask you what he needs to do to get a better grade. He simply volunteered to tell you how he was feeling. He wants you to listen and perhaps offer some sympathy. You might ask him what *he* thinks he needs to do to solve the problem. If he replies that he doesn't know and asks you for input, you might respond, "Well, perhaps there's a better way to study. Maybe you can try a new approach." You might let the child know that you are available to help him develop a more effective strategy. The next move is up to your child. Helping him, however, does not mean solving the problem for him. If you can not work with your child because of limited patience or knowledge about the particular subject matter, ask your child if he would like a tutor. Remember, your child owns his problems and his emotions. At best, you can only provide support for your child as he works at solving his problems and at sorting out his emotions.

The experience of failure can serve as an impetus for a child to develop the skills he needs to succeed the next time around. A child who goes into a batting slump and who continues to practice his batting in an effort to overcome the problem is demonstrating a basic belief in himself and his ability. Were he to quit the team or become emotionally distraught every time he struck out, he would be expressing a lack of faith in himself and his abilities. By discouraging your child from giving up and by encouraging him to develop the will to persevere and prevail, you are transforming the negative energy of failure and frustration into a positive, growth-oriented energy.

Striking the proper balance between protecting your child from excessive, demoralizing failure and frustration and allowing him to experience a controlled amount of failure and frustration can be heart-wrenching. As parents, you can only rely once again on your intuition as to what is appropriate. If you have doubts about your ability to handle the situation, the best investment you can make in your child's future is to seek professional advice.

THE EFFECTS OF LEARNING PROBLEMS ON BROTHERS AND SISTERS

Whenever one child is on the receiving end of a great deal of attention, there is the possibility that the other children in the family may resent the extra attention that their brother or sister is receiving. The child with a learning problem will be an obvious source of concern for his parents, and the child's problem can quickly become the focus of the entire family's emotional energy.

It is common for a child in distress to "act out," and the counterproductive behaviors that many frustrated and demoralized learning disabled children adopt can sorely test the patience and the endurance of everyone in the family.

The brothers and the sisters of the learning disabled child may also require special emotional support during the remediation process, especially if they are on the receiving end of the "acting out" behavior. Parents will need to explain to their children why the child with the learning problems is being given special attention. They will have to help their other children understand why their brother or sister requires extra love and patience from everyone in the family until the problem is resolved. Although there is no way to guarantee that your children will fully understand or appreciate the situation, every effort be made to help them understand as best they can.

Family council meetings offer an excellent opportunity to air resentments and misunderstandings. The expression of feelings and frustrations, and the expression of nonjudgmental acknowledgment of these emotions can be an invaluable means for defusing a difficult situation.

Children have a "right" to their feelings, even if these feelings are negative. Parents can best serve their learning disabled child and their other children by using family meetings as an opportunity to explore the tensions, the resentments and the misunderstandings that exist. Private discussions with each of your children may also be necessary.

Sometimes the brothers and sisters of the learning disabled child will also "act out." They may resent the special attention their brother or sister is receiving, and they may tease or make fun of the child. Teasing or "put downs" can only intensify the distress of the learning disabled child. This distress will in turn intensify the need that the learning disabled child has for his counterproductive defense mechanisms and compensatory mechanisms. Family meetings and private discussions are the primary means of identifying and discouraging this behavior which can only cause the learning disabled child additional emotional pain.

THE EFFECTS OF LEARNING PROBLEMS ON PARENTS

A child's learning problems can seriously strain the emotional resources of any family. The learning disabled child typically has a wide range of both educational and emotional needs. Meeting these needs can mis-align the emotional dynamics of the entire family. The learning disabled child can demand a seemingly unlimited amount of patience, understanding and love, especially if the child's problems are severe or resistant to remediation.

The behavior of the learning disabled child can test even the most exceptional parents. A child who is hurting emotionally may express his pain by misbehavior or by being inconsiderate, demanding or exceedingly shy. The relationship between the parents themselves is by no means invulnerable to the strains of having a child in the family who is unhappy in school.

It should be noted that many children with learning problems do not develop behavior problems. This is especially true when the learning problem is not particularly severe or when the problem is identified early in the child's life. When meaningful remedial treatment begins in kindergarten or first grade, much of the emotional scarring that typically is a byproduct of a learning problem can be avoided.

One of the primary sources of dissension between parents is agreeing that their child has a learning problem. One parent may be more aware that the child is struggling in school than the other parent, or one parent may be more willing to accept evidence of a learning disability than the other parent. It has been my personal experience that, fathers are generally less willing than mothers to acknowledge that their child has a learning problem. [7]

Ideally, parents will be able to discuss openly and forthrightly the emotional strains the family is experiencing. If a child is experiencing emotional distress parents will need each other's support. [8]

7.   Mothers are more frequently on the "front lines" and have to deal with the consequences of the child's learning problem on a daily basis. Teachers are also more likely to communicate with the mother than the father.

8.   Single parents will often not have access to this support system, and the strain of dealing with a learning disabled child will require great fortitude. Single parents should attempt to find or to create a parent support group in their local community.

Frequently one parent will assume the primary responsibility for dealing with the learning disabled child and the school. Although the primary responsibility may fall on one parent's shoulders, it is most important that both parents support each other in the remediation process (if there are two parents). The burden of responsibility can be very heavy when one parent is doing the work that should rightfully be shared by two.

FEELING GUILTY: AM I RESPONSIBLE FOR MY CHILD'S LEARNING PROBLEM?

Confronting a child's learning problem can be a painful experience for parents. Acknowledging that there is something wrong places a heavy responsibility on parents. Many parents would prefer not to be forced into the position of having to take responsibility for something that they may not entirely understand.

Denial is one way of avoiding this responsibility. Such denial may assume the form of refusing to look at the evidence or blaming others for the child's learning difficulties.

Parents who choose to deny that their child has a problem may give only marginal support to those who are attempting to provide help. They may go through the motions of giving the learning assistance "a try," but if their child does not quickly resolve his problems, these parents may blame the learning disabilities specialist, the program, the educational system or the classroom teacher for their child's lack of success. Some parents feel that if they admit that their child has special needs, they are admitting that their child is in some way "defective."

The child who senses his parents' lack of commitment to the teacher or the remedial program will also lack commitment. Without support and commitment from the parents and the child, no learning disabilities program can succeed.

Other parents will react to their child's learning problem with concern that far exceeds the nature of their child's problem. This excessive concern may interfere with their judgment and may cause them to overreact. Typically, these parents become overly involved in monitoring their child's performance. They may volunteer to help out in their child's classroom, to ostensibly help the teacher, but in reality they are checking up on their child's progress. If they enroll their child in an outside learning assistance program, they may attempt to get permission to observe each session. Although intellectually they may recognize that their concern is creating an unhealthy situation, emotionally they are not prepared to allow their child to own his problem, and they are not prepared to trust those who are providing help for the child.

When dealing with excessively concerned parents or with parents who deny that their child has a problem or needs help, I frequently become acutely aware of a barrier that exists between them and me. This barrier invariably interferes with the remediation process. For example, if I recommend that their child would benefit by being placed in a special learning assistance program in school, parents who are compelled to deny that their child has a problem often will argue that they do not want their child to be identified by the school as learning disabled. They contend that if their child is identified, he will be permanently labeled by the school system as handicapped. [9]

When I recommend to overly concerned parents that they not put added pressure on their child by "helping out" the classroom teacher, they will frequently argue that their child desperately needs their support. Unwilling to acknowledge that they are creating an emotional dependency which actually undermines the child's self-concept, they offer all sorts of rationalizations for their taking ownership of their child's problems.

When I have attempted to analyze why these parents respond as they do to their child's learning problem, I find a common denominator. That common denominator is guilt. The specific behavior patterns may vary, but in most cases those parents who are most difficult to deal with unconsciously feel that they are in some way responsible for their child's problems. They deny that a problem exists in order to repress these guilt feelings. By refusing to acknowledge their child's problem, they avoid the need to confront their fears. Other guilt-ridden parents attempt to compensate for their feelings by attempting to become surrogate teachers. Others become overly protective or overly harsh.

After I finally established a rapport with one "difficult" mother, she was able to reveal that her husband attributed their child's learning problem to her having smoked during pregnancy. Another parent feared that her child's learning problem was the result of her having gone back to work three months after her child was born. Many parents have acknowledged that they too had learning problems when they were children. These parents were deeply troubled by the fear that they had genetically transmitted this problem to their child.

Perhaps smoking can contribute to a learning problem, but to my knowledge this has never been documented. Placing a child in a child care situation may also in some way impede subsequent learning development, but to my knowledge such a causal link has never been established. Although the bonding between a mother and a child is a very important component in a child's development, a child who realizes that he is loved and who receives adequate sensory stimulation in the child care setting, is no more likely to be learning disabled than a child raised at home by his mother.

9. Schools do not use their records in the same way that the police use a criminal's "rap" sheet. Children are not "branded," and parents by law have access to their child's school records.

There does appear to be a genetic factor in the occurrence of learning problems. Parents who had learning problems have a greater statistical chance of having children who have learning problems. The transmission of genetic traits is a fact of life. Visual acuity, height, musculature, facial features, and coordination are all traits that are passed on from parents to child. Sometimes these traits are all positive. Most likely there will also be a few negative ones in the mix. There is nothing parents can do to prevent the genetic transmission of pattern baldness, less than perfect eyesight, or learning disabilities. All parents *can* do is provide their children assistance in instances where it will help.

A parent who has inadvertently passed on the trait that is responsible for learning problems need only remind himself or herself of the many other potentially more devastating traits that he or she might have transmitted. Eyeglasses or a tutor is a small price to pay for providing a child with the gift of life. [10]

Guilt is one of the most insidious of emotions. And the fear of guilt is equally insidious. Eight million children have learning problems in the United States. This represents the potential for creating as many as sixteen million guilt-ridden parents. Fortunately, most parents realize that they can either feel guilty about something which they could not prevent from happening, or they can take the initiative and do something constructive. Those that take the initiative and seek help serve their children far better than those who allow themselves to be paralyzed by guilt.

10.   Learning problems quite frequently are not inherited. Many parents who were themselves good students have children who have difficulty learning.

CHAPTER SEVEN_____

Communicating with Your Child

CRAIG: HE COULD HANDLE THE TRUTH

I was totally charmed by the little boy with the red hair and the freckles all over his face. His expressions ranged from intense seriousness to sparkling joy, especially when he did something correctly.

Craig was giving 100% as he worked at the diagnostic tasks I was asking him to do. When I flashed letters and numbers to determine if he could recognize the symbols and remember what he had seen, his face mirrored his total concentration. Despite his intensity, Craig appeared to be enjoying himself, and he proudly informed me that his special teacher in school did many of the same things with him.

When I began to check Craig's auditory processing skills, I noticed that his enthusiasm quickly disintegrated. It became quite apparent that he had difficulty with any task which involved listening. Craig was unable to reproduce the pattern when I clapped a simple rhythm with my hands. He became very frustrated with himself because he could not keep track of the number of beats and the rhythm at the same time. Although his hearing had been tested by a pediatrician and was normal, Craig could not distinguish between the different vowel sounds. My trests revealed that Craig's reading skills and math skills were approximately two years below grade level. He had problems sounding out phonetic words, and his reading was inaccurate.

No teacher had ever suggested to Craig's parents that he had a learning problem. But his parents could see that he was struggling and insisted that he be evaluated. A diagnostic work-up by the school psychologist confirmed their suspicions. Craig had a relatively severe learning disability. Because of his positive attitude, sunny personality and conscientiousness, his learning problems had simply been overlooked. Now that Craig was falling further and further behind, his academic problems could no longer be ignored. He had been placed in a special full-time learning disabilities program during the last month of fourth grade. He seemed to be happy with both the special program and his teacher. Unfortunately, he had made little progress.

My tests indicated no primary symptoms of a neurological disorder. [1] Craig's gross and fine-motor coordination were good, and he did not appear to have any difficulty paying attention. Although I did not administer an intelligence test, I was certain that Craig's I.Q. was in the normal range. On a scale of 1 to 10 (1 representing a very subtle learning problem and 10 representing a severe problem), I felt that Craig's learning problem was approximately a 6.

Craig's parents informed me that they had been reluctant to bring him to the center for fear that he might become demoralized. He had just recently begun his special program in school, and they felt that he might conclude that there was something profoundly wrong with him if they enrolled him in a special program at our clinic as well. His parents also expressed concern about putting too much pressure on him.

The learning assistance program in Craig's school appeared to be good, but I felt that he would benefit from additional help in the area of auditory processing. [2] Two additional hours of learning assistance did not seem an unfair burden to impose on Craig, especially if the training would speed up the remediation process. Rather than add to the pressure Craig was experiencing I felt that the additional help would actually reduce the pressure.

To avoid giving Craig the impression that he had a profound and insurmountable problem, I presented the idea of his receiving additional help positively. I knew that he needed to perceive the learning assistance as an exciting challenge and not as a punishment. My intuition told me that Craig liked challenges, and, my intuition proved correct.

When I explained to Craig why he was having difficulty in school and why he had difficulty remembering and distinguishing the things he heard, I could sense his relief. Despite his positive attitude and winning personality, he was painfully aware of his learning deficits. To understand at last why he was struggling and to hear that he could overcome his problem was a great relief. I proposed to Craig that we work with him at our center, and he responded enthusiastically. Craig intuitively realized that he was going to receive the help he needed to succeed in school. His parents' fears about him becoming demoralized or over-burdened proved unwarranted. Craig could see the light at the end of the tunnel.

HONESTY: THE FIRST STEP

Rarely is a child oblivious to his learning problem. Although the child may not be willing to admit to himself or to his parents that he needs help, he will recognize that he is "different" without anyone having to tell him so.

---

1. See Chapter 3 for a discussion of the symptoms of neurological disorders.
2. See Chapter 3 for a discussion of perceptual processing deficits.

Parents who explain to their child that he has a learning problem and assure him that with special help he can overcome it are lifting a great weight from the child's shoulders. The problem is out in the open, and now it can be dealt with positively and constructively. What a relief it is for a child to know that his parents understand and are on his side!

Conversely, a family which never openly discusses the learning problem can allow the problem to become distorted in the child's mind. Deprived of information and feedback, the child may erroneously conclude that his learning difficulties are more serious than they actually are, or that his parents are embarrassed by or ashamed of his learning problems.

Some parents are reluctant to discuss the learning problem openly with their child because they fear that to do so would make their child feel different from other children. Concerned that feeling "different" will cause the child to develop psychological problems, they expend a great deal of emotional energy trying to protect their child from reality. By building a protective (and essentially ineffective) shield around their child, these parents frequently impede any efforts by the school authorities to help their child.

Parents who believe that they can protect their child from pressure or from feeling inadequate by not discussing the learning problem or by pretending that it doesn't exist are deluding themselves. Trying to deny the reality of the learning disability to themselves and to their child only delays the day of reckoning. A child will benefit far more if his parents explain to him what his problem is and then let the child and his teachers get on with the process of correcting it.

The guiding principle for discussing learning problems with a child is honesty. The truth can have either a positive or negative impact on a child. The key is how the truth is presented. Parents who tell their child that he has a learning problem and imply that he will never be able to get a decent job unless he stops being "lazy" and starts working harder may indeed be telling the truth as they see it. In communicating their concern in this fashion, these parents are probably forcing their child to become defensive and resistant. Being honest with a child doesn't mean using the truth as a bludgeon. When the truth is used to assault the child, it will only elicit fear, anger and resentment.

Honesty does not preclude emphasizing the positive and deemphasizing the negative. When parents tell their child that he has a learning problem but that with help and effort the learning problem can be resolved, they are using the truth in a positive and supportive way. They are affirming their child's potential to prevail over his learning problems, and they are inviting his active participation in the remediation process. Children know when their parents are being honest with them and expressing confidence in them, and they will respond by tapping into their parents' optimism and positive expectations.

Some children with learning problems will deny that they are having difficulty in school. They do so for the same reasons that an adult might deny that he has a drinking problem or a gambling problem. Admitting a problem or a defect can be very difficult, especially when one's self-concept is tenuous. By pretending that the problem doesn't exist, it's possible to create the illusion that everything is okay.

A learning disabled child who denies that he has a learning problem may be psychologically unable to accept that reality. It could be counter-productive and emotionally damaging for parents to confront their child and insist that he accept the "facts" immediately. The truth can be very frightening and threatening to an insecure child. Children sometimes need time before they can accept and deal with the "facts." At first, some parents may even have to coerce their child into accepting help. Once the child realizes he is making headway, however, his resistance should diminish.

Each child will respond differently to confronting, accepting, and dealing with his learning problems. Older children with a history of un-resolved learning problems will often pose a special challenge to both parents and teachers. [3] Years of frustration tend to cause children to develop profound feelings of inadequacy and elaborate defense mechanisms.

The learning therapist must also confront the challenge of discussing the learning problem with the learning disabled child. The manner in which the therapist chooses to examine the subject with the child can have a profound positive or negative impact on the remedial program.

There are, of course, many different strategies for presenting and discussing a learning problem with a child. It has been my experience that children relate well to analogies. I often use two analogies that have proven effective in helping children to understand their learning problems and to accept learning assistance.

The Race Car Analogy

Me:	Do you know what a Ferrari is (or a Porshe or a Trans Am)?
Child:	Yes. A car.
Me:	What kind of car?
Child:	A fast car.
Me:	Yes, a fast car with a super engine. What happens when the car isn't running well?
Child:	You take it to a garage.

---

3. See Chapter Seven: "Dealing With Learning Disabled Teenagers."

Me:	That's right. You take it in for a tune-up. Do you know that you have a good engine, too? The engine is your brain. But you need a tune-up so that you can run better and do well in school. You don't want to run like a Pinto when you have a Ferrari engine, do you?
Child:	No.
Me:	But instead of adjusting your carburetor, we need to work on your concentration, your reading, your spelling, and your handwriting. When we're done giving you a tune-up, you should be able to run like a race car. And school will be easier for you because you will no longer have learning problems. How does that sound?
Child:	Good.
Me:	Do you want us to help you to do better in school?
Child:	Yes.
Me:	Super! Let's start next week.

The Athlete Analogy

Me:	If you wanted to be on the Olympics Swim Team, what do you think you would have to do?
Child:	I'd have to practice.
Me:	That's right. You would have to get up real early every morning and swim laps in the pool. And your coach would give you exercises to improve your speed and to make you a stronger swimmer. Do you think it would be hard doing all that practice?
Child:	No. Well, maybe sometimes.
Me:	Do you know how to swim?
Child:	Yes.
Me:	Even though you already know how to swim, do you think the coach might want to help you to learn to swim better so that you could make the team?
Child:	Yes.

Me:	Well, we want to help you learn better so that school will be easier for you. You already know how to read, but we feel that we can teach you to read better. Just like the swimming coach, we're going to do things with you to make you a stronger student and to help you with some of the things you're having difficulty with in school like concentration and math and reading. It'll be hard work just like swimming laps can be hard work, but in the end it will be worth it because you won't have to struggle so hard in school. How does that sound?
Child:	Good.
Me:	Great! Let's start next week.

There are many possible analogies or metaphors that you can use with your child to help him understand and accept his learning problem. The advantage of an analogy is that children can relate to it and remember it. If the child should falter during the therapy process, you can refer to the analogy again to help your child sustain his effort and commitment to overcoming his learning problem.

Communicating with a defensive, frustrated, resistant or unhappy child can be extremely difficult. Each parent will have to develop by trial and error a communication strategy which feels comfortable and natural. Although confronting the truth and accepting the facts may make a child feel sad at first, he will have to deal with the reality of the situation before he will be able to begin to resolve the problem.

Learning problems can create strains in any family. Parents who deal with the situation openly, who agree on a remediation strategy, who support each other, and who communicate openly with their child have a much better chance of prevailing over the strains.

COMMUNICATING VS. LECTURING

Being on the receiving end of a lecture is a passive experience for a youngster. Although some children may respond to the lecture, many will shift into cerebral "neutral" when they are being admonished. The child's primary concern is to get the lecture over with as quickly and painlessly as possible.

Sometimes a lecture is the appropriate remedy to a problem. Telling a five year old that he is not to wake you up at six in the morning unless he is ill is a reasonable way of communicating the rules of the house. The same

170

objective might also be achieved by communicating with the five year old in a different way. For example:

Parent:	After you go to sleep at night, do you know what mommy and daddy are talking about or what we might be watching on T. V.?
Child:	No.
Parent:	Why can't you tell what we're doing?
Child:	Because I'm sleeping!
Parent:	Do you think you would be happy if we woke you up to tell you it was raining outside?
Child:	No.
Parent:	Would you be mad?
Child:	Yes.
Parent:	Do you think mommy and daddy would wake you up to tell you it's raining?
Child:	No.
Parent:	You're right. We love you and we know that it would make you unhappy if we woke you up just to tell you it's raining. Well, mommy and daddy like to sleep in the morning until it's time for us to get up. We know you love us as much as we love you. And we also know that you wouldn't want to make us unhappy by waking us up when we are trying to sleep. Is that true?
Child:	Yes.
Parent:	What do you think you could do in the morning if you get up before we do?
Child:	I could play in my room.
Parent:	Yes, you could. Or you could go into the living room and watch TV. And if you're hungry you could go into the kitchen and have a banana or a glass of milk. Does that sound okay?
Child:	Yes.
Parent:	Good. Let's see if tomorrow you can take care of yourself until we get up. I'm betting that you can!

This hypothetical dialogue represents a communication strategy which actively involves the child in the process of recognizing, understanding and modifying his own unacceptable behavior. The dialogue is an alternative to the traditional approach in which a parent simply gives a command, delivers a lecture, or issues a warning with the threat of punishment for noncompliance.

Although the command/lecture/warning approach can be effective, children often respond to such an approach with active or passive resistance. Typically, children react on a reflex level to an angry parent. In the face of anger, a child's response might be: "Uh, oh, I'm in trouble again, and I'm going to get yelled at." A child's behavior may change as the result of a threat, but most likely he is acting out of fear.

Parent-child relationships which are based upon power are tenuous because the power base must inevitably shift to the child. At six years of age, a child has little real power. At sixteen, he has lot of power. If the teenager so choses, he can take the family car without permission or drink beer with his friends. His parents can, of course, punish him, but they really cannot control him if he doesn't want to obey. Exercising autocratic parental prerogatives is somewhat akin to bluffing in a poker game. If you do it too often, someone is going to call you on it.

Parents who show consideration for their child's feelings are encouraging their child to be considerate of other people's feelings. Parents who communicate their disapproval without eliciting a power struggle, resentment, or resistance defuse a potentially destructive situation. Once a child can understand the reasons why a particular behavior is unacceptable, he can begin to develop an appreciation for the rights and sensitivities of others.

At six o'clock in the morning, it may be totally appropriate and effective to yell "Quiet!" to a child who is making too much noise. It may also be appropriate to tell him the rules: "If you get up before mom and I do, you can either stay in your room, quietly watch TV or go to the kitchen and get something to eat. Unless you are sick, you are not to wake us." The ultimate goal is to help your child recognize the reasonableness of the behaviors you are requiring of him. Effective communication can make this possible.

The same communication strategy that is used to help children appreciate the effects of their behavior on others can be applied in communicating with a child about his learning problems. The key to making the process work is involving the child in examining the realities of his situation in school. By eliciting and acknowledging the child's feelings and perceptions, parents can help their youngster confront his problem and take ownership of it. For example:

Parent:	How do you think you are doing in school?
Child:	Okay.
Parent:	Are you sure?
Child:	Well, I'm having trouble with spelling.
Parent:	How about your other subjects?

Child:	They're all okay.
Parent:	Well, I just received an evaluation form from your teacher, and she says that you're having problems in several areas. Are reading and math difficult for you?
Child:	A little.
Parent:	I guess school is a real struggle.
Child:	Yeah.
Parent:	Do you have any ideas about what needs to be done?
Child:	Study harder.
Parent:	That probably would help, but maybe something else needs to be done.
Child:	Maybe I need extra help.
Parent:	That probably would help, wouldn't it?
Child:	I guess so.
Parent:	What do you think about taking some tests so we can find out what the problem is? If you don't know why you're having difficulty, you may start studying harder, but you may be studying the wrong thing. That wouldn't help very much, would it?
Child:	No.
Parent:	Good. Tomorrow I'll call the school and try to set up an appointment for some testing.

Honest, non-demeaning communication will enhance the relationship between parents and children. A supportive system of communication encourages the open and honest expression of feelings and ideas. Such a system is a preferable alternative to autocratic parental power. Although parents do have prerogatives, these prerogatives have far more influence when parents exercise them judiciously. The child whose parents reason with him learns to respect the power of reason.

Some parents feel that if they discuss a learning problem openly with their child, he may become discouraged and demoralized. It has been my experience that children deal far better with honesty than they do with subterfuge. If the "facts" are presented in a way which emphasizes the child's ability to prevail, the "facts" become a catalyst for getting on with the job of conquering the learning problem.

Parents who involve their child in the process of examining and finding solutions to problems are helping their child to learn how to deal more effectively with the realities of life. Once a child understands the challenge and recognizes that he has the support of his family, the process of overcoming the learning problem becomes far less awesome.

Below you will find a "Parent-Child Communication Checklist." This checklist will help you determine if you are willing and prepared to communicate with your child about his learning problem.

PARENT-CHILD COMMUNICATION CHECKLIST	YES	NO
Are you willing to express your feelings openly with your child?	☐	☐
Are you willing to permit your child to express his/her feelings openly to you?	☐	☐
Are you willing to admit that you may be wrong about something?	☐	☐
Are you willing to react objectively and non-judgmentally to your child's opinions and feelings?	☐	☐
Are you willing to enter into a discussion with your child which may involve ideas and feelings which contradict your own?	☐	☐
Are you willing to accept compromises when appropriate?	☐	☐
Are you willing to listen?	☐	☐
Are you willing to work at improving your communication with your child?	☐	☐

If your answers to these questions are predominantly "yes," you should have no problem establishing quality communication with your child. Remember, communication skills improve with practice. The more you work at communication, the better you and your child will become at it.

FEEDBACK: A TWO-WAY STREET

Telling someone how you feel or think can be risky, especially if what you are saying has the potential to trigger a negative or defensive reaction in the other person. Listening to someone tell you how he feels or thinks about you, your ideas or your work is equally risky. This is especially true when what the other person says is negative or contradictory.

Communication requires feedback, and feedback is like a ping pong ball — it needs to bounce on both sides of the net to be in play. Without feedback, what appears to be communication is simply monologue, lecture or diatribe.

Parents who have established a highly authoritarian relationship with their child may have a difficult time permitting him to express contradictions, anger, criticism, or intense emotion. These parents may perceive this type of open expression as undermining the traditional parent/child relationship. The more rigid a parent's attitudes, the more difficult it may be for that parent to tolerate any situation which might challenge his or her sense of propriety. Parents who consciously or unconsciously ascribe to such attitudes as: "Children should be seen and not heard" or "Spare the rod and spoil the child" will probably have a difficult time encouraging and handling open and frank feedback from their child.

To communicate openly with a child, parents *must* be willing to listen to their child. They must be willing to encourage their child to share his innermost feelings and be willing to create an environment in which the child is assured that he will not be punished or degraded for expressing himself. Candid communication involves risk. Parents who help their children to feel safe encourage such communication.

Imagine a child who is able to summon up the courage to tell his father, "You know, Dad, you never compliment me when I do something well. All you do is get upset with me when I make a mistake." Most children would probably feel that it is risky to make such a statement.

Were the child's father to respond by getting angry or by saying, "Well, it's not very often that you do something worth complimenting," it's unlikely the child will venture to share such feelings with his father again. The father has clearly signaled that he doesn't want feedback.

If the father were to respond, "Son, perhaps you're right. I frankly wasn't aware that I never gave you any compliments. Now I'm aware of how you feel, and I will be more conscious of acknowledging you for the good things you do," he would be clearly signaling his child that he, as a parent, is willing to look at his own behavior. The message is clear: "Thanks, son, for sharing how you feel." By modeling a reasonable response to valid criticism, the father is also signaling that feedback is a two-way street and that he will expect his son to respond with equal reasonableness to his feedback.

Parents who reject all criticism or who become defensive or autocratic defeat communication, as do parents who are highly critical or who place certain subjects "off limits" for discussion. Even under the best of conditions, children often find it difficult to express — or even understand — how they feel. When the conditions discourage communication, children will not even try to express their feelings.

Parents have the primary responsibility for creating an atmosphere conducive to communication. A child will often lack the perspective to recognize when he is being defensive or unreasonable. Parents have the burden of responsibility to perceive when communication is breaking down and impasses are developing.

175

Parents who want feedback from their child must resist the inclination to be excessively judgmental. Examining an issue and drawing conclusions is quite distinct from being judgmental. A child who feels his parents are continually judging him will most likely become defensive. When people are primarily intent on defending their respective positions, communication breaks down. Parents who react judgmentally to everything their child says convey a lack of respect for the validity and legitimacy of their child's position and, by implication, for the child himself.

Communication flourishes when parents and children feel mutual respect and trust. Even if such feelings do exist, parents must accept that there may be some subjects and feelings that their child will be unwilling to discuss. Many adolescents, for example, will have difficulty discussing their sexuality with their parents. Such reluctance to communicate does not indicate that the parents have failed as communicators. An adolescent may simply be unwilling to share certain feelings with his or her parent. There is nothing intrinsically "unhealthy" about such reticence, and the teenager's wish not to discuss this subject should be respected.

Receiving candid feedback is not always a pleasant experience. Feedback which is belittling or hurtful is of little value. Some parents will have a difficult time dealing with a child who expresses profound resentment or hostility. Expressing these intense feelings may be very therapeutic for the child but can also be very threatening to the person on the receiving end. Parents who have difficulty dealing with emotionally charged situations may find it advisable to seek the help of a professional or objective mediator. By helping the family to communicate more effectively and by helping each member of the family sort out his emotions, the counselor or therapist should be able to effect some positive changes in the family dynamics.

Ultimately, parents who want to communicate with their child must be willing to work at it. Communication is a skill and an art. Improving any skill or art requires desire and practice.

JIM: LEARNING TO DECIDE FOR HIMSELF

It was all but impossible to establish eye contact with the handsome fourteen year old sitting across from me. There were four of us at the conference: Jim, his mother, his teacher at our center, and me.

The boy had been receiving special help at our center for approximately three months. His learning problems were relatively severe, and they were compounded by his negative attitude toward school.

Jim's learning problems were first discovered in second grade. Because Jim's family had moved several times, he had received only sporadic learning assistance. Each time the family moved, Jim had to be reevaluated and placed in a new program.

176

Jim had been struggling since he had first entered school. At fourteen he was convinced that he didn't like school and never would. It was also apparent from the way he carried his body and from his facial expressions that he didn't like himself very much.

Jim had initiated the meeting in my office. He asked his instructor at the center if he could discontinue a particular aspect of the learning assistance program which he didn't enjoy. The instructor suggested that a conference be set up to discuss Jim's request.

Prior to the conference the instructor informed me that Jim definitely needed to learn how to concentrate, follow oral instructions, pay attention to details and develop his memory skills. Jim was deficient in all of these areas, and this was part of the program he wanted to discontinue.

I knew that we could not force Jim to continue the program. I also knew that if we simply tutored Jim in his academic deficit areas, we would probably not make any inroads into the source of his learning difficulties, which involved perceptual processing deficits. Unless we could help Jim function more efficiently in class, I had serious misgivings about his ever being able to overcome his learning deficiencies.

I began the conference by asking Jim how he felt he was doing in school. He replied that he was having problems with some of his subjects. The following is an approximate recounting of our conversation.

Me:	Do you know why you are having difficulty in some of your subjects?
Jim:	I guess I'm just not a good student.
Me:	Your teachers report that you are having problems concentrating in class and that you don't follow instructions. They also say that you don't hand in your assignments on time and that your work is sloppy. Do you think this is true?
Jim:	Yes. But one of the teachers is mean, and she's always yelling at me. I just tune her out like I tune out my mom when she starts yelling at me.
Me:	Tuning out the teacher and your mother makes the yelling more tolerable?
Jim:	Sometimes I just can't take any more yelling.
Me:	It makes you sad?
Jim:	Yeah.
Me:	And angry?
Jim:	I guess so.

Me:	Do you think tuning them out solves the problem?
Jim:	I don't know.
Me:	Do you feel your teacher and mother are being unfair when they yell at you?
Jim:	Yes. They yell at me when I'm not really doing anything wrong.
Me:	Why don't you tell your mom that? You can tell her now if you want.
Jim:	You're always yelling at me.
Me:	Good. I'm glad you got that off your chest. I sense that there are lots of things you need to tell your parents, and there are many things they need to tell you. Telling each other how you really feel clears the air. Silence about how you feel can hurt much worse than openess and honesty. Sometimes families need someone to help them learn to communicate openly. A family counselor is trained to do this, and I'm going to recommend family counseling. In the meantime we have to deal with your learning problem. Are you interested in sports?
Jim:	Yes.
Me:	Do you follow professional football or tennis?
Jim:	I'm more interested in football.
Me:	If you were a professional football player and had difficulty concentrating when you played, do you think this might affect your game?
Jim:	I don't know. What do you mean?
Me:	Well, I'm sure that you've heard the TV announcers comment about how the receiver was able to make a seemingly impossible catch because his concentration was so good. Have you ever heard them say that?
Jim:	Yes.
Me:	What do you think a football coach does?
Jim:	He teaches his team how to play better.
Me:	Right. He helps them to win. If a coach has a good player who has difficulty concentrating, he'll have to teach that player how to concentrate if the player is ever to become a star. That's the coach's job. He will assign exercises to develop the player's skills, timing *and* concentration. You've seen a high school team at football practice. Am I correct in what I'm saying?

Jim:	Yes.
Me:	Well, that's exactly what we're doing with you here during the perceptual training hour. We're your coaches, and we're teaching you how to be a better player, not on the athletic field but in the classroom. But we can't make you a great player unless you want to be one and unless you believe in us and are willing to work. Does that make sense?
Jim:	Yes.
Me:	Do you know what a game plan is?
Jim:	A plan a coach makes up for winning a game.
Me:	Exactly. Now, I believe *you* have the potential to be a good player, perhaps even a star. But you're playing with a losing game plan. You're using most of your energy to tune people out — your teachers in school, your mother, and your instructors here at the clinic. If this is your choice, there's no question that you can be successful in defeating us. In the process, however, I'm pretty sure that you're going to lose the game. It's sort of sad that someone can succeed at failing. Do you understand what I'm telling you?
Jim:	Yes.
Me:	You have to make a very important decision right now. You have to decide whether you are willing to accept us as your coaches or to reject us. You have to decide whether you trust us and think we know what we're doing, or whether you don't. You're too old for us to force you to do what you don't want to do. And if we tried to force you, I know that you could succeed in making us fail and you fail. So what do you say?
Jim:	I'd be willing to stay in the perceptual training part for six more weeks.

Me:	I really don't know if that will be enough time for us to correct your concentration problems. But I'm going to have to accept your offer because I think that's the best deal I can get from you right now. I know that if you give 100% for the next six weeks you could make tremendous strides. We'll have another conference in six weeks and we'll take a look at how you're doing. But if we're going to work with you for the next six weeks, we're going to need 100% from you. Is that a deal?
Jim:	Yes.
Me:	Super.

"Scripted" behavior is behavior which is predictable. Specific words, gestures and behaviors will trigger seemingly programmed responses. An example of a simple script might be:

Mother:	You misplaced your keys agin. You're always losing things.
Daughter:	I know someone moved them from the bookshelf! People are always moving my things.

Scripts that involve irresponsibility or self-defeating behavior can provide the illusion of protection from fears, vulnerabilities, and deficiencies. A person who is chronically irresponsible or who never finishes a project may be using a script to insulate himself from the possibility of failing or succeeding.

When a child attempts something and fails, he must deal with the emotional implications of having failed. Failure can sorely test the underpinnings of anyone's self-esteem.

When a child attempts something and succeeds, he then has to deal with the emotional implications of success. People's expectations of the child may begin to change. They may begin to expect more successes. Friends may become envious of his achievements, and the child runs the risk of having to find a new set of achievement-oriented friends. Success can be very unsettling to a child whose self-concept has been built upon an expectation of mediocrity or failure.

Taking responsibility for one's actions and completing a task involves taking risk. A child who chooses to take responsibility and who attempts to achieve a goal can no longer blame others for the consequences. The finished project represents his talents and will be judged upon its merits.

Jim had been able to create a semblance of security for himself by playing the role of victim in his own life's drama. His script consisted of resisting help, blaming others and feeling sorry for himself. By playing this role, he protected himself and avoided having to confront himself. Such a confrontation would require him to come face to face with all of his fears and insecurities about himself and his abilities.

Refusing to acknowledge his weaknesses had become a habit, and the habit had become an integral part of Jim's personality. When faced with the challenge of confronting and prevailing over his learning deficits, he chose to avoid the confrontation.

Although Jim did have significant learning problems, he could have prevailed over them had he wanted to badly enough. To do so he would have to deal with the source of his learning deficiencies: inattentiveness, irresponsibility and inefficient perceptual processing. Unless Jim were willing to confront the underlying problems, his prospects for succeeding in school were poor.

We were prepared to help Jim with the educational components of his problem. A family counselor would have to help the family sort out the emotional factors. Jim needed to make a commitment to *both* the remediation and counseling processes. If he didn't, he could easily spend two years going through the motions of working on his learning problems and, in the end, achieve nothing.

My function during the conference was to encourage Jim to make a commitment. There was no question in my mind but that Jim's decision would have a significant impact on the future course of his life. If he made the wrong choice and elected to run away once again, he would probably continue to fail in school. Before he could choose intelligently, Jim needed to understand the nature of his learning problem and the implications of his option to continue or to quit. Had I lectureed, coerced, scared or dictated to him, I would have only increased his resistance. My responsibility was to get the learning assistance program on track.

The conference produced a compromise. I was not fully satisfied with the result, but seldom are compromises totally satisfying. If I had tried to insist that Jim do it my way, I knew he would have been able to make things so miserable for his parents that ultimately they would have agreed to withdraw him from the entire learning assistance program. Jim would thus have failed one more time. By accepting Jim's compromise, I was giving him the opportunity to exert some legitimate power over his own life.

4. See Chapter 6 for a discussion of defense mechanisms and compensatory mechanisms.

Had Jim been seven years old, his parents and I probably would not have permitted him to make such an important decision. But Jim was fourteen, and he could no longer be forced to participate. If Jim had insisted on discontinuing the perceptual training, I would have been reluctantly forced to accept his decision. Jim knew this. There was no need for subterfuge. Jim had the option of simply saying: "I've made up my mind. I want to quit." Jim also knew that he was being given the option of making a critically important choice that might affect his entire life. We were taking a calculated risk in giving him this choice. Fortunately, Jim chose not to run away.

COMPROMISING VERSUS BEING COMPROMISED

Reaching a compromise is very different from being compromised. When a person is compromised, he is being coerced, forced or betrayed into doing something which is against his better judgment. When people reach a compromise, they are acknowledging each other's thoughts and feelings and are agreeing to work together toward solutions to mutual problems. A compromise requires that the parties involved be sensitive to each other's position and that they express their ideas and their feelings freely. Under the proper conditions, negotiating compromise with your child may be an effective and valid parenting strategy.

There is no universal formula for parenting. What may be appropriate in one situation may not be appropriate in another. Making compromises are one of the resources that parents have in dealing with their children. As is the case with most resources, this option must be used judiciously.

Compromising with a child is not always an effective course of action. Often parents must make unilateral decisions. Some of these decisions will not meet with the child's approval. A child who is misbehaving may need to be sent to his room as a punishment or simply because he needs some "time out" to think about his behavior. To try to compromise with the child under these circumstances might confuse the child about the family's guidelines for acceptable and unacceptable behaviors. Parents who negotiate too frequently risk sending a message to their child that everything is negotiable. Children who conclude that everything is negotiable tend to become manipulative and unwilling to accept parental authority.

Parents should be able to sense when it is appropriate to compromise. A mother who makes a "deal" with the child and lets him go to the movies with his friends *after* he straightens his room is negotiating a reasonable compromise. By agreeing to a "deal," the parent acknowledges her child's needs and affirms that they merit consideration. At the same time, the mother is upholding the validity and importance of her own needs. When parents and children are able to reach agreements which do not compromise either the parents or the children, they have developed an important communication skill.

Under the proper circumstances, compromises can facilitate agreement and cooperation. Whenever parents can achieve agreement and cooperation, they help neutralize the classic parent-child power struggle and consequently enhance the parent-child relationship.

ESTABLISHING EDUCATIONAL GOALS

If the learning disabled child is to participate in the remediation process, he needs to know what the score is. He needs to be aware of his problems, how he is doing, and what he must achieve before he can be considered "cured."

Ideally, a child should be involved in the process of establishing reasonable educational goals for himself. For example:

Parent:	Your reading teacher showed me your test scores. Your reading is about a year and a half below grade level.
Child:	Yeah, she told me.
Parent:	Do you think the tests are correct?
Child:	I guess so.
Parent:	You're finding reading difficult?
Child:	Yeah.
Parent:	The teacher feels that you could catch up by the beginning of school next September. What do you think?
Child:	I don't know.
Parent:	Are you willing to give it your best shot?
Child:	Yes.
Parent:	It's now October 10th. How many months in reading would you like to improve by Christmas?
Child:	Half a year.
Parent:	That sounds like a good goal to shoot for. I'll tell you what. If you improve six months in your reading by Christmas, you and I can celebrate by going skiing the first weekend in January. Do we have a deal?
Child:	Yeah!
Parent:	Now let's talk about how you are going to reach your goal.

183

When the learning disabled child becomes an ally in the remediation process, the prospects for resolving the learning problem increase significantly. Keeping your child informed about how he is doing and encouraging him to participate in establishing goals for himself are two of the most effective means of involving your youngster in the process. Structuring repeated opportunities for the child to experience success is also important. These successes do not have to be monumental achievements. They need only be symbolic of growth and improvement. Once a child begins to experience success and to achieve his objectives, he will start believing in himself and in his power to control his own destiny. Acquiring self-confidence is every bit as important as the learning therapy itself.

AVOIDING IMPASSES

A child's resistance can assume many forms. One child may manifest active resistance and refuse to cooperate. Another may be irresponsible or defiant. A third child may have temper tantrums or chronically misbehave. Passive resistance is generally less well-defined. A youngster may sabotage himself, or he may "shut down" and simply go through the motions of doing what is expected of him.

Resistance is common during the remediation process. This behavior may be symptomatic of an underlying problem or symptomatic of the "burn-out" we experience when we work hard for an extended period. Whether the resistance is active or passive, it is a misuse of energy and is counterproductive.

A child's experience of time is a very different experience than it is for an adult. Six months seems like it is forever. The prospect of having to work on resolving a learning problem for a year or more may seem like an eternity to a child. To expect an eight year old to remain actively involved in a program which may appear to him to be endless is asking a great deal. It is common for a learning disabled child to become discouraged periodically, especially if he feels he is not making any progress. Understandably, he may begin to think "Enough is enough!" Keeping the child informed about his progress is an antidote for this discouragement.

Children who do become convinced that their efforts are futile may respond by shutting down, resisting or giving up. If parents and teachers persist in pushing a child who is resisting, they risk creating an impasse. The more the parents and the teachers push, the more the child may resist or withdraw.

Parents and teachers need good instincts if they are to avoid impasses. Knowing when to push, when to back off, when to give a pep talk, and when to commiserate, is essential. Learning how to "read" a child is a

184

function of practice and sensitivity. A simple mannerism or statement can be a clue to a child's internal turmoil or increasing self-confidence.

A child's insistance that he no longer needs learning assistance should not necessarily be taken at face value. The child's perspective must be reconciled with that of the teacher. Although a child may state emphatically "I'm doing fine now!" or "That stupid class isn't helping me at all!", he may simply be trying to manipulate his parents into allowing him to quit.

Parents need to anticipate periods of resistance and burn-out and to plan in advance how they will deal with these situations. Parents who are unprepared may find themselves being manipulated into making "deals" with their child which are not in the child's best interests.

The desire to be finished with something painful or demanding is quite natural. Imagine how you would feel if you were in the hospital for an extended period of treatment. At times you might begin to question the effectiveness of the treatment. Each morning you might press your physician to tell you exactly when the treatment would be completed. Although you may want a specific release date, you would probably be content with reassurance and encouragement. Were your physician to discontinue the treatment before it was appropriate simply to placate you, the physician would be doing you a disservice.

Children who are receiving learning assistance will frequently press for a specific date when their program will be finished. Providing a child with such a date is very difficult. There are many unpredictable variables which must be considered. These include: 1) the child's performance in school; 2) the child's performance on standardized tests; and 3) the child's performance in his learning assistance program. A resource specialist may be able to predict that it should take approximately eight to twelve months to correct a child's problem, but no teacher can know positively that a child's learning problem will be corrected by May 18th.

Parents who provide their child with periodic updates and who support the child when he becomes temporarily discouraged can generally avoid impasses and showdowns. Letting a child know how he is doing, what he has already accomplished, and what he still needs to achieve, helps him make the critical transition from passive to active participation in the remediation process. Sometimes simply listening to a child express his frustration can provide invaluable emotional support.

Ironically, children are often the most resistant before they are about to make a major breakthrough. Sometimes children unconsciously sense that their lives are about to change dramatically, and they are frightened by the prospect of functioning without a learning problem. Although it may seem strange, children can actually become quite attached to their learning problems. The problems can become an integral part of the child's identity. Changing one's self-image can be as scary for a child as the prospect of functioning without alcohol can be for an addicted adult.

MIKE: A FRIGHTENED TOUGH GUY

From the moment the fifteen year old walked into my office, I knew that he wanted me to recognize that he was tough and street-wise. He also wanted me to know that there was nothing wrong with him and that the only reason he was flunking in school was because school was "dumb." Mike made it *very* clear that he was in my office under duress.

A juvenile court judge had instructed Mike's mother to have her son tested for a learning disability. Mike had been arrested three weeks previously for drinking beer in front of a movie theater and had also been picked up on two other occasions for truancy. The diagnostic evaluation for a learning disability was a court-imposed condition of his probation, and Mike's parents had been directed to submit my written summary of the test results to the court.

After talking with Mike for a few minutes, I realized that the tough, street-wise image that he projected was an affectation. The teenager came from a professional, middle-class home where he had access to anything he wanted. He attended an upper middle-class high school where the "bad guys" were in the distinct minority. Under the rough, swaggering exterior, I recognized an insecure, frightened, and unhappy kid who was convinced that he was dumb.

Mike was very angry at his parents, and it was obvious that they were quite intimidated by him. Whenever they said something that displeased him, he would become hostile, sarcastic or argumentative. His parents would then apologize and back down, clearly trying to avoid a confrontation.

The diagnostic tests revealed that Mike could barely read at a fourth grade level. His specific learning deficits were consistent with that of a typically learning disabled child: poor visual and auditory processing skills, poor phonics, and poor word-attack skills. Mike was also highly impulsive and disorganized. Despite his severe learning deficiencies, however, I sensed that he was very bright.

Mike desperately needed learning assistance, but I had serious misgivings about working with him. I knew that we could achieve very little without his cooperation. I also knew that even if Mike did agree to cooperate with us initially, he would need to work hard for perhaps two years to overcome his learning problems. His elaborate defense mechanisms and rationalizations would make it difficult for him to make or keep such a commitment.

Before discussing the possibility of learning assistance with Mike, I decided to give him an I.Q. test. Although I recognized that Mike's scores might be skewed by his emotional and perceptual problems, I felt that I needed some relatively objective assessment of the teenager's ability and potential. As I suspected, the test confirmed that Mike's I.Q. was considerably above average.

Mike looked at me incredulously when I told him that his I.Q. was 130. I could sense his ambivalent feelings of pride and fear. His pride was a natural response to hearing something positive about himself, and his fear was an equally natural response to the uncertainty that this information created in his life.

Over the years, pretense, affectation and rationalizations had become an integral part of Mike's life, and most of his energy was spent blaming, intimidating, making excuses, and compensating for his deficiencies. Mike's "act" had become his life.

Now that Mike had objective proof that he really was intelligent, he no longer needed his "act." For Mike to give up his "act," he would either have to establish a new "act" or be willing to risk simply being himself.

Mike's bravado was his security blanket. Like a child, Mike carried his "blanket" with him at all times. It was something to hold onto when he felt unsure of himself, and it helped make life a little less frightening.

I told Mike that I would not be willing to ask one of my staff to make a commitment to helping him overcome his learning problems unless he were willing to make an equivalent commitment. The learning assistance program would take a minimum of one year of intensive work and might take as long as two years. I told him that before I could consent to working with him, I would have to insist that he personally sign a one-year contract in which he commited himself to cooperating with us and giving 100% effort. [5]

I sensed that Mike was not ready to sign such a contract. He confirmed my suspicion. I then suggested to Mike that he might benefit from working with a counselor. I explained that the therapist would not take sides, but would simply help him figure out what was happening in his life.

To date, Mike has not made any decision about whether or not he wants learning assistance. He did, however, agree to see a counselor. At some point, I hope he will make the decision to conquer his learning problems. Once he does, I am certain that he will prevail.

DEALING WITH LEARNING DISABLED TEENAGERS

Convincing a learning disabled teenager that he would benefit from learning assistance can be a very challenging assignment. The emotional scars that result from years of academic struggle can create serious obstacles to remediation.

5. Such a contract would be symbolic and not legally binding.

The emotional scars that teenagers bear have certain features in common. Older students are often discouraged, defensive, unmotivated, and lacking in self-esteem. Despite these common denominators, each teenager develops his own distinctive pattern of psychological responses to his learning problem. After years of frustration, many students simply give up trying. Some students with severe learning problems, however, continue to "plug away." For reasons that are hard to explain, these teenagers possess an unflagging determination to prevail over their problems.

Factors which affect how a teenager chooses to deal with his learning problem include:

1. the severity of the learning problems
2. the type and quality of the learning assistance support that the student has received during elementary school
3. the quality of the communication system that exists between the teenager and his family
4. the teenager's strengths and weakness in other areas
5. the teenager's personality
6. the type and quality of the learning assistance programs that are available to the student in junior high school and in high school

Students with less severe learning problems generally have less serious emotional scars. Ironically, some teenagers with subtle to moderate problems develop serious self-concept problems while others with more serious learning problems somehow survive with their self-esteem relatively intact.

Some students may have difficulty with a particular subject but little or no difficulty with other subjects. Other students may have learning disabilities which affect their performance in all academic areas. A reading problem, for instance, which has not been remediated in elementary school will most likely cause serious problems for a high school student in any subject that involves reading. A student who is unable to read the material in his textbooks or who cannot understand what he reads will undoubtedly have difficulty with social studies, science, English and math.

Learning disabled high school students who received effective learning assistance in elementary school should be in a better position to handle the academic demands of high school. Although these students may still struggle with specific material or subjects, their learning problems should be less debilitating than had they not received learning assistance in elementary school. This assistance, if successful, will also reduce the risk of potential psychological damage.

Although learning disabled teenagers are often frustrated and discouraged, those who have a good communication system at home are less apt to become demoralized than those who do not have access to such a system. [6] Being able to discuss academic difficulties and feelings is an important emotional resource for learning disabled students. The school counselor can also be an important safety valve for the student. Sensitive and effective counselors can sometimes help students find solutions to problems which appear unsolvable.

The environment in a child's home during the formative years will probably influence how he responds to defeats, setbacks and frustration. The children of parents who model a positive attitude, responsible behavior and determination may adopt their parents' behavior patterns. But sometimes the converse is true. For reasons that are often difficult to explain, a child may react negatively to his parents' values and, with apparent purposefulness, do exactly the opposite. The child's behavior may be indicative of unhappiness in school or at home. The child may also be angry with his parents and express his anger by rejecting their values. When the teenager's behavior is self-defeating, it is essential that parents make every effort to identify what is causing the behavior. Professional assistance may be necessary.

The learning disabled student who has developed other interests and strengths is fortunate. These competencies can provide him with important ego support. A good athlete who doesn't do well in school will at least derive pride from — and acknowledgement for — his athletic achievements. This pride and sense of accomplishment can serve as an antidote to the negative experiences the student encounters in the academic arena.

Parents of learning disabled students who encourage their children to develop other areas of interest are helping to provide their children with alternative emotional support systems. A hobby or a skill can provide a comforting refuge from the academic "storm."

Another critical factor which affects how teenagers respond to their learning problems is the availability of quality remedial assistance in junior high school and high school. Students who receive academic and psychological support in school are less likely to develop counterproductive defense mechanisms. Unfortunately, many high school special education programs do not provide meaningful assistance. High school special education classes are often filled with badly scarred, turned-off, and highly resistant kids who are embarrassed by having been assigned to such classes. Many of the classes serve little more than a babysitting function, and the students know it.

---

6. Typically, students who are demoralized will claim school is "dumb" or irrelevant. This is a rather transparent defense mechanism.

The teenage years are difficult years. Even teenagers without learning or emotional problems will experience moments of insecurity and self-doubt as they make the first tentative steps toward establishing an adult identity for themselves. During this process, powerful social, physiological and emotional pressures will pull the teenager in many directions. A teenager whose self-concept is already tenuous because of a learning problem will find the pressure exerted by these forces all the more intense. This pressure may jeopardize the teenager's ability to cope successfully with the transition to adulthood and may undermine his resistance to negative influences such as alcohol and drugs.

Most learning disabled teenagers will learn to protect their "soft spots" in whatever way they can. The methods that they choose to protect their areas of vulnerability will vary and may include behaviors and attitudes which are self-defeating. Cutting classes, not completing assignments and resisting help are but a few of the typical defense and compensatory mechanisms that the learning disabled teenagers may use to insulate themselves from feeling inadequate. These methods provide only an illusion of security.

It is painful when parents recognize that their teenager is on a negative course, and even more painful when their child refuses to accept help. Young adults who engage in self-sabotage will probably require counseling or psychotherapy before they can reorient themselves. Parents are well advised to seek assistance for them before their self-destructive behavior becomes chronic. The sooner the emotional causes of the self-sabotaging behavior are resolved, the sooner the teenager can begin to permit himself to succeed. Conversely, the longer the self-sabotaging behavior continues, the more profound the emotional damage will be to both the teenager and to the entire family.

Parents who perceive that their child is making self-defeating choices will most likely find that their own emotional resources are being sorely tested. Watching a fifteen year-old sabotage himself can be an emotionally devastating experience for any parent. The natural instinct is to protect the child from making mistakes that could have serious consequences on his life. Resisting the temptation to offer protection to the child is one of parenting's greatest challenges. Sometimes direct and forceful intervention may be necessary, as in the case of a child stealing or taking drugs. But even in these situations, establishing effective communication is vital.

When parents respond to their teenager's self-defeating behavior by lecturing or admonishing him, they often elicit even greater resistance. Defensive teenagers tend to resist hearing "the truth." And the more parents attempt to push "the truth" as they perceive it, the more the child will resist.

The risk of an impasse is especially high when a teenager and his parents are primarily intent upon defending their respective positions. Communication breaks down when people become defensive. At best, parents can only listen and attempt to clarify. In the end, the teenager must decide what the "truth" is. Parents can, of course, forbid their teenager to do something, but if the teenager is determined to do what is forbidden, he will probably prevail. Parents cannot police an older child under all circumstances.

Suppose a learning disabled teenager has decided not to hand in his assignments. His parents have several options:

1. They can lecture their child.
2. They can threaten to take away privileges.
3. They can do nothing.
4. They can examine the issues objectively and empathetically.

Parents who elect to lecture their child about the need for being responsible will probably come to the realization that they have delivered this sermon in various forms on many different occasions. Rarely can a teenager be lectured into being responsible.

Threatening to take away privileges may serve as a deterrent, but deterrents are predicated on fear and are seldom successful in changing attitudes. A threat may work for a while, but unless there is a change in attitude, the undesirable behavior will re-emerge. The ultimate goal is for the teenager to develop a sense of responsibility, not because he's afraid he will lose access to the car, but because he sees the value of being responsible. Repeated threats become less and less effective as kids become accustomed to the consequences. Ultimately, the threats produce only bitterness and resentment.

An alternative is to do nothing about a teenager's misbehavior. Although doing nothing allows parents to avoid a showdown with their teenager, it also communicates to the child that his parents are either resigned to his self-defeating behavior or simply don't care. The message is clear: you do not have to answer to anyone for your behavior.

Examining the issues is by far the best strategy for dealing with a teenager's counterproductive behavior. This method provides you with an opportunity to hear and consider your child's perspective. At the very least your child's feelings and opinions deserve recognition and acknowledgement. For example:

Parent	I received a note from your counselor that you haven't been completing your assignments in English. What's up?
Teenager:	Why should I do them? I get bad grades on them anyway.
Parent:	The assignments are hard, I assume.
Teenager:	They're stupid. What does it matter if I know the parts of speech? I speak okay. Why do I have to know whether "going" is a participle or an infinitive or who knows what? How's that going to help me get a job?
Parent:	Knowing whether "going" is a participle or an infinitive probably won't help you get a job. What will help you get a job?
Teenager:	I don't know.
Parent:	What about your track record?
Teenager:	What do you mean?
Parent:	Your history of success and failure.
Teenager:	When I try to find a job after school I won't have much of a history. It'll be my first real job.
Parent:	I imagine there will be lots of kids competing for those jobs.
Teenager:	Yeah, I know.
Parent:	If you were the owner of an auto supply store, and you were going to hire an eighteen year-old high school graduate, how would you decide whom to hire?
Teenager:	I don't know. I guess I'd hire the kid I liked best.
Parent:	Me too. If you had to choose between one student who had good grades and who was in the school band and who had good recommendations from his teachers and from his previous bosses, and another who had gotten D's in school and who had never held a job before, whom would you hire?
Teenager:	The first guy, probably.
Parent:	Yeah, so would I. Think about that when you choose not to hand in your assignments. Your grade in that course and that teacher's recommendation might mean the difference between getting the job and not getting the job.

This hypothetical dialogue models a style of parent/teenager communication that will generally elicit less resistance than lectures, sermons or threats. The potential resistance is defused because the teenager does not perceive that he is being attacked or demeaned. The parent is simply presenting in a reasonable manner his or her perspective on an issue that affects the teenager and concerns the parent. Note that the parent resisted the temptation to lecture. Also note that the parent made his or her points succinctly and that the dialogue was kept intentionally short.

The resolution of the situation presented in this hypothetical dialogue is not certain. The teenager could still decide not to hand in his English assignments. Had the parent responded to the teenager's self-defeating behavior by threatening him with punishment, a "showdown" might have been created if the teenager were intent on contravening the parent's wishes. He could have chosen either to disobey the parent and suffer the consequences, or to hand in the assignments with the work incomplete or poorly done. Although the threat of punishment may deter a child from misbehaving, threats rarely effect meaningful changes in behavior or attitude. However, the repeated use of threats creates discord and resentment which often impede positive attitudinal and behavioral changes.

Parents who employ a communication strategy similar to the one shown in the dialogue are acknowledging a basic fact of life: their power to control the thoughts and actions of their teenage son or daughter will diminish as the teenager matures. Reality dictates that reason and cooperation must replace authority and prerogatives. The sooner this happens, the better.

Parents who help their teenagers achieve insight into their actions and appreciate the consequences of those actions are preparing their children to meet the challenges of adulthood. Teenagers who perceive the cause and effect relationship between their choices and the results of those choices will become more responsible than teenagers who do not perceive this relationship.

The preceding dialogue is, of course, contrived. It is intended only to model a communication system which can help parents and teenagers resolve contradictions, conflicts and disagreements. The communication strategy encourages the teenager to make choices and exert legitimate power over his life. By supporting the teenager's right to control his life, his parents are helping him make the transition from childhood to adulthood. Avoiding "war" is in the best interest of the parent and the teenager. By offering support rather than confrontation, parents sidestep battles which no one can win.

CHAPTER EIGHT _____

Building Self-esteem

JIMMY: DANCING ISN'T ALWAYS FUN

All the third graders from both classes filed into the gymnasium. The children were both excited and apprehensive. Today was the day they were going to learn how to square dance.

The teacher divided up the boys and girls into couples and then arranged the children in squares of four couples each. The teacher explained the steps, and the children practiced at first without the music. When the teacher turned on the music, most of the children responded to the commands of the caller as if they had been square dancing for years.

When the class was over, the teacher made an announcement: "Children, I just learned that Jimmy has been accepted at Brookview Academy." She paused and then added, "They must have lowered the standards in his case."

Jimmy's cheeks turned crimson with embarrassment. He couldn't believe what he had just heard. His partner, a little girl with black hair and freckles, stared at him as did the other third graders in the gymnasium. It had never before occurred to Jimmy that there was something wrong with him. Now for the first time he felt different from the other children. He must be dumb. The teacher couldn't be wrong!

Brookview Academy was a private college preparatory school with classes from kindergarten through twelfth grade. The students were all quite bright and in some cases brilliant. The entrance requirements were very high, and Jimmy's teacher was correct in her assumption that Jimmy had barely met them. Jimmy had not been an outstanding student in her class.

During the next seven years Jimmy struggled to keep his head above water at Brookview. The curriculum was highly accelerated, with emphasis on the traditional 3 R's and the memorization of information.

Jimmy was not very good at memorizing or retrieving data which was not particularly relevant to his life. Memorizing the phyla in biology or the dates of major battles in the Revolutionary War was difficult for him. His math and writing skills were only fair, as was his ability in Latin, French and Spanish. (At Brookview, students were required to take French in grades 3-6; Latin in grades 7-8; and Spanish, French or Latin in grades 8-12.)

Although Jimmy worked hard, he was consistently in the bottom quarter of the class. On those occasions when he did receive a *B*, the grade was the end product of 100% effort. But Jimmy knew that even the most brilliant of his classmates had to work very hard, so he didn't feel sorry for himself.

During Jimmy's senior year, Brookview hired a new headmaster who instituted major changes in the highly traditional curriculum. For the first time Brookview offered courses in psychology and philosophy. Jimmy was drawn to these subjects and found them highly stimulating. He also found that he was the best student in the class in these courses. For the first time in his school experience, he was getting *A*'s on his report card.

Jimmy did quite well on the college board exams, and on the National Merit Scholarship Exam he scored in the 99th percentile. When his teachers saw the results of the exams, they began to perceive him differently. Was it possible that Jimmy was simply a late starter?

Jimmy also began to perceive himself differently. He ultimately graduated from Stanford with a 3.6 grade point average.

Jimmy's experience in the gymnasium could have had a profoundly damaging effect on his perception of himself. And his subsequent experiences at Brookview might well have confirmed the perception that he was in some way defective or intellectually inferior. Despite this negative acknowledgment, however, Jimmy persevered. Perhaps he did so out of stubbornness. Perhaps he persevered because his parents communicated to him that they expected him to. Unquestionably, both Jimmy's temperament and his environment affected his reactions.

Jimmy was fortunate. Throughout his entire education at Brookview, his parents never once expressed disappointment with his grades. They continually supported and encouraged his efforts and repeatedly assured him that all they expected from him was that he do his best. Jimmy's parents recognized that school was providing him with little positive reinforcement, and they responded by clearly communicating to him their support for his efforts and their faith in his abilities. Jimmy's parents were also very clear about their value system and their priorities. They wanted their son to become the best person he was capable of becoming. They expected him to work hard and to give 100%. Whether he was an *A* student or a *C* student was not the critical issue for them. What mattered to them was that Jimmy learn to appreciate the value of effort. They were confident that accomplishment and success would inevitably follow, and they conveyed this confidence to Jimmy.

SUPPORT SYSTEMS

A child's self-concept will reflect his experiences in life. If he feels loved and accepted by those who are important to him and if his social and educational experiences are positive, he will probably feel good about himself. Conversely, if he feels unloved and rejected by the important adults in his life and if his social and educational experiences are negative, the youngster will probably feel negative about himself.

A child is extremely vulnerable and susceptible to the feedback he receives from the adults in his world. Although he may not appear to react to a negative or derogatory statement, such a statement may have a profoundly destructive impact on the child's perceptions of himself.

Derogatory statements from parents or teachers are like germs which invade the child's body. These statements may trigger an immediate reaction or a deferred reaction. If the emotional response to the derogatory statement is experienced immediately, the reaction may appear as pain, anger or shame. When the reaction is deferred, the child may seem to be unaffected. This lack of emotional response is deceptive. In most instances, "put-downs" cause an "infection" which may not be apparent until later. The infection in turn produces "antibodies" which take the form of misbehavior, manipulation, irresponsibility and generalized disharmony.

Jimmy's reaction to the devastating insensitivity of his third grade teacher and to the absence of positive reinforcement later in school was quite atypical. Many children in Jimmy's circumstances would have simply given up.

The reasons why some children "fight" and others give up is difficult to explain. Personality factors, environmental factors and, perhaps, genetic factors can all affect a child's reaction to derogatory statements. Although children will frequently react with a high degree of predictability to certain environmental conditions, their responses may also defy prediction. For instance, one child who is short may respond by becoming a bully and a tyrant. A second child may respond to his shortness by becoming shy and withdrawn. A third child may simply accept his shortness as a fact of life and show no apparent psychological ill effects. A child who is physically abused by his parents has a higher statistical chance of abusing his own children, but some abused children become very gentle and sensitive parents. Environment does affect and influence a child, but human beings do not necessarily respond like chemicals in a laboratory experiment. Human behavior often refutes statistical predictions and sociological tenets.

Although there is no guarantee that a positive, loving relationship between parents and their child during the formative years of his life will assure the child's emotional adjustment, such a relationship significantly

197

increases the probability of a child's being emotionally healthy. The bonding between parent and child is one of the most important factors that influences a child's personality and his emerging sense of himself and his abilities.

The cornerstone of self-esteem is self-acceptance. Children who possess a healthy self-esteem and a high level of self-acceptance are instantaneously recognizable. They radiate confidence and usually achieve their objectives. Rarely do children with a learning disability have an abundance of self-esteem. Such children have usually experienced too many defeats to have developed a sense of their own power and efficacy.

The role that both parents and teachers play in the development of a learning disabled child's self-esteem cannot be under-estimated. Parents who create an environment at home which supports the child emotionally while he is struggling to resolve his learning problems dramatically decrease the risk of damage to the child's self-concept. By creating an environment in the classroom which provides the learning disabled student with an opportunity to have successful experiences and by acknowledging the child for his accomplishments, teachers can significantly decrease the risk of self-concept damage.

The respective roles of parents and teachers in providing emotional support are extremely important. This is especially true when one or the other of the two critical support systems is not functioning adequately. Teachers who perceive that the learning disabled child's parents are not emotionally supporting the child have the added responsibility of attempting to compensate as best they can for this deficiency. Parents who perceive that the teacher is not making an effort to bolster the child's self-esteem will also have to try to compensate for this missing support.

IDENTIFYING SELF-ESTEEM DEFICITS

Parents of a child with low self-esteem will often recognize that their child is not happy with himself. They will see the child's unhappiness mirrored in his behaviors, attitudes and actions. Sometimes, however, children do such a good job of compensating for their deficiencies and camouflaging their vulnerabilities that their parents do not identify the behaviors and emotions which signal a self-concept problem. Some parents simply dismiss their child's nonadaptive behaviors as being "part of his personality" without realizing that the child's personality characteristics are a reflection of his feelings of inadequacy.

The following checklist will help you identify some of the specific behaviors that may indicate the presence of a self-esteem problem in your child.

SELF-ESTEEM INVENTORY

Code: 0 = Never 1 = Rarely 2 = Sometimes 3 = Often 4 = Always

Does your child have difficulty establishing eye contact?	_____
Does your child have poor posture?	_____
Is your child reluctant to experience anything new or different?	_____
Is your child shy around people he knows?	_____
Is your child shy around strangers?	_____
Does your child have difficulty making friends?	_____
Does your child have difficulty relating or playing with other children?	_____
Does your child feel he is "dumb"?	_____
Is your child convinced in advance that he will fail or have difficulty with new challenges?	_____
When you ask your child to draw a picture of a person, is the picture very small?	_____
Is your child generally fearful?	_____
Is your child unable to express his emotions openly?	_____
Is your child excessively resentful or jealous of his brothers or sisters?	_____
Does your child feel that other children do not like him?	_____
Does your child have difficulty accepting compliments or praise?	_____
Is your child derogatory about other people?	_____
Is your child derogatory about himself?	_____
Is your child frequently hostile or angry?	_____
Is your child frequently depressed?	_____
Is your child withdrawn or detached?	_____
Is your child a "loner?"	_____
Is your child defensive about his deficits?	_____
Does your child blame others for his problems?	_____

A pattern of 3's and 4's in your responses to these questions, may indicate that your child is manifesting symptoms of low self-esteem. A learning disability may account for many behaviors that are associated with low self-esteem, but the source of a child's poor self-concept may also involve other factors. These factors might include: family problems, emotional problems, and problems related to the transition from childhood to adolescence.

When your child's low self-esteem is the result of a learning disability, his self-concept should improve as the learning problem is remediated. If the behavior patterns persist, it is advisable to have your child evaluated by a competent mental health professional. Chronic anger, jealousy or resentment are signals that a youngster may need professional counseling.[1] If such intervention is necessary, the child should receive this help before his negative attitudes, behaviors and feelings become too entrenched.

SELF-ASSESSMENT SCALES

Learning disabled children frequently have a difficult time expressing how they are feeling about school and about themselves. Many children who struggle with learning problems are not consciously aware of their feelings. Other children may have trouble admitting to themselves or to their parents that they are hurting and unhappy.

Knowing how to help a child discover his feelings and share those feelings is a vital parenting skill. The parents of learning disabled children in particular need to acquire this skill because the repeatedly frustrated and demoralized child will often attempt to deny or repress his negative emotions. These emotions do not go away when they are repressed or denied; they simply become internalized and begin to contaminate the child's life.

The following self-assessment "scales" may help you communicate more openly with your child about his feelings and perceptions. A strategy for presenting the self-assessment scales is modeled below.

Parent:

I'm curious about how things are going in school. Let's try something. What's your best subject in school?

_____

Okay. What's your worst subject in school?

_____

1. See Chapter 4: "Common Symptoms of an Emotional Problem" and "Selecting a Therapist."

Now, take a look at this. At one end of the line is a sad face and at the other end is a happy face. [2] Do you see how the numbers run from 1 at the "sad" end to 10 at the "happy" end? The title at the top says "Quality of Work in the Best Subject." Now, what number do you think best describes how good a job you do in your best subject?

QUALITY OF WORK IN BEST SUBJECT

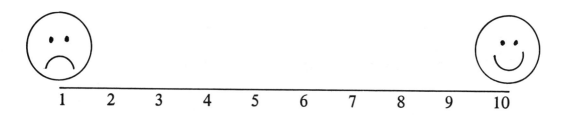

Parent: Fine. Now, let's try this one.

QUALITY OF WORK IN WORST SUBJECT

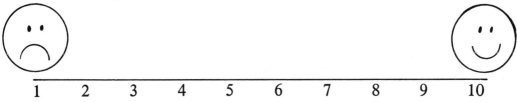

Parent: Okay. Now, this one is different. It says: "Smartness Scale." Let's say at the "happy face" end is the smartest kid in your class. Who do you think that is? Okay. Let's write Blair here. At the other end let's write the name of the "dumbest" kid in your class. Who do you think that is? Okay. Now if Blair is the "smartest" and Billy is the "dumbest," where would you write your name on the scale?

2. I don't recommend that you use "happy" and "sad" faces with children above 6th grade, who might find them demeaning. The numbers on the scale should suffice.

SMARTNESS SCALE

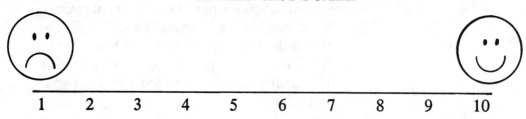

Parent: Good. Now let's look at the next scale.

AMOUNT OF EFFORT IN SCHOOL

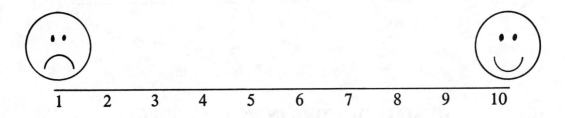

Parent: Now let's do this one.

HAPPINESS IN SCHOOL

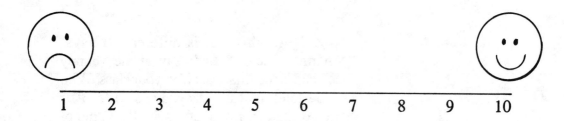

Parent:	And now let's do the last one.

HAPPINESS AT HOME

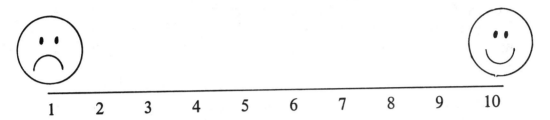

| 1 | 2 | 3 | 4 | 5 | 6 | 7 | 8 | 9 | 10 |

Some parents may choose to discuss each scale before proceeding to the next one. My experience has been that such a strategy can inhibit the child from responding to the subsequent scales. When parents simply acknowledge the child's response and proceed to the next scale, they can gather important information to use in subsequent discussion once the child has completed all the scales.

When discussing with your child his or her responses, resist the temptation to take ownership of the child's problems. For instance, your child may give himself a 2 on the smartness scale, and you may react by saying, "Oh, come on, Johnny. You're much smarter than that!" You may have the best of intentions, but you will probably not convince your child that he is intelligent.

An alternative strategy might be:

Parent:	It sure looks to me that you don't feel that you are very smart.
Child:	I'm not.
Parent:	You really are convinced, aren't you?
Child:	Yeah.
Parent:	What might help you to change your mind?
Child:	I don't know.
Parent:	Would doing well in school convince you that you are smart?
Child:	Yeah.
Parent:	Well, what do you think you have to succeed in school? Do you think tutoring might help?

Ideally, the conversation will evolve from this point into a discussion of possible ways for the child to improve his performance in school. Don't expect your initial discussion to convince your child instantaneously that he is intelligent. Changing a child's perceptions of himself takes time and patience. The child will need to become convinced of his own abilities. Helping a child experience success in school will provide the child with far more persuasive evidence of his own abilities than simply telling him he is smart.

The self-assessment scales are simply tools and are intended to serve as catalysts for communication. They are designed to help you and your child achieve greater insight into your child's feelings. They certainly aren't sacred, and I encourage you to change them or add to them as you see fit. [3]

If a child expresses doubts about himself or about his abilities, resist the natural inclination to give a "pep talk." Self-confidence is a function of achieving success. You can best serve your child by structuring opportunities for him to succeed. You may offer your help, but remember that your child's problems belong to him.

Ideally, the self-assessment scales will let children and parents identify and ventilate their feelings and perceptions. If the feelings which your child reveals appear to be highly distorted or if you feel incapable of dealing with the emotions that either you or your child are experiencing, don't hesitate to seek the assistance of a qualified mental health professional.

You may also want to use the scales to evaluate improvement in the child's self-concept. Compare how he feels about himself before and after receiving learning assistance. Ideally, your child will feel much better about his abilities and about school after making inroads into his learning deficits. If your child doesn't feel better about himself, he may need some form of counseling.

BREAKING THE FAILURE CYCLE

The origins of self-esteem and self-confidence are not very mysterious. The components in the equation that yields a happy, confident, harmonious child consist primarily of 1) love; 2) acceptance by others; 3) self-acceptance; and 4) success.

3. Be cautious about overusing the scales. If you do overuse them, your child may perceive them as being gimmicky.

Genetic factors may also play a role in a child's ability to handle life's challenges. The retarded child or the physically handicapped child will have to learn how to overcome or accommodate himself to his disabilities. Although children who have genetically-based disabilities may have a difficult time in certain areas of their lives, many disabled children not only cope with their deficits competently but actually prevail over them magnificently. In most instances, the key to this ability to prevail can be traced to an abundance of parental and professional support and love.

Parenting is not an easy job, and parents seldom receive any formal training to prepare them for the many challenges that they will face. It is simply assumed that somehow parents will rise to the occasion and know what needs to be done. No parent is perfect, and occasional errors in judgment are inevitable.

Parenting skills can be improved. To do so requires a willingness to take an honest look at the dynamics of your relationship with your child. Insight will permit you to defuse anger. Insight *and* effort will permit you to transform inconsistent child-rearing practices into more consistent child-rearing practices. Insight, effort *and* practice will permit you to resist manipulation and encourage authenticity.

The learning disabled child has the same emotional needs as any other child. The needs are universal: love, appreciation, acknowledgment and support. The learning disabled child, however, will probably require a bit more of these ingredients than the typical child.

Parents who are concerned about their child's self-esteem can intervene most effectively when they understand the dynamics of how self-esteem evolves. The components of self-esteem are interrelated and overlapping. The cycles represented on the following pages illustrate the reciprocal effects of the many factors which influence the child's sense of himself.

POSITIVE SELF-ESTEEM CYCLE

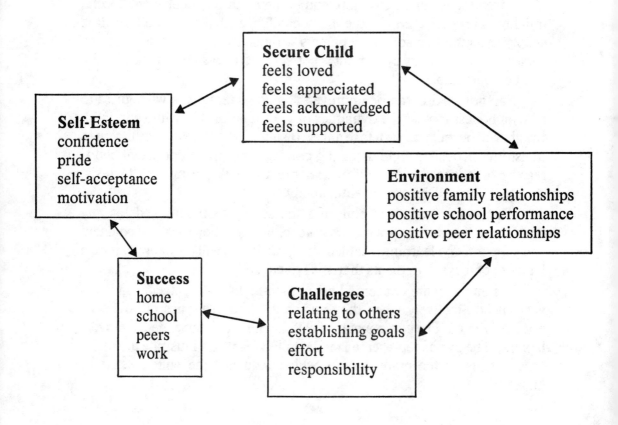

NEGATIVE SELF-ESTEEM CYCLE

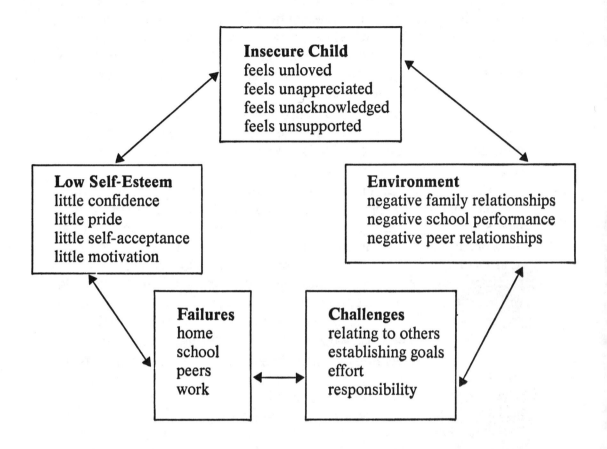

This somewhat simplistic representation of the self-esteem cycles illustrates the effect that any component in the equation can have on other components in the equation. Any negative factor can transform a positive self-esteem cycle into a negative self-esteem cycle. If a child should begin to have social problems, these social problems can affect his school performance and his family relationships. Problems with his school performance and family relationships can, in turn, affect his confidence and self-esteem. If the social problems persist and the child's peer relationships deteriorate further, increasing insecurity may result. The child may feel unloved, unappreciated, unacknowledged and unsupported. The emotional consequences can be disastrous. A child who could have previously been described by the first cycle is now more appropriately described by the second cycle.

In another hypothetical situation, a secure and capable student enrolls in a highly demanding private school with an accelerated curriculum. Although the child had previously been a good student in his public school class, he now finds that he is barely able to keep up. Despite continual effort, school becomes a monumental struggle. Because the child experiences little success, his confidence and self-acceptance begin to suffer. He becomes less and less motivated. He perceives for the first time that his parents are dissatisfied with his performance. The previously secure child has now become an insecure child.

A careful look at the self-esteem cycles reveals that there are two critical points in the cycle where parents and teachers can intervene and influence the evolution of a child's self-esteem: *Environment* and *Challenges*.

Effective intervention by parents requires effective communication, on-going emotional support, and firm, loving and sensitive parenting. As I have stressed repeatedly, the learning disabled child must understand what his problems are and what must be done to correct them. He will need to be assured that, despite his learning problems, he is loved, accepted and appreciated as an important and cherished member of the family. The child will also need to know that his parents have full confidence in his ability to prevail over his learning problems. Finally, the child must be helped to realize that he will be expected to work hard at solving his problems.

Effective intervention by teachers requires competent learning assistance, effective communication, encouragement, and firm, loving and sensitive teaching. The learning disabled child will need support not only from his special education teacher, but also from his regular classroom teacher. The child must be apprised of how he is doing and what he still needs to achieve. He will need to understand that his teacher fully expects him to attain his objectives and truly believes that he can do so. Finally, the learning disabled student must recognize that his teachers will not accept work that is inferior to what he is capable of doing and will not accept irresponsible, manipulative behavior.

Parents who attempt to influence the type of challenges a child experiences must determine their child's current level of achievement, and they must strive to understand the nature and implications of their child's particular learning problems. Positive expectations for a child can be an inspiration. Unrealistic expectations can be a nightmare. Parents who expect a learning disabled child two years below grade level to catch up in six months are probably setting up their child and themselves for a major disappointment. The result can be another significant defeat for the child, one that can have serious emotional consequences for a child whose self-esteem is already tenuous.

Parents can most effectively improve their child's self-esteem by reducing the child's chances of failure. By carefully directing realistic challenges and by attempting to insure their child's success at these challenges, parents can have a profound influence on the formation of a positive self-concept. Each new success, however modest, will reinforce and support the child's self-esteem.

Engineering opportunities for your learning disabled child to experience success and acknowledging that success builds self-esteem. Teaching or encouraging your child to do something that other children might not normally do helps your child to develop pride. For example, you might encourage your child to collect something or to use a lathe or to do needlepoint. By helping your child become competent and letting him know how proud you are of his accomplishments, you create a context for the development of self-confidence. The child who can actually see his achievements will be much more convinced of his ability than the child who is simply told that he is smart and capable. Nothing builds self-esteem more effectively than tangible success.

Teachers play a vital role in determining what constitutes realistic and unrealistic challenges for each student. Like parents, teachers walk a fine line between expecting too much from a child and expecting too little. The level of their expectations will affect the level of a child's achievement and his self-esteem.

An often-cited experiment that is purported to have occurred at a well-respected university offers an excellent illustration of the influence that expectations can exert on academic achievement. A professor in the school of education informed some selected graduate students that they were being assigned to teach several severely learning disabled students who had enigmatic learning problems which had not responded to traditional learning assistance. Although the children were very bright, no one had been successful in developing an effective teaching strategy for them. The professor expressed complete confidence that *his* graduate students would be able to find the key that would help the children learn at a level commensurate with their intelligence.

During the next several months the graduate students tried every conceivable teaching method. Although progress was slow, the children began to respond positively to their teachers' efforts and achieved relatively significant academic gains. Only after the graduate students had documented these results did the professor inform them that the children were retarded. The test results confirmed that the children had progressed at a far faster rate than is customarily expected from students of their tested intelligence level.

209

Because the graduate students believed that the children they were teaching were bright, they approached the challenge of teaching them with positive expectations. The students were undeterred by the "fact" that other teachers had been unsuccessful. Knowing that others had tried and failed only inspired them to push themselves to the limit and somehow make a breakthrough. Their efforts were prodigious, and the results they achieved directly reflected their positive expectations and extra effort.

Miraculous things can happen when human beings choose to test themselves and their capabilities. Man's history is one of breaking records and overcoming limitations. To do so, a person needs only inspiration and the conviction that he *can* succeed.

In order to overcome the effects of a learning disability, children must be inspired to learn and convinced that they can learn. Initially, adults who are charged with the responsibility of parenting and teaching will have to provide this inspiration and conviction. They will know that they have been successful in their efforts when the child begins to develop his own faith in himself and his abilities.

JODY: LEARNING TO BELIEVE IN HIMSELF

The third grader had made up his mind. He didn't want to be promoted to the fourth grade. He was convinced that he wouldn't be able to handle the work.

Neither my staff nor the principal of his school were as convinced as Jody appeared to be. Jody had made remarkable progress during the five months that he had been attending our center, and there was every reason to expect that he would continue to improve during the remaining three months of the school term. We were all certain that by the end of the summer he would be reading at least a year above grade level. Given Jody's remarkable improvement, his retention could not possibly be justified.

As I chatted with Jody, I sensed that he was very apprehensive about being assigned to either of the fourth grade teachers at his school. He had heard that they were both very demanding. Jody told me that he was afraid of being embarrassed in front of the other children if he made a mistake while reading aloud or if he asked a question about something he didn't understand.

Jody's relationship with his third grade teacher was excellent. The teacher liked Jody and was very supportive. Jody felt very secure with her and desperately wanted to stay in her class for another year.

Although I could understand Jody's anxiety about fourth grade and his trepidations about having a demanding teacher, I knew that retention would be a mistake. I felt certain that not only would Jody be able to handle fourth grade, but that he would have a very successful year.

A child's fears and anxieties may appear irrational or unwarranted to an adult. But to the child, these emotions are very real and can have a paralyzing effect. We could not dismiss Jody's concerns about fourth grade as "silly." Making the transition from the security of a class where he felt appreciated and successful to the potential insecurity of a class where he might not feel as successful was a frightening prospect for Jody. He needed more than just simple assurances to feel confident about making the transition. He needed proof that he could make it in fourth grade.

To allay his anxiety, I told Jody that no decision would be made until August. In the meanwhile we would continue to work with him. Jody seemed greatly relieved to put off the decision.

During the next five months, my staff developed a series of challenging tasks that tested Jody's academic and reasoning skills. The tasks were sequential and were designed to become increasingly more difficult. Each task or test had been carefully selected so that Jody would be able to succeed. Jody was very aware that the work was getting more and more difficult, but because he was succeeding, he became very involved in the process and eagerly looked forward to the next "test" of his ability.

In August we informed Jody that the "tests" he was taking were at the seventh grade level. Jody was stunned. He believed us only after we showed him the manual and the textbooks from which we had taken the material.

I called Jody into my office and told him that I had decided to skip him up to sixth grade the following year since he was clearly able to do sixth grade work. Jody's mouth dropped open. I then smiled and told him that I would agree to placing him in fourth grade if he preferred. A big grin spread across Jody's face. I asked him if we had a deal, and he nodded his head in agreement.

Jody made the honor role in fourth grade. When he was tested with the other fourth graders in his class on the national achievement tests, he scored at the ninth grade level in both reading and math.

CHANGING PERCEPTIONS

Most children who are not successful in school expend a great deal of emotional energy protecting themselves from feeling inadequate. Their protective walls can be very thick and hard to penetrate. Guiding a child from behind the walls that protect his fragile ego demands careful planning and execution on the part of both parents and teachers.

The unknown "dangers" on the other side of the wall were very frightening to Jody. In third grade he was assured of success and nurturing. Beyond the wall, in the fourth grade, Jody saw himself exposed to potential failure and shame. Although his learning problems were never severe, they seemed monumental to him. Jody convinced himself that he would not be able to succeed in the fourth grade. Because of his low self-esteem, he clung desperately to the security that the third grade represented.

Jody's self-esteem and self-confidence would improve only if Jody were able to deduce that he was capable of success. To arrive at this deduction, he would have to experience repeated success at tasks and projects which he himself recognized as difficult.

The dynamics of Jody's "transformation" had to be carefully orchestrated. The tasks with which he was challenged had to be difficult, but not too difficult. The reinforcement he received in the form of acknowledgment and encouragement had to be honest and appropriate, but not so effusive that he would begin to discount it. The help we provided in the form of learning assistance had to be sufficient, but not so supportive that it would encourage emotional dependency.

The strategy proved successful. Jody realized that he could succeed at virtually anything we asked him to do. Jody began to derive more satisfaction from testing himself and "winning" than he did from protecting himself and being nurtured by his well-intentioned third grade teacher.

Jody had been "set up" to succeed. We had cultivated his self-esteem like a carefully planned garden. As Jody experienced more and more success, he began to accept himself and to appreciate his many talents. He also began to expect further success and to believe that he not only could achieve such success but that he deserved to. This attitude is the very essence of self-esteem and self-acceptance.

STRUCTURING SUCCESS

For most couples, producing a child is relatively easy. Helping that child to become happy, self-accepting and self-confident can be far more difficult. The process demands love, dedication and a lot of skillful parenting.

Structuring success for a child with a learning problem requires three prerequisites: concern, insight, and information. Helping a learning disabled child who has a poor self-concept can be one of the most difficult and emotionally demanding challenges a parent can face. But it can also be one of life's most rewarding experiences. What could possibly be more exciting and meaningful for a parent or a teacher than to witness and participate in the transformation of a despairing and defeated child into a confident and achieving child!

No wonder children who fail in school become kids who hate school! Failure is the key to this tragic waste of human potential. It is the key which locks doors to careers, self-fulfillment, financial rewards and self-esteem.

Once you acquire sufficient information and insight, you can play a significant and vital role in the process of assuring that your child experiences success rather than failure in school. To do so, you must be willing to participate actively in your child's education, especially if your child has a learning disability. The quality of your participation and the quality of the education provided by your child's teachers will be the two primary factors which will ensure that your child becomes one of the kids who love school, and not one of the kids who hate school.

GLOSSARY OF EDUCATIONAL TERMS

Aphasia	A complete inability to use language to communicate effectively. (This communication disorder is not the result of a physical impairment such as damage to the vocal cords or larynx.) (See Dysphasia).
Apraxia	Complete inability to make purposeful motor movements when there is no paralysis. (See Dyspraxia).
Associative Skills	The ability to relate a new concept or new material to previously mastered material. *For example:* A child seeing the word "cat" must associate the letters that make up this word with the furry animal that purrs.
Ataxia	An inability to coordinate muscles. (See Dystaxia).
Auditory Discrimination	The ability to hear the difference between sounds. *For example:* "pig" and "peg".
Auditory Memory	Remembering what is heard. *For example:* A teacher tells the class to get out their science books, turn to page 145 and do problems 1-6. The student is expected to remember all three directions. If a child is unable to remember this information, he may have auditory memory deficits.
Auditory Perception and Processing Skills	The ability to recognize and interpret things that are heard. This term includes auditory discrimination, auditory memory, auditory sequencing and figure-ground discrimination.
Auditory Sequencing	Remembering the proper sequence in which things are heard. *For example:* 12345 and not 12435.
Behavior Modification	A technique used to change a child's behavior by setting up a system of positive rewards and/or negative consequences. The positive rewards might consist of food, money or tokens, while the negative consequences might consist of punishment or denial of privileges.
Blending	The ability to "sound out" and put together the separate sounds that make up a word. *For example:* A child would blend the "c" sound, the "a" sound and the "t" sound to form the word "cat".
Closure	The act of bringing an experience or a concept to a conclusion. When everything is stated and the child understands and has integrated the information into his store of knowledge, then closure has been achieved. Some material (such as grammar or syntax) may require months or even years before a child fully understands the concepts involved and is able to achieve closure.
Convergence	The ability of both eyes to coordinate their movement and focus on an object or a written word.
Decoding	The basic process of responding to auditory or visual symbols. An example of decoding is reading words aloud; that is, using the knowledge of the sound that each letter makes to figure out how to pronounce a word.

Differential Diagnosis	A relatively comprehensive testing procedure designed to pinpoint areas of strength and weakness and, where possible, to locate the exact cause of the child's learning difficulties.
Directionality	Being aware that there is a right and left side to the body and being able to relate this internal awareness to external objects. Children with directionality problems will frequently reverse letters and/or numbers ("b" for "d") because they cannot perceive that the letters are pointed to the right or to the left.
Discrimination Skills	Skills that help a person tell the difference between two or more things. (See Auditory and Visual Discrimination.)
Dyslexia	Generally, a visual perception problem commonly characterized by letter and word reversals ("p"/"q" or "saw"/ "was"). Dyslexic children frequently have directionality problems (right/left confusion) and visual tracking problems (difficulty seeing letters and words accurately when reading). Sometimes the word "dyslexia" is used simply to describe a reading problem.
Dysphasia	Difficulty in using language to communicate which is not the result of a physical impairment such as damaged vocal cords or larynx. *For example:* a child may have difficulty finding the appropriate word to complete a sentence or a thought even though the word is part of his/her everyday vocabulary. (Aphasia is more severe).
Dyspraxia	Great difficulty in making purposeful motor movements when there is no paralysis. *For example:* a child playing hopscotch may remain poised on one square trying to make his/her muscles work correctly in order to hop to the next square. Less severe than apraxia.
Dystaxia	Difficulty in coordinating muscles. The condition is less severe than ataxia.
Encoding	The process of writing or speaking by retrieving the written and spoken symbols (or words) from memory and using those symbols to express oneself.
Far Point Deficits	Difficulty copying or reading something in the distance. *For example:* difficulty copying from the blackboard.
Figure-Ground Deficits	Difficulty in distinguishing a specific shape or sound from the background. *For example:* a child may be unable to screen out distractions and background noises when trying to listen to the teacher talking.
Fine-Motor	Referring to the specialized muscles in the hands. These muscles develop more slowly than the large skeletal muscles and are needed specifically for good handwriting.
Gross-Motor	Referring to the large skeletal muscles used for crawling, walking, lifting, balancing, etc.
Hard Neurological Signs	Specific measurable deviations in brain functioning that usually indicate organic brain damage. Hard signs are usually revealed by an E.E.G. exam that is performed by a neurologist.

Kinesthetic Techniques Methods of teaching reading that involve movement of the fingers, arms or whole body. Children who are taught by this method receive input from the muscles which is intended to reinforce the association of the visual symbol with its sound. *For example:* a child learning the letter "b" might trace over a "b" with his fingers on sandpaper, trace a giant "b" in the air or form a "b" with his whole body.

Language Disabilities Difficulty expressing oneself in either written or spoken form. *For example*: a child who knows the answer to a question but has trouble finding the words to express it may have a language disability. (See Encoding).

Laterality Being aware of and being able to use both sides of the body.

Linguistic Approach A teaching method that emphasizes learning to read whole words and word families. *For example:* if the child can read "dog", then he should be able to read "log".

Math Skills The ability to use numbers effectively to solve problems. Math skills involve 1) the ability to do basic computations (adding, subtracting, multiplying, dividing); 2) the ability to apply those skills to everyday situations (word problems); 3) the ability to understand the mathematical concepts involved in the computations (adding mixed fractions).

Mental Retardation A condition in which a child's I. Q. is determined to be below 70 and where the child has deficits in adaptive behavior, motor coordination, communication, self-help, and/or socialization skills.

Mid-Line An imaginary vertical line which divides the right and left sides of the body. The left half of the brain controls the right side of the body, and the right half of the brain controls the left half. Skipping, or drawing a line from the left side of a paper to the right side involves crossing the mid-line. Difficulty crossing the mid-line (*for example:* difficulty coordinating both sides of the body) can be a symptom of a perceptual or neurological problem.

Minimal Brain Dysfunction (M. B. D.) A medical term applied to children who show "soft" neurological symptoms of perceptual deficiency but who show no organic evidence of brain damage as measured by an E.E.G. (see Perceptual Dysfunction).

Motor-Coordination The ability to perform with dexterity tasks involving movement of the body, such as walking or swimming. Specific components of coordination include: balance, synchronized upper-lower body movement, fine-motor skills, eye-hand coordination, and depth perception.

Motor Planning	Thinking through the movements that the body must make to perform a task before attempting the action. An example of basic motor planning is a child thinking of how to move his muscles in order to jump over a rope. More complex motor planning might involve looking at a set of instructions for building something and then purposefully planning how to move one's hands to follow the directions.
Motor Skills	Skills which involve the coordinated movement of the body, such as jumping, balancing, or drawing. (see Gross-Motor and Fine-Motor).
Near Point Deficits	Difficulty copying or reading something that is close at hand (*for example:* copying from a book on the desk.)
Neurological Disorders	A condition resulting from damage to the brain or central nervous system. The damage may be so slight that there are no observable symptoms or there may be more serious damage that can be measured by neurological tests (see Soft Neurological Signs and Hard Neurological Signs).
Neurological Impress Method	A reading method in which the teacher and student read out loud simultaneously at a fairly rapid pace while the student follows the printed word with his/her finger. The child has input from the printed page, and the movement of his/her finger and the sound of the two voices reading help him master the words.
Perceptual Decoding	See Decoding.
Perceptual Learning Disabilities	An inability to process sensory data efficiently resulting in specific learning problems such as letter reversals, spelling problems, and reading comprehension problems.
Perceptual-Motor Activities/Perceptual-Motor Training	Activities designed to train the child to process information coming from the senses efficiently and to make appropriate responses to that sensory information. *For example:* a physical activity which requires children to follow a series of command strains them to listen carefully to the directions and remember what was said.
Perceptual Processing	The instantaneous sorting and analysis by the brain of sensory data from the five senses and the association of this data with past sensory experiences. *For example:* a child sees a "b", recognizes it, associates it with the letter "b" and says, "This is a 'b'."
Phonics Approach	A method of teaching reading which emphasizes learning the sound of each letter and then blending the sounds together to say words. To read "hen", the child would first say the sounds "h", "e", and "n", then put them together to say "hen".
Reading Comprehension	The ability to understand and remember what one has read.
Self-Concept	A person's view of him/herself. Children who have good self-concepts see themselves as generally able to succeed in many areas. Children who have a poor self-concept often perceive themselves as unpopular or inadequate.

218

Sensory Impairment	Physical damage to one of the sensory receptors (*for example:* the eyes) resulting in partial or complete loss of the use of that sensory receptor. Blindness and hearing loss are two examples of sensory impairments.
Sensory-Motor Integration/Sensory Integration Therapy	A procedure designed for children with relatively severe perceptual problems in which perceptual processing skills are enhanced by means of activities and exercise which stress central nervous system development. This procedure is usally implemented by trained occupational therapists.
Sight-Word Approach/ Sight-Word Recognition	In reading, learning to recognize words by memorization. There are many words, such as "thought", which do not follow phonic rules and which must be learned "by sight".
Soft Neurological Signs	Deficits in gross-motor and fine-motor coordination, balance, and concentration which are associated with minimal brain dysfunction and perceptual learning disabilities. "Soft signs" involve less severe neurological symptoms and can be distinguished from "hard signs" which generally indicate a neurological disorder involving organic brain damage.
Sound/Letter/Word Retrieval	In reading, the ability to remember a previously learned sound, letter, or word.
Spatial Judgment/ Spatial Concepts/ Spatial Skills/ Spatial Relationships	The awareness of one's body in space and its relationship to other things around it. Judging distance, size and location all involve spatial skills. A child may have difficulty with prepositions (such as "above", "next to", and "behind") because he/she has difficulty understanding spatial concepts.
Tracking	See Visual Tracking.
Visual Decoding Skills	See Decoding.
Visual Discrimination	The ability to tell the difference between things one sees, *for example:* differentiating "b" and "d". Poor visual discrimination is frequently responsible for poor reading skills.
Visual Memory	Remembering what one has seen. *For example:* a child with poor visual memory who is shown a series of numbers will have difficulty repeating the numbers from memory.
Visual-Motor Skills/ Visual-Motor Integration	Skills that involve making a motor response (speaking, writing, or moving) to a visual stimulus. A child copying or reading from the blackboard or following written directions is using visual-motor skills.
Visual Perception/ Visual Processing Skills	The ability to recognize and interpret the things one sees. This includes figure-ground discrimination, visual discrimination, visual memory, and visual sequencing. *For example:* finding matching pictures or letters.

Visual Sequencing	Process of remembering and then placing what one has seen in the correct order. *For example:* when copying the word "milk" from the board, a child with poor visual sequencing skills might remember all the letters but put them in the wrong order and write "mlik".
Visual Tracking Problem	Difficulty reading with precision the letters and words which make up printed text. Typically, children with visual tracking problems will confuse "b" and "d" (a static tracking problem) and/or will omit syllables, mispronounce words and drop word endings (a kinetic tracking problem). Children with visual tracking problems often lose their place when reading and may skip words, phrases or entire lines.
Word Attack Skills	Skills that help a child to pronounce and understand words that are read. These skills primarily involve phonics, but also include recognizing context clues (how was the word used in the sentence) and structural clues (prefixes, suffixes, syllables).

GLOSSARY OF TESTING TERMS

Ability Test A test designed to measure what a person can do.

Achievement Test A test designed to measure how much a person has learned after instruction in a specific content area. Generally, these tests are standardized and normed.

Aptitude An ability, capacity or talent in a particular area such as music or mathematics. Aptitude is a specialized facility to learn or understand a particular skill.

Criterion-Referenced Test A test, usually designed by a teacher or publisher, which measures the student's mastery of a specific subject he/she has studied. The scores are not standardized but can provide the teacher with useful information about what the child has and has not learned.

Diagnostic Test A test which pinpoints a student's strengths and weaknesses. The results are generally used in planning specific strategies designed to correct the weaknesses.

Grade Equivalent A statistical ranking of a child's performance based on his raw score which compares the child's performance level to the score which could be expected statistically from an average child at that same year and month in school. This score is expressed in terms of years and months, (9 months making up each school year). *Example:* a score of 2.8 would mean that the student's score is the same as an average child in 2nd grade, 8th month.

Intelligence Quotient (IQ) An index designed to predict academic success. The IQ test compares a person's intelligence (or learning potential) with that of others the same age. This comparison yields a derived score called IQ. The score does not measure creativity, talent or motivation. Any IQ score between 85-115 is considered to be in the average range. A score between 70-85 is low average, while 115-130 is high average. A score below 70 indicates possible mental retardation and a score above 130 indicates possible giftedness. These scores may vary slightly depending on the IQ test that is administered and the scores can be influenced by emotional, cultural, and perceptual factors.

Mastery Test See Criterion-Referenced Test.

Mean Score The mathematical average of all students' test scores in a particular test.

Mental Age	A score on a mental abilities test which ranks the performance level of a child in relation to the score which could be expected statistically from a child at that same age. The mental age score is used to distinguish between a child's chronological age and his actual performance. *Example:* if a child's chronological age is 10-6 (10 years, 6 months) and his mental age is 11-4, then his performance on the test is comparable to the average performance of children whose chronological age is 11 years, 4 months. The child's mental age would thus be "above average."
Norms	A frame of reference for a standardized test which shows the actual performance on the test by pupils of specific ages and grades. Through the use of norms, the score of an individual student can be compared to the scores of other students of a similar age or grade across the country.
Percentile	A score which states a student's relative position within a defined group by ranking all students who have taken a particular test.
Personality Test	A test that measures character traits and the way a person acts rather than specific knowledge or intelligence.
Power Test	An untimed test with items usually arranged in order of difficulty that determines a student's level of performance in a particular subject area.
Raw Score	The total number of correct answers on a test.
Readiness Test	A test that measures a student's maturity or mastery of prerequisite skills which are needed before going on to a new content area. This kind of test is typically used in preschool or kindergarten to determine whether the child is academically and developmentally prepared to function effectively at the next academic level.
Reliability	How well a test consistently produces the same results.
Scaled Score	A ranking system, chosen by the publisher of the test, which is derived from the raw scores obtained on that test. A different scale is established for each test. For example, one test could have a scale from 1-19 while another might have a scale from 1-70. In order to interpret a scaled score, you must know the mean score and the standard deviation for that test.
Standard Deviation	A measure of how much one student's score varies from the mean score of all the students taking the test.
Standard Score	A statistical ranking, with respect to the performance of a large sample of students of the same age and/or grade level, of a child's performance on a standardized test, based on the raw score he achieved on the test.

Standardized Test	A test which has specific and uniform instructions for administering, timing and scoring. It is given to large numbers of children at one time and statistically compares one student's performance with that of a large sample of students of the same age and/or grade level. The norms established by the standardization process are used by teachers and school psychologists to determine a child's relative level of performance or achievement.
Stanine	A statistical ranking of a child's performance on a standardized test on a scale of 1 through 9. A mean score is 5 and any stanine score from 3 to 7 is generally considered to reflect average performance. Frequently, the results on a standardized test will be given by means of both a stanine score and a percentile score. The higher the stanine score, the higher the percentile score will be.
Survey Test	Test which measures general achievement in an academic area. It is not as comprehensive or specific as a criterion-referenced test.
Validity	The accuracy with which a test measures what it has been designed to measure.

TESTING APPENDIX

BERRY-BUKTENICA DEVELOPMENTAL TEST OF VISUAL-MOTOR INTEGRATION

Function:	Measures visual perception and fine-motor coordination.
Age range:	2-15 years.
Scores:	Age level.
Procedure:	Students copy geometric forms that range from straight lines to complex designs.

BENDER VISUAL MOTOR GESTALT TEST

Function:	Measures visual-motor integration, perceptual maturity, and emotional disturbances.
Age range:	5-11 years.
Scores:	Age level, percentile.
Procedure:	Students copy 9 abstract designs.

BRIGANCE DIAGNOSTIC INVENTORY OF BASIC SKILLS

Function:	Measures readiness, reading, language arts, and mathematics skills and pinpoints specific areas of academic strengths and weaknesses.
Age range:	K-6th grade. Separate inventory for older children.
Scores:	Grade level.
Procedure:	Examiner asks student questions and records the answers in a record book.

DENVER DEVELOPMENTAL SCREENING TEST

Function:	Detects developmental delays in young children.
Age range:	Birth-6 years.
Scores:	Age level.
Subtests:	Personal/social (getting along with people).
	Self-help skills (dressing).
	Fine-motor adaptive (using hands to pick up objects; drawing).
	Language (following commands; speaking).
	Gross-motor (sitting; walking; jumping)

DETROIT TESTS OF LEARNING APTITUDE

Function: Measures general learning abilities.
Age range: 3-19 years.
Scores: Mental age and I.Q. Test also indicates the student's strengths and weaknesses.
Subtests: Reasoning and comprehension
Practical judgment
Verbal ability
Time and space relationships
Numerical ability
Auditory attentive ability
Visual attentive ability
Motor ability

GOODENOUGH-HARRIS DRAWING TEST

Function: Measures intellectual and emotional maturity.
Age range: 3-15 years.
Scores: Standard, percentile, quality scale.
Procedure: The child draws a complete picture of a man, woman, and then of himself.

ILLINOIS TEST OF PSYCHOLINGUISTIC ABILITIES (ITPA)

Function: Measures visual-motor and auditory-vocal skills (listening, then responding by speaking).
Age range: 2-10 years.
Scores: Age level, scaled (scaled from 0-68 with a mean score of 36. Anything below 26 is considered to be a potential danger signal).
Subtests: **Auditory reception**—Measures how well the child understands verbal questions; Example: "Do caterpillars fly?"

Visual reception—Measures how well the child understands visual pictures; Example: matching similar pictures.

Auditory association—Measures how well the child links ideas that are presented orally; Example: A bird has wings; a dog has _____ .

Visual association—Measures how well the child links ideas that are presented visually; Example: finding a picture of a spoon that goes with a picture of a bowl of soup.

Verbal expression—Measures how well the child describes familiar objects; Example: a button is round, has four holes, etc.

Manual expression—Measures how well the child shows how objects are used; Example: the child makes a sawing motion when shown a picture of a saw.

226

Grammatic closure—Measures how well the child uses correct grammar. Example: Here is a house. Here are two _____.

Visual closure—Measures how well the child identifies pictured objects when parts are missing. Example: a child is shown a picture of a junkyard scene with many dogs in it, some partially obscured. The child must find all the dogs.

Auditory sequential memory—Measures how well the child remembers what he has heard. Example: the child is told a series of numbers and must repeat them in order.

Visual sequential memory—Measures how well the child remembers (in order) what he has seen. Example: the child is shown a series of shapes and must reproduce them in order.

Auditory Closure—Measures how well the child identifies a word when part of it is not said. Example: __asketball.

Sound blending—Measures how well the child blends individual sounds into a word; Example: "c", "a", "t" into "cat".

KEY MATH DIAGNOSTIC ARITHMETIC TEST

Function: Measures a wide range of mathematical skills.
Age range: K-6th grade.
Scores: Grade level.
Subtests: Numeration, fractions, geometry and symbols, addition, subtraction, multiplication, division, mental computation, numerical reasoning, word problems, missing elements, money, measurement, time.

MARIANE FROSTIG DEVELOPMENTAL TEST OF VISUAL PERCEPTION

Function: Measures visual perception and visual-motor skills
Age range: 3 to 8 years
Scores: Age level, scaled (ranging from 0-20, with 10 as average), and perceptual quotient (scores lower than 90 suggest high risk of learning disabilities for children entering first grade)
Subtests: Eye-motor coordination (tracing within boundaries)
Figure-ground
Constancy of shape (picking out one shape from other similar shapes)
Position in space (finding identical figures)
Spatial relations (copying designs by connecting dots)

MEETING STREET SCHOOL SCREENING TEST (M.S.S.S.T.)

Function: Identifies children with potential learning disabilities and identifies developmental maturity.

Age range: 5-7½ years.

Scores: Scaled scores (for each subtest, from 1-19; total test score from 20-80. Cutoff for kindergarten children is 39, for 1st grade, 55).

Subtests: Subjective behavior rating scale.

Motor patterning (hopping, clapping).

Visual-perceptual-motor (matching shapes, copying forms, remembering forms and letters).

Language (repeating words and sentences, telling a story).

PEABODY PICTURE VOCABULARY TEST

Function: Measures understanding of word meanings.

Age range: 2-18 years.

Scores: Mental age, percentile, IQ equivalent.

Procedure: The examiner pronounces a word. The child must select the picture that represents that word.

PURDUE PERCEPTUAL-MOTOR SURVEY

Function: Measures perceptual-motor, gross-motor and fine-motor skills.

Age range: 6-10 years.

Scores: None, profile only.

Subtests: Balance and posture, body image (knowledge and movement of body parts).

Perceptual-motor match (rhythmic writing and chalkboard tasks involving directionality and laterality).

Ocular control (visual tracking activities).

Form perception (copying geometric forms).

SLINGERLAND SCREENING TESTS FOR IDENTIFYING CHILDREN WITH SPECIFIC LANGUAGE DISABILITIES

Function: Measures visual, auditory and kinesthetic skills which are related to reading and spelling.

Age range: 6-12 years.

Scores: None, provides guidelines for prescriptive teaching.

Subtests: Copying, visual memory, visual discrimination, auditory memory, initial and final sounds, auditory discrimination, following directions, word finding, story telling.

SLOSSON INTELLIGENCE TEST FOR CHILDREN AND ADULTS

Function: Measures mental ability.
Age range: 5 months-adult.
Scores: Mental age, IQ.
Procedure: The examiner asks the student a variety of questions dealing with general knowledge, mathematical reasoning, vocabulary, and auditory memory.

SPACHE DIAGNOSTIC READING SCALES

Function: Measures a wide range of reading skills.
Age range: 1-8th grade, 9-12th grade for students with reading problems.
Scores: Grade level.
Subtests: Word recognition, oral reading, silent reading, auditory comprehension and phonics.

STANFORD-BINET INTELLIGENCE SCALE

Function: Measures general intelligence.
Age range: 2 years-adult.
Scores: Mental age, IQ.
Procedure: The examiner asks the student to answer questions or perform tasks which assess a variety of abilities including vocabulary, memory, abstract reasoning, numerical concepts, visual-motor skills and social competence.

WECHSLER INTELLIGENCE SCALE FOR CHILDREN REVISED—(WISC-R)

Function: Measures general intelligence.
Age range: 6-17 years.
Scores: Verbal IQ, performance IQ, full scale IQ, scaled score, test ages.
Subtests: **Verbal section**

Information (What day comes after Tuesday?)

Similarities (How are a shoe and a boot alike?)

Arithmetic (word problems involving mental computation)

Vocabulary (What is a stadium?)

Comprehension (What should you do if you cut yourself?)

Digit span (remembering a series of numbers)

Performance section

Picture completion (identifying what's missing from an incomplete picture of an object)

Picture arrangement (putting pictures in a logical order)

Block design (copying a design with blocks)

Object assembly (putting puzzle pieces together to form a familiar object)

Coding (associating a symbol with a particular shape)

Mazes (following a maze without lifting the pencil)

WEPMAN AUDITORY DISCRIMINATION TEST

Function:	Measures auditory discrimination.
Age range:	5-8 years.
Scores:	Rating scale ranging from "very good development" to "below the level of the threshold of adequacy"
Procedure:	The examiner pronounces two words and the child must determine if they sound the same or different. Example: "bad-bat".

WIDE RANGE ACHIEVEMENT TEST

Function:	Measures achievement in reading (word recognition only), spelling and arithmetic.
Age range:	5 years to adult.
Scores:	Grade level, standard, percentile and stanine.
Procedure:	The student reads word aloud, writes down dictated spelling words and writes down the answers to printed arithmetic problems.

WOODCOCK READING MASTERY TEST

Function:	Measures a wide range of reading skills
Age range:	K-12th grade
Scores:	Grade level, percentile, relative mastery, achievement index, reading range.
Subtests:	Letter identification, word identification, word attack, word comprehension, and passage comprehension.

REFERENCES

Bannatyne, A. *Language Reading and Learning Disabilities.* (2nd ed.) Springfiedl, IL: Charles C. Thomas, 1971.

Compton, C. *A Guide to 65 Tests for Special Education.* Belmont, CA: Pittman Learning, Inc., 1980.

Durkin, D. *Teaching Them to Read.* (2nd ed.) Boston: Allyn & Bacon, Inc., 1974.

English, H. and English, A. *A Comprehensive Dictionary of Psychological and Psychoanalytical Terms.* New York: David McKay Company, Inc., 1958.

Hinsie, L. and Campbell, R. *Psychiatric Dictionary.* (3rd ed.) New York: Oxford University Press, 1960.

Johnson, D. and Myklebust, H. *Learning Disabilities.* New York: Grune & Stratton, 1967.

Kauffman, J. *Characteristics of Children's Behavior Disorders.* Columbus: Charles E. Merrill Pub. Co., 1977.

Lerner, Janet, *Learning Disabilities.* (3rd ed.). Boston: Houghton Mifflin Co, 1981.

Levinson, Harold N., *A Solution to the Riddle of Dyslexia.* New York: Springer-Verlag, 1980.

MacMillan, D. *Mental Retardation in School and Society.* Boston: Little, Brown & Co., 1977.

Mercer, C. *Children and Adolescents with Learning Disabilities.* Columbus: Charles E. Merrill Pub. Co., 1979.

Olson, J. and Dillner, M. *Learning to Teach Reading in the Elementary School.* New York: MacMillan Pub. Co., Inc., 1976.

Telford, C. and Saurey, J. *The Exceptional Individual.* (3rd ed.) Englewood Cliffs, NJ: Prentice-Hall, Inc., 1977.

Test Service Notebook. "A Glossary of Measurement Terms." New York: Harcourt, Brace Jovanovich, Inc.

Wiig, E. and Semel, E. *Language Disabilities in Children and Adolescents.* Columbus: Charles E. Merrill Pub. Co., 1976.

INDEX OF CHECKLISTS

Copies for your individual use of the checklists included throughout this book are available from:

Humanics Limited
P.O. Box 7447
Atlanta, Ga. 30309
(404) 874-2176

Please write or call for ordering information.

INDEX OF ANECDOTES

GENERAL INDEX

237

Self-sabatoge, as symptom of 10
Sensory deprivation 23-24
Severe 34, 35, 73, 92, 123, 160
Sloppiness, as a symptom of 98, 107, 123, 125, 177
Structure, importance of in remediating 21, 128-129, 144-148
Subtle 45, 73, 90-91, 123
Symptoms 41-42, 44-45, 47-48, 52, 56, 57, 58, 60, 62, 76, 90-92, 101
Testing for (See Diagnosis)
Unusual (See Atypical)
Yoga, as treatment for 20, 123-125
Learning Disabilities Specialist 2, 11, 12, 33, 34, 82, 96, 119, 161, 168
Learning Potential 30-32, 35, 90-92, 95, 110-111
Learning Problems (See Learning Disabilities)
Learning Proficiency 30-32, 35, 90-92, 95, 107
Letter Reversals 28, 34, 35, 74
Level of Learning, Determining 24-26
Lisping (See Speech Disorders)

– M–

Manipulative Behavior 37, 140, 150-154
Marginal Learning Problems 34, 35
Math Problems 40, 85-86
Computational skills deficiency 41, 85-86
Conceptual skills deficiency 85-86
Math Skills 33, 41, 85, 86, 89
Medical Components of Learning Problems
Allergies 49
Amphetamines 44, 76
Auditory impairment 47-48, 56, 57, 69, 118
Balance 44, 75
Downs Syndrome 64
Ear infections 48

Electroencephalogram (E.E.G.) 36, 43-44, 75
Genetic influences 56, 64, 75, 162-163
Medication 20, 43-44, 76, 77, 96
Neurological disorders 27, 36, 41, 42-47, 71, 75, 76
Phynlketonuria (P.K.U.) 64
Ritalin 96
Sensory impairment 27, 47-48, 56, 57, 69, 116, 118
Special diets 20, 45
Visual impairment 47, 48, 116
Medication 20, 43-44, 76, 77, 96
Mental Delay (See Mental Retardation)
Mental Retardation 31, 39-40, 41, 61, 71, 209, 212
Causes 64
Definition 61-62
Diagnosis 61-62
Educable Mentally Retarded (E.M.R.) 39-40, 63-65
Profoundly Mentally Retarded (P.M.R.) 63-64
Symptoms 61-62, 64
Trainable Mentally Retarded (T.M.R.) 63-64
Minimal Brain Dysfunction (See also Perceptual Dysfunction) 45, 75
Diagnosis 75
Distinguishing from minimal brain damage 45, 75
E.E.G. 36, 75
Neurological examination 36, 44
Symptoms 75
Treatment 45, 73-74, 100
Motor-coordination Deficits 36, 42, 44-45, 56, 72, 155, 166
As indicator of organic brain damage 36, 42, 44-45, 75, 166
Fine-motor development 67, 86-88, 98, 166
"Hard" or severe symptoms 36, 42, 44, 76
Necessity for neurological examination 36, 43, 44
"Soft" or moderate symptoms 36, 37, 75

242

249

I.Q. 30-32
  Sample test question 32
Multi-discipline 36, 37, 42
Necessity for 36, 37, 42, 71, 82, 116
Possible distorting factors 32-33, 66-67
Requesting 18, 36, 92, 116
Scores 82-85, 119
  Effect of learning problems on 30-31, 33
  Interpretation 25, 31-32, 82, 91, 119
  Understanding 25, 91
Standardized 22, 24, 25, 35, 91, 107, 118, 132, 185
  Facsimile test result 25
Trainable Mentally Retarded (T.M.R.) (See Mental Retardation)
Tutors 10, 23, 73, 74, 96, 114, 140-143, 147, 158, 177, 203
  Parents as 140, 141-143
  When appropriate 73

– U–

Unrealistic Expectations 128-130, 136-138, 139, 209
Unusual Learning Problems (See Atypical Learning Problems)

– V–

Visual Impairment 27, 47-48, 116
Visual Memory 28, 34, 76, 80, 83, 84, 89
Visual Tracking 28, 74, 82, 98
Vocabulary Skills 25, 82-83
  Facsimile test result, standardized test 25

– W–

Written Language Arts Problems 58-60
  Language Arts Checklist 61

Symptoms 60
Written Language Arts Skills 58-60
  Components 60

– Y–

Yoga 20, 124, 125

J E S -

$24.00

192/month -